The Art
of
Elixir

elegant, functional programming

Jeff
Hajewski

building fault-tolerant
and self-healing
distributed systems

Jeff Hajewski
Olympia, WA
jeff@parkereverett.com

The Art of Elixir

iv

Contents

Chapter 1

Why Elixir?

1.1 What is Elixir?

Elixir is a dynamic, functional language designed for building scalable and maintainable applications. It runs on top of the BEAM VM, the same VM that powers Erlang, which is known for being incredibly fault-tolerant, fast, and supporting a huge level of concurrency. Elixir is widely used in domains such as web development, multimedia processing, data ingestion, and large-scale distributed systems. The language was heavily influence by some of the best features from Ruby, Erlang, and Clojure and provides a powerful yet friendly language for developers.

Elixir's out-of-the-box support for concurrency, fault-tolerance, and functional programming is one of the main draws to the language. If you are looking for a language to build a large, highly concurrent, and performant Elixir should be at the top of your list of languages. Elixir also has the added benefit if being a simple (and functional) language, which helps keep your code easy to understand. In fact, companies like Discord, Pinterest, Pepsi, Moz, and Toyota use Elixir to power some of their highest traffic/highest demand systems.

Part of Elixir's power comes from its concurrency model. Elixir provides lightweight processes that get executed concurrently. These processes help developers to better leverage modern multi-core processors without worrying about many of the challenges of traditional thread-based concurrency. Processes are isolated and only communicate with each other only through message passing. This eliminates common concurrency issues like race conditions and deadlocks.

Another major selling point for Elixir is that it is a functional language. This means functions are first class citizens and data is immutable by default. They can be assigned to variables, passed to other functions, and in general treated like data in many respects. Functions are generally pure, meaning they don't have side effects (e.g., modifying their input data).

Many proponents of functional programming claim it leads to pre-dictable, simpler to reason about, and maintainable code. In my experience, this is true for languages like Elixir. Elixir takes all the best parts of functional programming without requiring you to spend hours playing type Tetris like you do in Haskell or highly-functional Scala codebases.

Elixir's syntax was heavily inspired by Ruby. This gives Elixir a rather intuitive syntax and makes the language very readable. Elixir also includes pattern matching and a hygenic macro system. Pattern matching is a powerful tool that allows developers to elegantly destructure data and manage control flow. The macro system enables developers to easily extend the language, creating domain-specific languages and constructs.

Elixir is built on top of the BEAM VM (Bogdan/Björn's Erlang Abstract Machine), the VM that powers Erlang, which brings with it incredible fault-tolerance and concurrency capabilities. For decades, BEAM has served as the foundation for many massively scalable and self-healing systems for telecommunications, banking, and social media. Because Elixir is built on top of BEAM, Elixir applications are generally reliable and performant, even in the face of hardware failure and network partitions.

Whether you are building a web server, distributed system, or all of the above, Elixir is a great choice. As a functional programming language it is incredibly expressive and productive. Its concurrency, scalability, and fault-tolerance characteristics make it a performant language, capable of handling just about everything you throw at it. Elixir also has a vibrant and growing ecosystem, containing a number of libraries for testing, database management, and web frameworks. In addition to getting your local environment set up, the rest of this chapter will dig a little deeper into some of the topics covered in this introduction.

1.2 Why Choose Elixir?

Elixir is an excellent choice for a wide range of applications, from web development to large-scale distributed systems, due to its unique blend of functional programming, concurrency support, and fault-tolerance. With the prevalence of multi-core processors and increasing complexity of distributed systems, Elixir's ability to make efficient use of hardware resources gives it a major leg up on languages like Python and Javascript, while keeping (and often exceedingly) the level of productivity provided by those languages. Elixir's lightweight processes and message-passing concurrency model result in far simpler code than its Java, C++, and Kotiln counterparts.

One of the reasons Elixir is such a popular language is how easily it promotes developer productivity and code maintainability. Elixir code is an incredibly expressive language, resulting in readable and concise code. Its functional roots (e.g., pattern matching and immutability) lead to more predictable and easy-to-reason-about code. Code that is easy to read and understand has fewer bugs and generally more performant. The language comes with built-in testing tools and documentation features that further contribute to maintainable code.

Elixir's resilience and fault-tolerance characteristics come from the Erlang VM, and are primary motivations in organizations choosing it as a language. The Erlang VM has a rich history in the implementation of highly available, fault-tolerant systems in industries where uptime is critical. Because it is built on top of the Erlang VM, Elixir has built-in support for process supervisors, which automatically restart failed processes. Leveraging the Erlang VM also makes it easy to build applications that can withstand hardware failures and network partitions as well as being distributed applications across multiple servers.

One of the most important considerations when choosing a language for a project is the community support. A language with no community has fewer quality libraries, fewer resources for learning, and generally harder to work with. Elixir has a vibrant, supportive, and, most importantly, growing community of developer aross the world. This community is an excellent resource for asking questions. Be sure to checkout the Elixir Forums, Elixir Slack, and Elixir Discord for support.

Elixir also comes with a built-in package manager, Hex. Hex

provides access to thousands of libraries and frameworks, such as Ecto, a popular ORM, and Phoenix, Elixir's Rails-like web framework. You can also host private packages on Hex (though this isn't free). Hex integrates with the default Elixir build took, Mix, making it easy to get started.

1.3 Elixir's Core Benefits

There are three core areas in which Elixir excels. Elixir is built for concurrency. This makes it an excellent choice for web applications and distributed systems. Elixir is a functional language with dynamic typing. This makes it both safe *and* productive. Elixir's focus on immutability makes it trivial to build safe, concurrent programs. Because Elixir is built on top of the BEAM VM, it inherits all of the advantages the BEAM provides. This includes the BEAM's incredible fault-tolerance and performance characteristics.

Concurrency

One of the main reasons people reach for Elixir is its support for concurrency. Many view Elixir as Erlang but with a friendlier syntax. What made Erlang so popular was its native support for massive concurrency and Elixir is no different. Elixir can support tens of thousands of processes on a single machine.

An Elixir process is different from an OS thread. Processes consume minimal resources. They are fast to create and manage, and they can even communicate with eachother through message passing. The use of message passing, and Elixir's immutability by default, means common problems in concurrent programs like race conditions and deadlocks are much easier to avoid.

Immutability

Elixir is a functional language[1]. This means functions are first-class citizens; they can be passed around as arguments to other functions just as you would pass a variable. You can even store functions in

---

[1]The definition of a "functional language" is actually somewhat poorly defined. In general though, it means some level of immutability and the ability to treat functions as data. Some languages, like Haskell, take immutability and functional design to the extreme. Others, such as Scala, are less militant about immutability and combine the best of functional programming and object oriented programming.

variables. It also means data and variables are immutable. When you add an element to a list, you aren't appending to the original list[2] but, rather, creating a new list.

A pure function is one that returns the same output for a given input. That is, it doesn't mutate any internal or external state. Pure functions are a core tool in the functional programmer's toolbox. Building software with immutable data and pure functions makes for surprisingly simple and easy to understand code. The functions are trivial to test as they have no internal or external state to worry about. This makes your code predictable and simpler to reason about.

Fault-tolerance

The BEAM VM is the foundation of Elixir's fault-tolerance and what makes it such a great language choice for building distributed systems. The BEAM VM and OTP provide utilities and tools for building fault-tolerant and self-healing systems. This is through a combination of Supervisors (which we will learn about later in the book), and process isolation.

Supervisors are the watchdogs of your Elixir system. You tell them which processes to watch and how to respond when a process fails. Once run, they sit and watch, making sure everything is running as expected. With Supervisors, you can build supervision trees that manage and self-heal with thousands of processes. This means as unexpected states or inputs occur, causing your system to crash, you will have already put into place the pieces that will repair your system, just by writing idiomatic Elixir.

1.4 The BEAM VM

Elixir's power and performance come from the Erlang Virtual Machine (VM), also known as the BEAM (Bogdan/Bj"orn's Erlang

---

[2]This isn't entirely true. There are what are known as "functional data structures." These data structures are designed in a way that give you immutability (that is, appending to a list gives you a new list) while avoiding unnecessary copies. For example, appending an element to a list *typically* involves creating a new pointer to the head of the list, using the body of the old list, and updating the tail of the list to point to the new element. Although a second list is created, it shares most of its data with the original list. If you find this interesting, I recommend checking out *Purely Functional Data Structures* by Chris Okasaki.

Abstract Machine). The BEAM VM has been used for decades to build massivively scalable, fault-tolerant systems across a wide range of industries, including banking, social media, and telecom. Becase Elixir runs on top of the BEAM VM, it inherits BEAM's strong concurrency and fault-tolerance capabilities. It's heavily Ruby-inspired syntax makes the language more approachable and expressive syntax for developers.

Elixir's lightweight, isolated processes are one of its key features. These processes are Erlang's version of green threads. They are analogous to goroutines in Go, fibers in D and Crystal, asyncio in Python, coroutines in C++ and Lua. Erlang's processes are managed by BEAM. Each process runs in its own isolated memory space, with its own stack and heap, and communicates with other processes via message passing. This isolation ensures that processes cannot directly access or modify each other's state, eliminating many common concurrency issues such as race conditions and deadlocks. The BEAM VM's scheduler is highly optimized to manage millions of these lightweight processes efficiently, enabling Elixir applications to achieve massive concurrency with minimal overhead.

The BEAM VM is also what gives Elixir its strength in distribution and fault-tolerance. It allows Elixir apps to run across multiple nodes, either on the same machine or over several networked matchines, without extra work for the developer. This lets Elixir apps scale up easily by adding nodes to handle more traffic. The VM's resilience comes from its built-in safety features. Elixer processes have supervisors, which spot and restart failed processes. Because these processes are self-contained, it is rare that a failure in one process impacts another process. This keeps things running smoothly in the face of failures.

The BEAM VM also offers hot code reloading and tracing. To the uninitiated, these may not seem like major features. But for those who have used these features in other languages, they are amazing tools. Hot code reloading allows developers to modify and update running Elixir applications without the need for downtime. This enables seamless deployments and reduces the impact of maintenance on system availability. It also speeds up local development and iteration. There is nothing worse than making a minor change and waiting several minutes for your code to build, only to realize you forgot another change (Rust, Java, and C++ programmers know this feeling all too well).

Tracing being a first-class citizen within BEAM greatly simplifies monitoring and debuging in Elixir systems. This is done at the process event level, making it easy to debug both logic and performance issues.

Although BEAM VM is a key factor in Elixir's success, Elixir is not just a wrapper around Erlang. Elixir builds upon the strengths of the Erlang by providing a more expressive and developer-friendly language. This includes a cleaner and more consistent syntax, powerful metaprogramming capabilities, and an active ecosystem of libraries and frameworks.

The BEAM VM is the machine behind which Elixir's concurrency, scalability, and fault-tolerance features. Elixir is a great choice for building systems that require high levels of concurrency and resilience. It is continually evolving and its ecosystem is constantly growing. The combination of its expressiveness and BEAM's robustness make a compelling option for buidling modern distributed systems.

1.5 Who Uses Elixir?

There is a pretty active community of Elixir users. The main forum, elixirforum.com, is incredibly active. The r/elixir reddit community is equally as active, with over 30,000 members. Though Elixir isn't as widely used in industry as languages like Go or Python, it is used by quite a few large companies. Heroku and Discord are two major companies with extensive Elixir codebases. You will also find Elixir at places like Meta, Google, Mozilla, and even Pepsi. There is also a pretty active job board on the Elixir Forum, with at least one or two posts every week.

1.6 Conventions used in this book

The examples in this book will alternate between being done in IEx and just being shown as plain code. IEx is great for experimenting, especially in the early chapters as we explore the language. However, we will quickly reach a point where it is easier to show examples as pure code, rather than within IEx. For example, demonstrating list manipulation is simpler in IEx because you can play with the examples on your.

```
iex> xs = [1, 2, 3]
[1, 2, 3]
iex> [head | tail] = xs
[1, 2, 4]
iex> head
1
iex> tail
[2, 3]
```

More complex code deserves its own listing, without IEx.

```
def probably_prime(n, k \\ 50) do
  is_fermat_probable_prime = fn a -> rem(pow(a, n - 1), n)
  ↪   == 1 end
  cond do
    n == 2 -> true
    rem(n, 2) == 0 -> false
    true -> Enum.find(
      1..k,
      :prime,
      fn _ -> not is_fermat_probable_prime.(:rand.uniform(n
      ↪   - 1)) end
    ) == :prime
  end
end
```

In this case, the code will be on its own and it is up to the reader to decide how they'd like to run it. As we will discuss later in the book, all functions must be defined in a module. For most code listings, we will omit the module.

Behavior and Behaviour

As you read through the book you may notice I spell behavior two different ways. As an American, I spell *behavior* without the u, rather than the British spelling *behaviour*. In Elixir, there is a concept of *behaviour*, and it is spelled with a u. To avoid confusion, when I refer to a *behaviour* in the Elixir context, I will always use a u (the British spelling). When I am using the word *behavior* to describe how something acted or behaved, I will generally use the American spelling.

By the end of this I will surely be as confused about which way I should spell behavior and as I am gray (or is it grey? I can never remember...).

Chapter 2

Setting Up Your Environment

2.1 Setting Up Your Environment

Before we dive into the language we need to setup our environment. In this section, we'll walk through the process of installing Elixir and configuring your development environment.

To get started with Elixir, you'll need to install it on your machine. On macOS, you can use the Homebrew package manager to install Elixir by running the command `brew install elixir`. For Linux, you can use your distribution's package manager, such as apt-get on Ubuntu or yum on CentOS, to install Elixir. For example, `apt-get install elixir`. On Windows, you can download the installer from the official Elixir website and follow the installation wizard.

Now that you've installed Elixir, let's verify the installation. Open up your terminal and runn the following command:

```
$ elixir --version
Erlang/OTP 26 [erts-14.2.5] [source] [64-bit] [smp:10:10]
↪  [ds:10:10:10] [async-threads:1] [jit] [dtrace]

Elixir 1.17.2 (compiled with Erlang/OTP 26)
```

NOTE

We use the notation $ to indicate your shell prompt. The text that follows indicates the command being executed. With the exception of line continuation characters \, text on the following line represents the output.

We will typically use words enclosed in angle brackets to represent something you need customize. For example, $ cd <project path> represents using the cd command with the path of your project. You should not type the angle brackets in the command. Instead, the command you actually type would look something like cd path/to/my/project assuming your project is in the directory path/to/my/project relative to your current working directory.

This command will display the version of Elixir installed on your system. You can also start an interactive Elixir shell, called IEx, by simply running:

```
$ iex
Erlang/OTP 26 [erts-14.2.5] [source] [64-bit] [smp:10:10]
↪   [ds:10:10:10] [async-threads:1] [jit] [dtrace]

Interactive Elixir (1.17.2) - press Ctrl+C to exit (type h()
↪   ENTER for help)
iex>
```

IEx provides a REPL (Read-Eval-Print Loop) environment where you can execute Elixir code and experiment with the language features. For example, we can define variables, functions, etc.

```
Erlang/OTP 26 [erts-14.2.5] [source] [64-bit] [smp:24:24]
↪   [ds:24:24:10] [async-threads:1] [dtrace]

Interactive Elixir (1.17.2) - press Ctrl+C to exit (type h()
↪   ENTER for help)
iex> defmodule Hello do
...>    def hello(name) do
...>      "Hello " <> name
...>    end
...> end
{:module, Hello,
 <<....>>, {:hello, 1}}
iex> Hello.hello("Reader")
"Hello Reader"
```

```
iex> say_something = fn -> IO.puts("Something!") end
#Function<43.105768164/0 in :erl_eval.expr/6>
iex> say_something.()
Something!
:ok
```

The weird syntax say_something.() is specific to lambda functions. Normal function calls (that is, named functions) omit the ..

We will use IEx extensively as we learn and explore the Elixir language.

We also need an IDE or text editor. There are a number of options when it comes to choosing an IDE or text editor. We will briefly cover Visual Studio Code and Neovim. Visual Studio Code is one of the most, if not the most, popular text editors/IDEs. I'm adding Neovim because that's what I generally use. Many IDEs, such as IntelliJ, offer Elixir plugins as well.

For Visual Studio Code, I recommend installing the ElixirLS plugin. You can find this by searching plugins for "elixir".

For Neovim, I recommend elixir-ls. If you are using the Kickstart Neovim you can simply add elixirlsp to your language server config. If you aren't using Kickstart, you probably know more about Neovim configuration than I do.

2.2 Running Elixir Code

There are several ways to run Elixir code. The usecase and amount of code will dictate which choice is best. Sometimes it will be clear from the example that we are using a particular approach. Many of the code examples early in the book are clearly run from IEx (indicated by the prompt iex >). Scripts (Elixir source files ending in .exs) will always have the name of the scripts at the top of the code as a comment. Anything else is almost always a Mix project.

In some cases, I may just show a code sample with no indication of how to run it. In this case, it's up to you how you would like to run the code (if at all). Generally it will be between IEx and a script file, though more often it will be a script file. Let's take a look at how to to run our code.

IEx

IEx is usually the correct choice for or quick, one-off experiments or small amounts of code. For example, as you read through the initial chapters of this book it's a good idea to have a computer with you and a terminal open running IEx. This makes it easy to quickly test out new ideas and concepts.

For example, suppose you are reading about comprehensions. IEx can be perfect for experimenting.

```
iex> squares = for x <- 0..5, do: x * x
[0, 1, 4, 9, 16, 25]
```

Script Files

IEx becomes unweildy once you have to write much more than a few lines. Even with a few lines, every time you make a mistake you have to retype *all* the lines in IEx again. That becomes tedious and annoying *very* fast. The solution is to move to a script file, which uses the .exs extensions.

Script files are run using the elixir commond from the terminal. As stated at the beginng of this section, we will always have the script name at the top of the file. These are available on the book's GitHub for download.

Let's look at an example

```
# src/introduction_to_elixir/sample_script.exs
defmodule ExampleModule do
  def say_hello(name) do
    IO.puts("Hello, #{name}")
  end

  def factorial(0), do: 1
  def factorial(n) when n > 0, do: n * factorial(n - 1)
  def factorial(n) when n < 0, do
    raise(ArgumentError, "n must be a non-negative integer")
  end
end

ExampleModule.say_hello("world")
IO.puts(ExampleModule.factorial(5))
IO.puts(ExampleModule.factorial(-1))
```

To run this, we call elixir from the terminal

```
$ elixir src/introduction_to_elixir/sample_script.exs
Hello, world
120
** (ArgumentError) n must be a non-negative integer
    src/introduction_to_elixir/sample_script.exs:8:
    ↳  ExampleModule.factorial/1
    src/introduction_to_elixir/sample_script.exs:13: (file)
```

Mix

Mix is the official build tool for Elixir, and it comes bundled with the language. If you haven't used a build tool before, they help you create, compile, test, and manage dependencies for your project. To create a new Elixir project using Mix, navigate to the directory where you want to create your project and run the command `mix new <project name>`. This command will generate a new directory with the basic structure of an Elixir project, including a `mix.exs` file for configuring your project and managing dependencies.

With your Elixir installation and editor set up, you're ready to start writing Elixir code. To create a new Elixir project, type the following command:

```
$ mix new <project name>
```

This creates a project with the following structure:

- `README.md`
- `mix.exs`
- lib
  - `intro.ex`
- test
  - `intro_test.exs`
  - `test_helper.exs`

There are two main ways to run your project. You can run your project as an application, or you can define and run a specific task from your project. There's a lot to learn about how to manage projects with Mix – we will dig into that in a later chapter. For now we will just give you a brief overview of how you can use Mix to run your Elixir code. Let's look at the application approach first.

If you have used other languages like Go, Java, C, C++, Python, etc. you will be familiar with the idea of a `main` funciton. In Elixir we need to tell Mix which module is our application. Mix will then run that module's start function. Update lib/intro.ex with the following content:

```
# lib/intro.ex
defmodule Intro do
  @moduledoc """
  Documentation for `Intro`.
  """

  use Application # We have added this

  @doc """
  Hello world.

  ## Examples

      iex> Intro.hello()
      :world

  """
  def hello do
    :world
  end

  # This is also new!
  def start(_type, _args) do
    IO.puts "Application started"
    IO.puts "Hello, world!"
    Supervisor.start_link [], strategy: :one_for_one
  end
end
```

We also need to update mix.exs. Your mix.exs file should be updated to match this:

```
defmodule Intro.MixProject do
  use Mix.Project

  def project do
    [
      app: :intro,
      version: "0.1.0",
      elixir: "~> 1.17",
      start_permanent: Mix.env() == :prod,
      deps: deps()
    ]
  end

  # Run "mix help compile.app" to learn about applications.
  def application do
```

```
    [
      mod: {Intro, []}, # <-- this is what we have added
      extra_applications: [:logger]
    ]
  end

  # Run "mix help deps" to learn about dependencies.
  defp deps do
    [
      # {:dep_from_hexpm, "~> 0.3.0"},
      # {:dep_from_git, git:
      ↪  "https://github.com/elixir-lang/my_dep.git", tag:
      ↪  "0.1.0"}
    ]
  end
end
```

Note that version may vary slightly, the key piece is adding the
mod: line. From here we can run the application using `mix run`.

```
$ mix run
Application started
Hello, world!
```

Alternatively, we can run a specific task. To do this, let's define a
new task module. Task module are prefixed with `Mix.Tasks` and
the filename uses . instead of underscores or dashes. Create the
following file `lib/mix/tasks/my.task.ex` with the following content.

```
defmodule Mix.Tasks.MyTask do
  use Mix.Task

  @impl Mix.Task
  def run(_arg) do
    IO.puts("Hello world, from a task!")
  end
end
```

Compile the task by running

```
$ mix compile
```

and then run it via

```
$ mix MyTask
Hello world, from a task!
```

This last approach, with tasks, should feel a bit confusing and overwhelming. We will cover these in greater detail later in the book. For now just know that this is *one* way you can get your code to run. I suggest you stick with script files for the earlier chapters until we start learning more about modules and Mix.

Chapter 3

Basic Syntax and Data Types

This chapter will give you just about everything you need to know to start writing some basic Elixir code. The more experience you have with programming, the more you will get out of this chapter. By the end of the chapter you will know how to do everything from iteration, branching, comments, basic pattern matching, and defining functions. If you are new to programming, take your time with this chapter. If you are a seasoned programmer, feel free to skim through it, spending more time on areas where the syntax is less familiar.

3.1 Syntax Basics

Elixir is a dynamic, functional programming language. This means it does not have static type checking like languages such as C++, Go, or Rust. Instead, the type of a variable is bound at runtime.

For example, consider the following ternary expression

```
iex> x = if false, do: 1, else: "hello"
"hello"
iex> y = if true, do: 1, else: "hello"
1
```

We can use the i command to inspect these two variables.

```
iex> i x
Term
  "hello"
Data type
  BitString
Byte size
  5
Description
  # Omitted

iex> i y
Term
  1
Data type
  Integer
Reference modules
  Integer
Implemented protocols
  IEx.Info, Inspect, List.Chars, String.Chars
```

Notice that even though the variables were assigned using the same expression, they have different types. This type of expression is also valid in Python (another dynamically typed language) but is not valid in languages like C++ or Rust, which are statically type-checked languages.

Languages are described as functional when they are designed to support and encourage functional programming paradigms. These paradigms first and foremost encourage immutable data and functions as first-class citizens. Immutable data means, for example, adding an element to a hash map results in a *new* hash map, rather than updating the original one. Functions as first-class citizen is a phrase to describe the ability to treat functions as data. You can assign them to variables, pass them into other functions, etc.

As a language built on top of the BEAM VM, Elixir shares some syntactic similarities with Erlang. However, it also introduces its own unique features and conventions. In this chapter we will cover the basics of Elixir syntax.

In Elixir, variables are declared using the equals sign (=), and their names must start with a lowercase letter or an underscore. For example

```
iex> x = 1
1
```

Elixir has a strong emphasis on immutability, which means that once a variable is assigned a value, it cannot be changed. Instead, you create a new variable with a different name to hold a new value. Within IEx, this can be a point of confusion for beginners.

Consider the following example:

```
iex> x = 1
1
iex> x = 2
2
iex> x
2
```

This seems to demonstrate the mutability of x. In fact, x is rebound. It may seem like splitting hairs between rebinding and mutability, but it's an important distinction. The original value of x is unchanged, but the reference for x has changed. Extending this example helps clarify the distinction:

```
iex> x = 1
1
iex> my_fun = fn -> x end
#Function<43.105768164/0 in :erl_eval.expr/6>
iex> x = 2
2
iex> my_fun.()
1
```

The original x remains unchanged, but at the outerscope, the reference x has been rebound to a different value. In other words, the original x and the rebound x can be thought of as different variables.

Let's contrast this to Python.

```
>>> x = 1
>>> def f():
...     return x
...
>>> f()
1
>>> x = 2
>>> f()
2
```

Elixir supports the standard arithmetic, comparison, and logical operations. Arithmetic operators include +, -, *, and /. Note that Elixir does not include the binary operators += and -= (like Python) nor does it include the unary operators ++ and -- (like C++). Remember, variables in Elixir or immutable and these operations are mutations. Comparison operators include ==, ===, !=, !==, <, >, <=, and >=. The operators === and !== are strict comparison operators. These really only differ from the standard operators when comparing integers to floats. The standard comparison operators == and != will perform a type case while the strict operators do not. For example

```
iex> 1 == 1.0
true
iex> 1 === 1.0
false
```

Logical operators include and and && for logical AND, or and || for logical OR, and ! and not for logical negation.

Bitwise operators are slightly different from what you might expect coming from a language like C or C++. Elixir uses &&& for bitwise AND, ||| for bitwise OR, ~~~ for bitwise negation, and <<< and >>> for left and right shift operators, respectively. As with most languages, these operations only work on integers.

Elixir expressions are typically written using parentheses to specify the order of evaluation. For example, (9 + 1) * 3 evaluates to 30.

Elixir also supports pipe operator |>. The pipe operator takes the result of the expression on its left side and passes it as the first argument to the function on its right side. Since data is immutable in Elixir, functions we think of as mutations return the new data, rather than mutating the original data. It is more natural to refer to these functions as transformations, rather than mutations. Let's look at a contrived example of transformation functions and the pipe operator.

```
iex> x = [1, 2, 3]
[1, 2, 3]
iex> x ++ [4, 5, 6]
[1, 2, 3, 4, 5, 6]
iex> x
[1, 2, 3]
iex> List.replace_at(x, 0, 42)
[42, 2, 3]
```

```
iex> x
[1, 2, 3]
```

Note how the call to List.replace_at(x, 0, 42) didn't mutate x but returned a new list. Now suppose we wanted to update our list twice. This is where the pipe operator comes in. We are also going to use an import to avoid having to prefix replace_at with List every time.

```
iex> import List
iex> x = [1, 2, 3]
[1, 2, 3]
iex> x |> replace_at(0, fn _ -> 42 end) |> replace_at(1, fn
↪    _ -> 43 end)
[42, 43, 3]
iex> x
[1, 2, 3]
```

Once again, notice that while replace_at/3 produced an updated list, it did not modify the original list referenced by x.

Aside

By the way, you will notice the notation List.replace_at/3 looks a little strange if you are coming for any language other than Erlang. The List. prefix is easy to guess – it's the module name. The /3 suffix indicates the number of arguments the function takes, also known as the function's *arity*.

What happens if you want to pipe data into a function, but not as the first argument? You can use then/2, which takes its first argument and passes it to its second argument. Suppose we defined the wrapper function Wacky.replace_at\3 as

```
defmodule Wacky do
  def replace_at(idx, xs, replace_fun) do
    List.replace_at(xs, idx, replace_fun)
  end
end
```

We've just swapped the positions of the list and the index. We can still pipe to this, but we have to use then/2

```
iex> [1, 2, 3] |> then(&Wacky.replace_at(0, &1, fn _ -> 42
↪   end))
[42, 2, 3]
```

We will talk about the weird & usage in a later section.

3.2 Comments

Comments in Elixir start with a hash symbol #. Elixir also supports documentation comments, which start with @moduledoc and @doc , followed by a triple-quoted string """(similar to Python multiline strings). The @moduledoc annotation generally follows defmodule and is used to provide module-level documentation. The @doc annotation comes *before* the def and is used to provide def documetnation. There is also @spec, which typically comes after the docs and provides the type signature of the def that follows.

```
defmodule Hello do
  @moduledoc """
  Contains a single function to tell the user hello.
  """

  @doc ~S"""
  Print hello

  ## Parameters
    - name: String of the name to print

  ## Examples
  The following is a doctest. We will learn more about this
  in the chapter on testing

    iex> say_hello("Alice")
    hello Alice!

  """
  @spec say_hello(String.t()) :: :ok
  def say_hello(name) do
    IO.puts("hello " <> name <> "!")
  end
end
```

Documentation comments support Markdown formatting. You will find the community somewhat split on the use of @spec. It is quite useful if you are using a language server. However, using guards in your function definition also makes the correct usage quite clear.

3.3 Functions

Elixir provides a number of ways for defining functions.

```
iex> add_3 = fn x1, x2, x3 ->
...>   x1 + x2 + x3
...> end
#Function<40.105768164/3 in :erl_eval.expr/6>
iex> add_3.(1, 2, 3) # note the . between the variable and
↪   the parentheses
6
```

The use of fn here is as an anonymous function (also referred to as a lambda function). The function itself has no name (hence "anonymous") but is referred by the variable add_3. Calling the anonymous function requires using a . between the variable name and the arguments. We can write this function even more concisely using the following notation

```
iex> add_3 = &(&1 + &2 + &3)
...>#Function<40.105768164/3 in :erl_eval.expr/6>
iex> add_3.(1, 2, 3)
6
```

This is referred to as capture syntax.

Aside from references to anonymous functions, there are no free functions in Elixir. Functions defined using def or defp must occur within a module. Modules are declared using defmodule.

Let's look at an example.

```
iex>def hello() do
...>"hello"
...>end
** (ArgumentError) cannot invoke def/2 outside module
    (elixir 1.17.2) lib/kernel.ex:6811:
    ↪   Kernel.assert_module_scope/3
    (elixir 1.17.2) lib/kernel.ex:5300: Kernel.define/4
    (elixir 1.17.2) expanding macro: Kernel.def/2
    iex:53: (file)
iex> defmodule Hello do
...>    def hello do
...>      "hello"
...>    end
...> end
{:module, Hello,
 <<70, 79, 82, 49, 0, ...>>, {:hello, 0}}
```

```
iex> Hello.hello()
"hello"
```

Note that we used def here instead of defp. defp is used for declaring private functions.

```
iex> defmodule Hello do
...>    defp private_hello do
...>      "a private hello"
...>    end
...> end
warning: function private_hello/0 is unused

{:module, Hello,
 <<70, 79, 82, 49, 0, ...>>, {:private_hello, 0}}
iex> Hello.private_hello()
** (UndefinedFunctionError) function Hello.private_hello/0
↪   is undefined or private
    Hello.private_hello()
    iex: (file)
```

There are two interesting things to note here. When we defined the module with an unused private function, Elixir warned us that this was unused. We didn't see this warning when we used def, because it was possible for that function to be used outside the module scope. In the defp case, Elixir was able to determine that private_hello will never be called. Also notice that we get an error when trying to call that function outside the module.

We will cover functions and modules in greater depth later in the book. This is the minimum information to get you started with playing around with functions.

3.4   Primitive Types

Elixir provides the same set of primitive data types that every other language provides. Primitive types include integers, floating-point numbers, booleans, atoms, and the special nil value. These types can be combined together in structs to create more complex data types.

Integers in Elixir are whole numbers that can be positive, negative, or zero. They can be written directly as literals, such as 42, −17, or 0. Elixir supports arbitrary-precision arithmetic, which means that integers can be as large as memory allows without any fixed limit. This is particularly useful for applications that require high precision or deal with very large numbers.

Floating-point numbers, or floats, represent real numbers with decimal points. In Elixir, floats are written with a decimal point, such as 3.14, −0.5, or 2.0. Floats are IEEE 754 double-precision floating-point numbers, providing a wide range and precision for representing fractional values.

Atoms are constants whose values are their own name. They are often used to represent named constants, finite states, or as keys in key-value data structures. Atoms start with a colon : followed by a sequence of letters, digits, underscores, or at signs. For example, :apple, :red, and :user_id are all valid atoms. Atoms are internally represented by an integer in a special atom table, which makes atom comparison and equality checks very efficient. However, atoms persist throughout the entire life of a program, so they should generally not be created en masse.

Booleans in Elixir are a special case of two atoms: :true and :false. That is, true is an alias for :true and false is an alias for :false. Elixir provides a set of logical operators, such as and, or, and not, to perform boolean operations and combine boolean expressions. Unlike other languages, Elixir does not treat empty collections or zero values as being falsey. Only false and :false evaluate as false.

```
iex> if true do "true" else "not true" end
"true"
iex> if false do "true" else "not true" end
"not true"
iex> if 0 do "true" else "not true" end
"true"
iex> if nil do "true" else "not true" end
"not true"
iex> if [] do "true" else "not true" end
"true"
```

The special nil value represents the absence of a value. Similar to true and false, nil is an alias for the atom :nil. As demonstrated above, nil is treated as a falsey value, meaning it evaluates to false in boolean contexts. This behavior is useful for conditional checks and default value assignments.

In addition to these primitive data types, Elixir also provides a range of composite data types, such as tuples, lists, and maps, which allow you to structure and organize data in more complex ways. These composite types are built upon the primitive types and offer powerful abstractions for working with collections and structured data. We will explore these in greater depth in the following sections.

3.5 Strings

Strings are one of the most fundamental and versatile data types in Elixir. They are used to store and manipulate text, such as user input, output messages, and data read from files or external sources. Elixir provides a rich set of functions and operators for working with strings, supporting operations like concatenation, splitting, and pattern matching.

In Elixir, strings are represented as a sequence of Unicode characters enclosed in double quotes. For example, `"Hello, world!"` is a valid string in Elixir. Like most things in Elixir, strings are immutable. That is, once a string is created, its contents cannot be changed. Instead, any operation that modifies a string returns a new string, leaving the original string unchanged (just as we saw with our list example earlier). This immutability ensures that strings are safe to use in concurrent and parallel programming scenarios. Multiple processes can access and manipulate strings without the risk of unexpected side effects.

One of the most common string operations is concatenation, which involves joining two or more strings together. In Elixir, string concatenation is performed using the <> operator. For example, `"Hello, " <> "world!"` evaluates to `"Hello, world!"`. The <> operator is efficient for concatenating small strings, but for building large strings incrementally, it's recommended to use the `IO.iodata_to_binary/1` function or the string interpolation syntax.

`IO.iodata_to_binary/1` takes a list of strings and concatenates them together. For example, `IO.iodata_to_binary(["Hello, ", "World!"])` returns the string `"Hello, World!"`.

String interpolation is a convenient way to embed expressions and variables within a string. In Elixir, string interpolation is done using the `#{}` syntax. Any valid Elixir expression can be placed inside the curly braces, and its value will be interpolated into the string. For example, `"Hello, #{name}!"` will replace `#{name}` with the value of the name variable. String interpolation is a powerful feature that allows for dynamic string construction and formatting.

Elixir provides a wide range of built-in functions for manipulating strings in the String module. Some commonly used functions include:

- `String.length/1` – Returns the number of Unicode graphemes in a string.
- `String.split/2` – Splits a string into a list of substrings based on a given pattern or delimiter.
- `String.replace/3` – Replaces occurrences of a substring within a string with another substring.
- `String.trim/1` – Removes leading and trailing whitespace from a string.
- `String.upcase/1` and `String.downcase/1` – Convert a string to uppercase or lowercase, respectively.

These functions, along with many others in the String module, provide a comprehensive toolset for working with strings in Elixir.

In addition to the String module, Elixir also supports sigils, which are a shorthand syntax for creating strings with specific characteristics. Sigils start with a tilde ~ followed by a letter and are delimited by a pair of matching characters. Some commonly used sigils include ~s for strings, ~c for character lists, and ~r for regular expressions. Sigils provide a concise and expressive way to create strings with special properties or behaviors.

The ~s sigil can be used to create multiline strings.

```
iex> ~s"Here is an
...> example
...> of a multiline
...> string"
"Here is an\nexample\nof a multiline\nstring"
```

You can also use ~s to delineate a string *without* double quotes, which lets you use double quotes within the string.

```
iex> ~s/Hello, "world!"/
"Hello \"world!\""
```

We use ~c to create character lists. For example, ~c(this is a character list). These are typically used when interoping with Erlang.

The ~w sigil is an interesting one. It is used to create a word list, where words whitespace separated.

```
iex> ~w(hello world)
["hello", "world"]
```

The ~r sigil changes the character escaping characteristics of the string, which is useful when dealing with regular expressions. Let's use the String.match?/2 function to demonstrate the use of ~r.

```
iex> String.match?("Hello", ~r/ello/)
true
iex> x = ~s/This
is a multiline
string/
"This\nis a multiline\nstring"
iex> String.match?(x, ~r/\n/)
true
```

Elixir provides a rich set of functions and capabilities when it comes to string handling and manipulation. It is out of the scope of this book to cover all functionality. Checkout the String module documentation to get a complete picture of what you can do with strings in Elixir.

3.6 Tuples and Lists

Tuples and lists are two fundamental data structures in Elixir. They allow you to group multiple values together. While they share some similarities, tuples and lists have distinct characteristics and use cases that make them suitable for different scenarios. Understanding the differences between tuples and lists is crucial for choosing the right data structure for your needs and writing efficient and idiomatic Elixir code.

Tuples are fixed-size collections of values enclosed in curly braces {}. They are typically used to group a fixed number of elements together, often representing a cohesive unit or structure. For example, you can use a tuple to represent a point in 2D space: {x, y}. You can think of tuples as fixed sized arrays. They are used in scenarios where they are storing fixed-lengthed data (e.g., a point in 2D space will *always* have only two components). Tuples are immutable (like all data in Elixir). In other languages, such as Python, the contents of the tuple can change but not the number of elements. Tuples are often used for destructuring data. This is true in many languages, such as Python.

To create a tuple, you simply list the desired elements within curly braces, separated by commas. For instance, {1, 2, 3} creates a tuple with three integers, and {:ok, "Hello"} creates a tuple with an atom and a string. You can access individual elements of a tuple using the Kernel.elem/2 function, which takes the tuple and the zero-based index of the element you want to retrieve. For example, elem({1, 2, 3}, 1) returns 2.

One handy feature of tuples is the ability to use them to destructure data. Consider the following example.

```
iex> x = {1, 2}
{1, 2}
iex> {a, b} = x
{1, 2}
iex> a
1
iex> b
2
```

This is paricularly useful when combined with pattern matching and case expressions, which we will cover later.

Lists, on the other hand, are dynamic, linked data structures that can hold any number of values. They are represented using square brackets [] and are commonly used for storing and manipulating collections of related data. Lists in Elixir are implemented as singly-linked lists That is, each element in the list contains a value and a pointer to the next element. This structure allows for efficient insertion and deletion of elements at the head of the list, but accessing elements by index requires traversing the list from the beginning, resulting in linear time complexity.

Creating a list is as simple as enclosing the desired elements within square brackets, separated by commas. For example, [1, 2, 3] creates a list with three integers, and ["apple", "banana", "orange"] creates a list of strings. Elixir provides the cons operator | for constructing lists by prepending an element to the head of an existing list. For instance, 1 | [2, 3] creates a new list [1, 2, 3]. You can also use the ++ operator to concatenate two lists together, like [1, 2] ++ [3, 4], which results in [1, 2, 3, 4].

One of the most powerful features of lists in Elixir is pattern matching. You can use pattern matching to destructure lists and bind variables to specific elements or sublists. For example, [head | tail] = [1, 2, 3] binds head to 1 and tail to [2, 3]. This allows you to easily extract elements from a list and work with them separately. Pattern matching is a fundamental concept in Elixir and is extensively used when working with lists and other data structures.

```
iex> my_list = [1, 2, 3]
[1, 2, 3]
iex> [head | tail] = my_list
[1, 2, 3]
iex> head
1
iex> tail
[2, 3]
```

It is worth pointing out that this idiom is quite common among functional languages. Just about every functional language supports this general operation of getting the head or tail of a list. A few languages, like OCaml and Haskell, support this exact syntax.

Elixir provides a rich set of functions for working with lists in the List module. Some commonly used functions include:

- List.first/1 and List.last/1 – Retrieve the first or last element of a list.
- List.delete/2 and List.delete_at/2 – Remove a specific element or an element at a given index from a list.
- List.flatten/1 – Flatten a nested list structure into a single-level list.
- List.foldl/3 and List.foldr/3 – Perform a left or right fold operation on a list, useful for reducing a list to a single value.

Let's try these out

```
iex> x = [1, 2, 3]
[1, 2, 3]
iex> List.first x
1
iex> List.delete(x, 1)
[1, 3]
iex> x
[1, 2, 3]
iex> List.flatten [x, x]
[1, 2, 3, 1, 2, 3]
iex> List.foldl(x, 0, &(&1 + &2))
```

6

The last example uses the capture operator to create the anonymous function. The function `List.foldl/3` takes a list, a starting value, and a function that combines two values, the element and the accumulator. The syntax `&(&1 + &2)` is equivalent to `fn x, acc -> x + acc end` where `&1` refers to the first argument and `&2` refers to the second.

The List module provides a powerful toolset for manipulating and transforming lists in Elixir. We will explore tuples and lists in greater detail, later on in this book.

3.7 Comprehensions

Comprehensions use the `for` special form[1] followed by a generator expression. A generator takes the form

```
some_var_or_pattern <- some_enumerable
```

That is, on the left-hand side of `<-`, we use either a variable or pattern matching expression. On the right-hand side we use any enumerable.

When using a pattern on the left-hand side, all elements that *don't* match the pattern are skipped.

The `do`-block of the `for` form specifies what you want to do with the matched values.

By default, comprehensions return a list. We will see later in this section that you can use comprehensions to create just about any collection.

```
iex> for x <- 0..5, do: x
[0, 1, 2, 3, 4]
```

---

[1]Special forms in Elixir are part of the `Kernel` module. They are a core set of keywords and symbols that have a fixed implementation. For example, as we just learned, `for` is apparently a special form that, and its implementation is fixed (it is used to create comprehensions). The pin operator, `^`, is also a special form. Special forms don't need to be imported because they provide a large portion of Elixir's core functionality.

Let's look at another example where we filter out some values based on their pattern.

```
iex> for {:ok, x} <- [{:ok, 1}, {:error}, {:ok, 42},
↪ {:error}], do: x
[1, 42]
```

We can also filter using a boolean expression to the right of the enumerable

```
iex> for x <- [0..5], rem(x, 2) == 0, do: x
[0, 2, 4]
```

We can also stack generators.

```
iex> for x <- 0..2, y <- 3..5, do: {x,y}
[
  {0, 3},
  {0, 4},
  {0, 5},
  {1, 3},
  {1, 4},
  {1, 5},
  {2, 3},
  {2, 4},
  {2, 5}
]
iex> for y <- 3..5, x <- 0..2, do: {x,y}
[
  {0, 3},
  {1, 3},
  {2, 3},
  {0, 4},
  {1, 4},
  {2, 4},
  {0, 5},
  {1, 5},
  {2, 5}
]
```

In both cases we cover the same values, just in different orders. That is, as you stack generators, they act as nested for-loops from other languages. The first generator is the outer scope (or for-loop). Each generator below gets nested. For every value in the first generator, the succeeding generators will get completely executed. This is most obvious in the first example.

Comprehensions and Strings

Iterating over the characters of the string require us to use bit strings. As with most modern languages that support various character encodings such as UTF-8 or UTF-16, the concept of a *character* is not always straight forward. Let's look at a trivial example.

```
iex> for <<c <- "hello world">>, do: <<c>>
["h", "e", "l", "l", "o", " ", "w", "o", "r", "l", "d"]
```

:into

If you are coming from a language like Python or Ruby, the idea of comprehensions will be familiar. At this point in the section you might be wondering about comprehensions into data structures other than lists, such as maps. Unsurprisingly, Elixir supports this as well. All that is required is using the :into option with your comprehension. Let's look at an example where we use a comprehension to create a `Map`.

```
iex> for n <- 0..10, into: %{}, do: {n, "#{n}"}
%{
  0 => "0",
  1 => "1",
  2 => "2",
  3 => "3",
  4 => "4",
  5 => "5",
  6 => "6",
  7 => "7",
  8 => "8",
  9 => "9",
  10 => "10"
}
```

This can also be combined with filtering

```
iex> for n <- 0..10, rem(n, 2) == 0, into: %{}, do: {n,
↪    "#{n}"}
%{0 => "0", 2 => "2", 4 => "4", 6 => "6", 8 => "8", 10 =>
↪    "10"}
```

Any data structure that implements the `Collectable` protocol can be used with :into.

:uniq

The :uniq option guarnatees that the values returned from the comprehension are unique. There's not much else to say about this option. Let's just look at an example and move on.

```
iex> for _ <- 0..10, do: 1
[1, 1, 1, 1, 1, 1, 1, 1, 1, 1, 1]

iex> for _ <- 0..10, uniq: true, do: 1
[1]
```

:reduce

The :reduce option is similar to :into, but offers greater flexibility. Similar to usage of Enum.reduce/3 we saw earlier in this chapter, this works on the idea of an accumulator.

Let's consider an example. Suppose we wanted to determine if two words were anagrams of eachother.[2] Two words are anagrams if you can rearrange the letters of one word to spell the other word. This is true when the frequencies of their letters are equivalent.

```
defmodule Words do
  def char_freqs(word) do
    for <<c <- word>>, reduce: %{} do
      acc -> Map.update(acc, <<c>>, 1, &(&1 + 1))
    end
  end

  def are_anagrams(word1, word2) do
    char_freqs(word1) == char_freqs(word2)
  end
end
```

3.8   with

with is yet *another* special form. It is an incredibly useful tool in keeping your code linear, simple, and easier to read. with lets you stack match clauses sequentially, only moving on to the next pattern if the previous pattern matched. The result is you can avoid nesting

---

[2]Why would you want to do this? Anytime you want to interview for a job I guess. Otherwise you'd really only do this if you were trying to come up with a mildly interesting example while writing a book.

pattern matching expressions and instead user a single expression. Let's take a look at some examples.

Let's define two toy modules representing two services. The first service, UserService fetches a user object (represented by a map). The second service, ApiService, takes the user object and performs an API request on its behalf.

```
# src/basics/with.exs
defmodule UserService do
  def get_user(id) do
    if id == 1 do
      {:ok, %{name: "Alice"}}
    else
      {:error, :not_found}
    end
  end
end

defmodule MyAPI do
  def get_data(user, should_fail \\ false) do
    unless should_fail do
      {:ok, %{user: user, data: "[some data]"}}
    else
      {:error, :internal_server_error}
    end
  end
end
```

The problem we frequently encounter with pattern matching is that our code can get very "branchy" with each pattern we need to match or destructure. Code branches can be bad for two reasons. A common issue people cite is each branch incurs a performance penalty. Technically true, but it's unlikely most readers of this book will ever encounter a situation where too many if statements impact the performance of their code (plus CPU branch predictors are incredibly good!).

The real problem with "branchy" code is it can be quite difficult to read. This adds to the visual and logical complexity of the code. If you take nothing away from this book that the following, it will be well worth the money. *Always* strive for visual and logical simplicity. No one will ever see your terse, information dense, hard to read code and think "wow this guy is a genius!" Quite the opposite. They will likely sigh, contemplate their life choices, check reddit, and then decide to suck it up and try to figure what the hell your code is doing and why in God's name you decided to make it so hard to understand.[3] Before I get off my soapbox, just remember this: the easier your code is to read (it should look clean and elegant!) the easier it will be to understand. The engineers I've worked with whose code was understood by everyone were also the engineers that earned the most respect from their peers.

Building on our example, here's what it would look like if we first get the user, handling a potential error, and then make the API call, also handling the potential error.

```
case UserService.get_user(1) do
  {:ok, user} ->
    case MyAPI.get_data(user) do
      {:ok, %{user: user, data: data}} ->
        IO.puts("got data: #{data} for user: #{user.name}")
      {:error, :internal_server_error} ->
        IO.puts("Internal server error")
    end
  {:error, :not_found} ->
    IO.puts("User not found")
end
```

That's two function calls and we are already dealing with two different error paths in two different blocks. This is workable, but it leaves less space in your brain to figure out the remaining parts of the code.

Forutnately, Elixir gives us with for exactly this kind of scenario. Let's re-write this example using with.

```
with {:ok, user} <- UserService.get_user(1),
     {:ok, %{user: user, data: data}} <-
     ↪ MyAPI.get_data(user),
     %{name: name} = user do
  IO.puts("got data: #{data} for user: #{name}")
else
  {:error, :not_found} -> IO.puts("User not found")
  {:error, :internal_server_error} -> IO.puts("Internal
  ↪ server error")
end
```

The result is dramatically cleaner code. Each match clause inside with gets matched in order, its results available for the following

---

[3]I really think all of us have been here. But in case you haven't there are two possibilities. You are either incredibly lucky or you are the one writing this obscure code. I've worked with engineers like this on a number of occasions and they are the bane of every other engineer's existence.

clauses. The other benefit of this form is the error block is linear. That is, each error we might encounter is grouped with all the others.

3.9 import, require, and use

Functions are the basic building blocks of Elixir. As we saw in an earlier section, you cannot define functions outside of modules in Elixir. One question we haven't addressed is how we access functions from other modules.

The simplest approach to access functions from other modules is to use the fully-qualified name of the function. The fully-qualified name is the complete chain of modules, separated by dots, followed by the function name. For example, if you have a module `MyModule` with a public function named `my_function`, the fully-qualified name is `MyModule.my_function`. If you use this fully-qualified name when calling a function, you do not need to import anything.

What if you don't want to use the fully-qualified name? You have two options. You can import the module using `import`. This imports *all* functions from the module.

```
defmodule SomeOtherModule do
  import MyModule # <- imports all public functions from
  ↪  MyModule

  def some_function() do
    some_other_function()
  end
end
```

`import` is lexically scoped, meaning the imports will only be visible within the context (think code block) in which the import is done. If you `import` at the module level, the imported functions are available to the entire module. If you use `import` within a function body, the imported functions are only available within the function body.

Sometimes this is what you want, though in general, it probably isn't. We have three different techniques to avoid importing everything.

The first is to only import the specific functions we need.

```
defmodule SomeOtherModule do
  import MyModule, only: [some_other_function: 0]
```

```
def some_function() do
  some_other_function()
end
end
```

Here we use the only:, followed by a keyword list of function name to arity mapping. As you might have guessed, this *only* imports the functions named in the keyword list. Alternatively, we could use except:, followed by a keyword list of function name to arity to import everything from the module *except* the listed functions.

A final approach to avoiding a fully-qualified name is to alias the module using alias. *Most of the time* this is what you want. Using alias requires the fully-qualified module name followed by a comma, as: and the alias name (which should start with a capital letter). Let's look at an example.

```
defmodule SomeOtherModule do
  alias MyModule, as: MM

  def some_function() do
    MM.some_other_function()
  end
end
```

You will also commonly use the require keyword . As we mentioned earlier, public functions are globally available. That is, as long as you use the fully-qualified name you can access a public function anywhere without having to import it. This is not true of macros. If you want to use a macro define in a module, say MyModule, you must first first require the module. Once you have required the module, you still need to fully-qualify the macro. For example

```
defmodule SomeOtherModule do
  require MyModule

  def some_function
    MyModule.my_macro()
  end
end
```

Like import, require is also lexically scoped.

The use macro is a little different from import and require. First, it is *not* lexically scoped. Second, use injects code into your module, which can (and typically does). This is what happens when you add lines like use GenServer or use Supervisor to your modules. Those lines inject some code into your module, changing its behavior.

3.10 Immutability

Immutability is a core aspect to functional programming languages like Elixir. Once a value is assigned to a variable, that value cannot be changed. Operations in Elixir create new versions of the data instead of modifying existing data. This immutability applies to all data types in Elixir, including primitives, tuples, lists, and more complex structures.

Immutability offers a number of benefits. Code is easier to reason about. Once a value is set, you can be confident it won't change. Immutability also enables safer concurrent programming, as multiple processes can access shared data without the risk of race conditions or inconsistent states.

In Elixir, when you perform an operation that seems to modify a data structure, it is actually returning a new version of that structure with the changes applied. We have seen this a number of times throughout this book. For example, consider adding an element to a list:

```
list1 = [1, 2, 3]
list2 = [4 | list1]
```

In this code, list1 remains unchanged as [1, 2, 3], while list2 is a new list [4, 1, 2, 3] that shares some structure with list1. This sharing of underlying structure is an optimization technique known as structural sharing, which allows efficient memory usage and fast creation of new versions of data. Figure 3.1 shows an example of structural sharing.

Immutability is particular important here. If the data *was* mutable, then changing list1 would have the side-effect of changing list2. One of the main goals of immutability is to eliminate side-effects.

Immutability also influences how you approach problem-solving in Elixir. Instead of relying on mutable state and in-place modifications, you often use recursion and higher-order functions [4] to

---

[4]A *higher-order function* is a function that either takes one or more functions

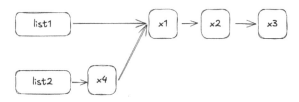

Figure 3.1: An illustration of structural sharing.

transform data. Recursive functions, which call themselves with updated arguments until a base case is reached, are a natural fit for working with immutable data structures. Higher-order functions like map, filter, and reduce allow you to express complex operations on collections in a declarative and immutable way.

While immutability is the default in Elixir, there are times when you need to manage mutable state, such as in system interactions or performance-critical code. Elixir provides mechanisms like the Process dictionary and ETS (Erlang Term Storage) tables for these situations. Just remember to use mutable state sparingly and judiciously, as it can introduce complexity and make reasoning about the code more difficult. If you are working on a team, others will expect immutability from your code. Violating that will eventually lead to bugs and heartache.

3.11   Finding Help

Hex Docs (hexdocs.pm) is the official documentation on Elixir. The documentation is simple, clear, and well written. This should generally be the first place you look when looking for documentation.

When using IEx, there is the h function, which prints the documentation for the respective function.

```
iex> h Enum.map

                    def map(enumerable, fun)

  @spec map(t(), (element() -> any())) :: list()

Returns a list where each element is the result of invoking
  ↪    fun on each
```

as input, or returns a function.

corresponding element of enumerable.

For maps, the function expects a key-value tuple.

Examples

```
iex> Enum.map([1, 2, 3], fn x -> x * 2 end)
[2, 4, 6]

iex> Enum.map([a: 1, b: 2], fn {k, v} -> {k, -v} end)
[a: -1, b: -2]
```

There is also the Elixir Forum (elixirforum.com), which is very active, in addition to reddit (r/elixir), Slack, and Discord communities.

Chapter 4

Collections

4.1   Lists

Lists are a fundamental data structure in Elixir. Since Elixir is
dynamically typed, you can store elements of different types in an
array. This may be strange coming from a statically type-checked
language like C++ or Java, but familiar if you are coming from
Ruby or Python. As we saw earlier, lists are defined with square
brackets [].

Lists in Elixir are implemented with linked lists. If you are unfa-
miliar with linked lists, they are chain of nodes where each node
contains a value and a link to the next node. They are a very
popular data structure in functional languages. Linked lists work
well when you don't need random access to the list. Operations like
inserting or deleting at the head of the list are $O(1)$ operations while
random access is $O(n)$ (the list must be traversed to the respective
element).

Elixir provides the typical set of list operations. The ++ operator
concatenates two lists together, creating a new list that contains
all the elements from both lists. For example, [1, 2, 3] ++ [4,
5] yields [1, 2, 3, 4, 5]. The -- operator, on the other hand, is
used to subtract elements from a list, creating a new list with the
specified elements removed. For example, [1, 2, 3, 4, 5] -- [2,
4] yields [1, 3, 5]. Note that if the array on the right hand side of
-- contains elements not in the left hand side array, thos elements

are ignore.

Elixir also provides the pipe operator |. This is used to prepend a fixed number of elements to the head of a list. For example

```
iex> xs = [3, 4]
[3, 4]
iex> [1 | 2 | xs]
[1, 2, 3, 4]
```

The advantage of the pipe operator (|) is that it is much faster than appending. Remember, lists in Elixir are backed by a linked list data structure. Linked lists support constant time ($O(1)$) insertions at the head, but linear time ($O(n)$) appends on the tail.

As you have seen earlier in the book, a common pattern for pattern matching with lists is matching on the head and tail. The head refers to the first element in the list. The tail refers to everything after the first element. The head refers to the first element of the list, while the tail represents the rest of the list (i.e., all elements except the head). Elixir provides two functions, hd/1 and tl/1, to retrieve the head and tail of a list, respectively.

```
iex> x = [1, 2, 3]
[1, 2, 3]
iex> hd(x)
1
iex> tl(x)
[2, 3]
```

As we saw earlier, we can also pattern match on the list with the pattern [head | tail] (note you can use whatever variable names you want).

The other piece that may not be immediately obvious is the ordering of the parameters to the reducer function used in Enum.reduce. The parameter acc, which is short for accumulator, holds the accumulated value. The first reducer, fn x, acc -> 2 * x + acc end doubles the elements of xs and sums them. The second reduce, fn x, acc -> x + acc end simply sums the elements.

4.2 Tuples

Tuples are another fundamental data structure in Elixir. We use tuples to group a fixed number of related elements together. For example, this could be an status and element when getting a value from a function (e.g., {:ok, 42}). It could also be coordinates, such as {x, y, z} in 3 dimensional space. Tuples are represented using curly braces {}, with elements separated by commas. For example, {1, 2, 3} is a tuple of three integers, and {"Alice", 25, "New York"} is a tuple containing a string, an integer, and another string.

One of the key characteristics of tuples is that they have a fixed size. This size is determiend when the tuple is created. Tuples cannot change their size once they are defined. Lists, on the other hand, can dynamically change their size. This fixed size property makes tuples useful for representing fixed collections of related data, such as a date {year, month, day}.

Accessing elements in a tuple is done using pattern matching or the Kernel.elem/2 function. We can extract the first element of a tuple via x = elem({1, 2}, 0). With pattern matching, we can destructure a tuple and bind its elements to variables. For example, {x, y} = {1, 2} binds x to 1 and y to 2. You will most likely find yourself reaching for destructuring rather than Kernel.elem/2.

Tuples are often used to return multiple values from a function. In Elixir, as in many languages, functions can only return a single value. Returning a tuple can be an effective way to return multiple values. However, it's generally good to keep returned tuples small. When you need to return a more complex data structure it is better to reach for a map or struct.

Another common use case for tuples is to represent tagged values. By convention, the first element of the tuple is used as a tag or label, describing the meaning or type of the data stored in the following elements. For example, {:ok, result} and {:error, reason} are commonly used to represent the success or failure of an operation, respectively.

Tuples are also used in pattern matching to selectively match and extract values based on their structure. You can use the _ placeholder to match any value in a specific position, or use variables to bind values to names. This makes tuples powerful for handling different cases or conditions based on the structure of the data.

Note that, unlike lists, tuples are stored contiguously in memory. This means that accessing elements in a tuple is a constant-time operation. However, modifying a tuple requires creating a new tuple with the updated values, as tuples are immutable.

4.3 Maps

Elixir also provides a key-value data structure called a map. This data structure lets you associate a name (key) with a value. You can reason about them as hash tables, though they don't share the same time complexity. Similar to hash tables, maps in Elixir are unordered.

Maps are represented using the %{} syntax, where keys and values are separated by the => operator. Keys in a map must be unique, ensuring that each key maps to a single value. Unlike statically typed languages, Elixir maps can have different types for the values. For example, %{"name" => "Alice", "age" => 25} is a valid map. When the key of the map is an atom, you can use key: value shorthand. Let's look at some examples.

```
iex> %{"hello" => "world"}
%{"hello" => "world"}
iex> %{hello: "world"}
%{hello: "world"}
iex> %{42 => "world"}
%{42 => "world"}
```

The main advantage of maps is that they provide fast key-based access to values. Unlike lists, where you need to traverse the entire list to find a specific element, maps allow you to directly access a value by its corresponding key.

For small maps (less than 32 keys), these are implemented as a sorted array of tuples. Large maps are implemented as hash array mapped tries (HAMTs). The access complexity is $O(\lg_3 2n)$. HAMTs are a data structure that combines the benefits of hash tables and tries, allowing for fast insertion, deletion, and lookup operations. This makes maps efficient even when dealing with large amounts of data.

You can access values in a map using bracket notation [], Map.get/3, or Map.fetch/2. If the key doesn't exist in the map, Elixir returns nil. Let's look at some examples.

```
iex> m = %{hello: "world", forty_two: 42}
%{hello: "world", forty_two: 42}
iex> m[:hello]
"world"
```

```
iex> m[:world]
nil
iex> Map.get(m, :forty_two)
42
iex> Map.get(m, :world)
nil
iex> Map.fetch(m, :hello)
{:ok, "world"}
iex> Map.fetch(m, :world)
{:error}
```

Both square bracket access and `Map.get/3` work similarly. Fetching an key that doesn't exist in the map returns `nil`. However, `Map.get/3` takes an optional third argument that provides a default value when the requestsed key doesn't exist.

```
iex> m = %{}
%{}
iex> Map.get(m, "hello", 42)
42
```

On the other hand, `Map.fetch/2` returns the status of the fetch along with, optionally, the element (when it exists). If you've used maps in Go, this will feel familiar.

Assertive vs Non-assertive Map Access

One more access pattern you can use with maps is the so called `map.key` notation. We refer to this as assertive access. It indicates that `key` is expected to be a key in the map `map`.

For example

```
iex> m = %{hello: "world"}
%{hello: "world"}
iex> m.hello
"world"
iex> m.world
** (KeyError) key :world not founc in: %{hello: "world"}
```

If you expect a value in a map, whether due to convention, or prior logic, you should prefer assertive access.

Updating values in a map is also straightforward. You can use the `%{map | key => value}` syntax to update the value associated with a specific key. This creates a new map with the updated value, leaving the original map unchanged.

```
iex> m = %{forty_two: 42}
%{forty_two: 42}
iex> m2 = %{m | forty_two: "forty two"}
%{forty_two: "forty two"}
```

We can also use `Map.put/3` for inserts, returning a new map.

```
iex> m = %{}
%{}
iex> Map.put(m, "hello", "world")
%{"hello" => "world"}
iex> m
%{}
```

Two other commonly used functions are `Map.delete/2` for deleting key-value pairs, and `Map.merge/2` for merging two maps. These work exactly as you might expect.

```
iex> Map.delete(%{hello: "world"}, :hello)
%{}
iex> Map.merge(%{one: 1}, %{two: 2})
%{two: 2, one: 1}
```

Maps are often used to represent structured data or configurations in Elixir. They provide a clean and readable way to organize related data, making the code more expressive and self-explanatory. Maps are also commonly used in Elixir libraries and frameworks for configuration purposes, such as specifying application settings or defining environment-specific values.

4.4   Keyword Lists

Keyword lists are a special type of list that consists of key-value pairs, where the keys are atoms. Keyword lists are defined using the syntax [key: value, ...]. For example, [name: "Alice", age: 42] is a keyword list with keys :name and :age. Keyword lists are commonly used for passing options to functions, as they provide a convenient and flexible way to represent optional parameters.

One of the main characteristics of keyword lists is that they are ordered. Unlike maps, which are unordered key-value data structures, keyword lists maintain the order in which the key-value pairs are defined. This means that the elements in a keyword list can be accessed by their index, just like in a regular list. What is unique about keyword lists is they can also be indexed via their key. Let's look at a few examples.

```
iex> l = [one: 1, two: 2]
[one: 1, two: 2]
iex> l[:one]
1
iex> Enum.at(l, 1)
2
iex> Keyword.get(l, :two)
2
iex> l[:three]
nil
iex> Keyword.get(l, :three, 3)
3
```

Another important property of keyword lists is that they allow duplicate keys. Unlike maps, where each key must be unique, keyword lists can have multiple key-value pairs with the same key. When duplicate keys are present, the value associated with the first occurrence of the key is used. This behavior is useful in scenarios where you want to pass multiple values for the same option.

Elixir provides a number of functions in the Keyword module for working with keyword lists. Some of the more commonly used functions include:

- `Keyword.put/3` – Adds a new key-value pair to the keyword list.
- `Keyword.delete/2` – Removes a key-value pair from the keyword list.
- `Keyword.merge/2` – Merges two keyword lists, with the values from the second list taking precedence.
- `Keyword.keys/1` – Returns a list of all the keys in the keyword list.
- `Keyword.values/1` – Returns a list of all the values in the keyword list.

Since keyword lists are implemented as lists, accessing a value by its key requires a linear search through the list, which has a time complexity of $O(n)$. This means that keyword lists are not as performant as maps when it comes to key-based access for large lists. For small lists, there will not be a material difference in performance.

How do you know when to use a keyword list versus a map? As with most things, use what makes sense. Do you need to handle duplicate keys? Use a keyword list. Are you using the data structure to pass options to a function? Again, you probably want a keyword list. Building a frequency map over a large collection of items? You most certainly want a map.

4.5   Sets

Sets are another useful data structure that allow you to store unique elements in an unordered fashion. You can think of a set as a hash map without the values. Sets are represented using the MapSet module, which provides a variety of functions for working with sets. The key characteristic of sets is that they only contain unique elements, meaning that duplicates are automatically removed when added to a set. This property makes sets ideal for scenarios where you need to ensure the uniqueness of elements and perform operations like membership tests, unions, intersections, and differences.

To create a set in Elixir, you can use the `MapSet.new/0` function, which returns an empty set. You can also create a set from an existing enumerable (such as a list) using the `MapSet.new/1` function. Let's look at a couple of examples

```
iex> MapSet.new
MapSet.net([])
iex> MapSet.new([1, 2, 3, 3, 3])
MapSet.new([1, 2, 3])
```

Adding elements to a set is done using the `MapSet.put/2` function. This function takes a set and an element as arguments and returns a new set with the element added. If the element already exists in the set, the set remains unchanged.

```
iex> s1 = MapSet.new
MapSet.new([])
iex> s2 = MapSet.put(s1, 3)
MapSet.new([3])
iex> s3 = MapSet.put(s2, 4)
MapSet.new([3, 4])
iex> s4 = MapSet.put(s3, 3)
MapSet.new([3, 4])
```

Sets in Elixir support various set operations, such as union, intersection, and difference.

- `MapSet.union/2` – returns a new set that contains all the elements from two sets combined.
- `MapSet.intersection/2` – returns a new set that contains only the elements that are common to both sets.
- `MapSet.difference/2` – returns a new set that contains the elements from the first set that are not present in the second set.

One of the most common actions taken on a set is determining set membership. You can do that with the `MapSet.member?/2` function.

```
iex> s = MapSet.new([1, 2, 3])
MapSet.new([1, 2, 3])
iex> MapSet.member?(s, 2)
true
```

Under the hood, MapSet is implemented using Map. This means insertion, deletion, checking membership, and fetching elements takes $O(\lg n)$ time. For small sets (fewer than 32 elements), similar to Maps, MapSet is backed by an array and the time complexities degrade to linear ($O(n)$). At these sizes, however, the impact of linear search is negligible (and in many cases better).

There are a few other functions from the MapSet module worth mentioning.

- `MapSet.size/1` provides the size of the set.
- `MapSet.subset?/2` takes two sets and returns `true` if the first argument is a subset of the second argument, and `false` otherwise.
- `Mapset.equal?/2` returns `true` when the two sets are equal (i.e., they contain the same elements), and `false` otherwise.
- `MapSet.disjoin?/2` return `true` when the to sets do not overlap (i.e, their intersection is empty), and `false` otherwise.

Admittedly, outside of `MapSet.size/1`, you will use these other functions less frequently. The most common uses of sets (and by extension, `MapSet`) are deduplication of values or keeping track of previously processed values.

4.6   Erlang Collections

Elixir has access to everything in Erlang. You can access Erlang functions just like you would Elixir function, you just prefix the module name with a colon (`:`). There are two modules in Erlang that are useful to know in Elixir: `array` and `queue`.

array

Erlang arrays are largely the same as other array implementations you have used. For example, they are 0 indexed (meaning the first element is at index 0). Arrays are dynamically sized, meaning they will grow as needed. This is similar to how arrays work in other languages like Java, Python, and Ruby.

You create a new array via `:array.new/0`, which will create an empty array. If you want to create an array that has a given size, simply provide the size to `:array.new/2`.

There is one aspect the Erlang's array that will feel weird for just about everyone: you can insert into any index in the array, regardless of array size. Inserting into an index that is larger than the current array size will simply cause the array to allocate enough space to hold the value. A natural question at this point is "what does Erlang put in all the allocated but unused spots in the array?" The atom `:undefined` is used as a placeholder.

Let's take a look:

```
iex> a = :array.new()
{:array, 0, 10, :undefined, 10}
iex> a = :array.set(0, 1, a)
{:array, 1, 10, :undefined,
 {1, :undefined, :undefined, :undefined, :undefined,
 ↪ :undefined, :undefined,
  :undefined, :undefined, :undefined}}
iex> :array.size(a)
1
iex> a = :array.set(11, 42, a)
{:array, 12, 100, :undefined,
 {{1, :undefined, :undefined, :undefined, :undefined,
 ↪ :undefined, :undefined,
  :undefined, :undefined, :undefined},
 {:undefined, 42, :undefined, :undefined, :undefined,
 ↪ :undefined, :undefined,
  :undefined, :undefined, :undefined}, 10, 10, 10, 10, 10,
 ↪ 10, 10, 10, 10}}
```

```
iex> :array.size(a)
12
```

Notice that when we set the value at index 11 to 42, the array size grows to 12. This is not surprising since we are using 0-based indexing. The 11 index is the twelfth item.

The internal representation of Erlang's array is a tree of tuples. Each tuple stores 10 elements or it stores tuples. This means that although random access is faster than using a list, it is not $O(1)$ like in typical array implementations (e.g., Python, Ruby, C++, etc. arrays).

For most tasks, you probably want a list. If you are going to be making a lot of random accesses, then array makes sense. If you are in a situation where you start to care about cache effects, specific memory allocation patterns, etc. then you are probably using the wrong tool (Elixir) for the job (or you should explore Elixir's NIFs).

queue

The queue module provides a double-ended queue. The API for queue is quite extensive and I encourage you to check it out on . We will cover a few of the essentials.

Before we dive into the API, I should briefly touch on performance. *Most* operations are $O(1)$ amortized. The notable exception to this is the function :queue.len/1, which, surprisingly, is $O(n)$ (for good reason, apparently). The other functions that are not $O(1)$ are functions you would not expect to be $O(1)$. For example, functions like :queue.all/2 or :queue.any/2 or not $O(1)$, but that's not too surprising.

First things first, how do we insert?

- :queue.in/2 - takes an item and a queue and appends the item to the rear of the queue.'
- :queue.in_r/2 - same as queue:in/2, but the item is added to the front of the queue.

Similarly, we get items from the queue using:

- :queue.out/1 - takes a queue and returns a 2-tuple {{:value, elem}, new_q} where elem is the element at the end of the queue and new_q is the old queue without the last element. If the queue is empty, the returned 2-tuple is {:empty, q}.

- `:queue.out_r/1` - same as `:queue:out_r/1` but returns the last element.

Chapter 5

Modules and Structs

5.1 Modules

Modules are the fundamental unit of code organization and reusability in Elixir. They provide a way to group related functions, macros, structs, and other modules together into a single, cohesive unit. They also serve as namespaces, preventing naming conflicts between functions and allowing for better organization of code.

The `defmodule` keyword keyword is used to define a module in Elixir.

```
defmodule MyModule do
  # Module contents
end
```

Module names are typically written in PascalCase, with each word capitalized. For example, a module for handling user authentication might be named `UserAuthentication`. Inside the module definition, you can define functions, macros, structs, and even nested modules.

One of the key benefits of using modules is that they provide a way to encapsulate related functionality. Modules make it easier to group related functions and macros, which makes it easier to reasona about and maintain your codebase. This encapsulation also promotes code reuse, as modules can be easily shared across different parts of your application or even across different projects.

A Note on Naming

Recall that there are no free functions in Elixir. Every function must be associated with a module. When naming your module, name it with consideration to how it will be used. Let's look at the standard library `Map` module. Perhaps it's an unfair example because there aren't too many alternatives for naming a map. Regardless, when paired with its functions, there is a very clear and concise flow: `Map.insert`, `Map.get`, and so on.

Where am I going with this? Well, suppose you were to create a module to manage a connection with some external service. You might name it `MyConnection` and that's probably a reasonable name. When it comes to function names within that module, they should create a similar, simple flow like we saw with `Map`. Functions like `MyConnection.start`, `MyConnection.init`, or `MyConnection.new` are all pretty good. On the other hand, `MyConnection.connect` does not read well.

Naming is one of the hardest parts of programming. My best advice is to not over think it, use proper grammar, and always welcome feedback.

5.2   Attributes

Module attributes allow developers to annotate modules with metadata and define compile-time constants. Attributes are key-value pairs that are specified within a module using the @ symbol prefixing the attribute name. The attribute value follows the attribute name. These attributes can serve various purposes, such as providing documentation, specifying module-specific settings, or defining constants that can be used throughout the module.

Elixir provides a number of attributes for you, many of which are used to provide documentation of some sort. The `@moduledoc` attribute allows you to provide a high-level description of the module's purpose and functionality. You typically see this documentation at the top of the module definition. This documentation can be accessed using the `h` function in IEx or through documentation generation tools like ExDoc.

There is also the `@doc` attribute, which provides documentation on a function or macro. This is located right before the function clause, similar to javadoc (if you are familiar with that) or how functions are documented in languages like C++, Go, etc. The @doc attribute describes what the function does, its parameters, return values, and so on.

Both @moduledoc and @doc use multiline strings (triple-quoted strings similar to Python's multiline strings). These are referred to as heredocs.

```
defmodule JeffsModule do
  @moduledoc """
  Provides a number of functions that allow Jeff to interact
  ↪  with the reader.

  ## Examples
    iex> JeffsModule.say_hello()
    "Helo, my name is Jeff!"

  """

  @doc """
  Says hello to the reader
  """
  def say_hello() do
    IO.puts "Hello, my name is Jeff!"
  end
end
```

There is the @spec attribute , which is used to provide a typespec for the respective function. However, keep in mind that Elixir is a dynamically typed language so the typespecs are only used for documentation. The Elixir compiler will never use type information for any kind of compile-time optimization.

Typespecs using the @spec attribute have the pattern @spec <function_name>(<function_args>) :: <return_type>. I recommend spending some time looking at the typespec documentation (https://hexdocs.pm/elixir/typespecs.html). There is some disagreement within the community as to whether typespecs are good or not. Some argue that proper guards on your functions can communicate the function contract just as clearly, if not more clearly, than the typespec.

I generally find them helpful when reading through the documentation. But typespecs are noticeably absent from this book. In a dynamic language like Elixir, I think learning the language *before* worrying about typespecs is a better approach (same with Python). You can quickly get lost in trying to correctly describe the type of your function or struct.[1]

Module attributes can also be used to specify module-specific settings or configuration. This allows for easy configuration and customization of module behavior without modifying the module's code directly. For example

```
defmodule APIClient do
  @default_timeout 5

  def make_api_call(timeout // @default_timeout) do
    # ...
  end
end
```

The constant @default_timeout is replaced with the literal 5 during compilation and cannot be changed during runtime. Attributes are not visible outside the module in which they are defined. In this example, @default_timeout is local to the APIClient module.

Using module attributes as constants is generally not recommended. Instead, the recommended approach is to use functions. The above example is best written as

```
defmodule APIClient do

  defp default_timeout(), do: 5

  def make_api_call(timeout // default_timeout()) do
    # ...
  end
end
```

On the surface, this may seem verbose or less efficient. In some cases, that may be true. Module attributes are replaced at compile-time with their respective value, which is fine for small constants like a default timeout. But consider the case where the attribute value is much larger, for instance a large map. In this scenario, the constant is copied throughout your codebase. In comparison, using a function results in a single instance of the value referenced throughout your codebase. This can be a very subtle footgun.

---

[1]I spend a lot of time working on systems written in Python. Almost all the code includes type-hints. I recently got bit by a subtlety in how Pydantic handles the type Optional[str]. The point is, no matter how experienced you are, sometimes typing discussions are not so straightforward.

The other advantage to using functions is that they require less change as your requirements become more complex. For example, maybe we want the default timeout to be configurable:

```elixir
defmodule APIClient do
  defp default_timeout() do
    System.get_env("DEFAULT_TIMEOUT")
  end
end
```

There are more idiomatic approaches to storing application configuration, such as configuration files, but those are beyond the scope of this chapter.

5.3 Structs

Elixir structs are defined within modules and serve as a blueprint for creating instances of a specific data structure. They provide compile-time checks, default values, and the ability to pattern match on specific fields. This makes them a valuable tool for working with structured data in a more reliable and expressive way.

To define a struct, you use the `defstruct` macro within a module. The `defstruct` macro takes a list of field names and their default values (if any) as its argument. Each field *must* have a default value. Let's create a `User` struct.

```elixir
defmodule User do
  defstruct name: "", age: 0, email: ""
end
```

We could also create the same struct without default field values.

```elixir
defmodule User do
  defstruct [:name, :age, :email]
end
```

When you don't provide default values, Elixir will default to `nil`.

In our original example, the `User` struct is defined with three fields: `name`, `age`, and `email`. The `name` and `email` fields have default values of empty strings, while the `age` field has a default value of `0`. These default values are used when creating a new instance of the struct without providing explicit values for those fields.

To create an instance of a struct, you use the %<StructName>{} syntax, where <StructName> is the name of the struct. You can provide values for the fields using the key-value pair syntax. For example:

```
user = %User{name: "John Doe", age: 30, email:
↪  "john@example.com"}
```

This creates a new User struct instance with the specified values for the name, age, and email fields. Any fields not explicitly provided will take their default values as defined in the struct.

One of the main benefits of using structs is that they provide compile-time checks. Elixir will raise a compile-time error if you attempt to access a field that is not defined in the struct or if you pass an invalid field name when creating a struct instance. This helps catch mistakes early in the development process and ensures that the code is using the struct correctly.

Structs also support pattern matching. You can pattern match on struct instances to extract specific field values or to conditionally match based on the values of certain fields. This allows for concise and expressive code when working with structured data.

For example:

```
def greet(%User{name: name}) do
  "Hello, #{name}!"
end
```

Here we match on a User struct and extract the value of the name field. Let's look at a slightly more complex example.

```
def process(x) do
  case x do
    %Result{value: value} -> # handle the value case
    %Error{msg: message} -> # handle the error
  end
end
```

By encapsulating related data fields within a struct, you can create meaningful and self-documenting data types that represent concepts specific to your application domain. This improves code readability and makes it easier to reason about the data being passed around in your program.

If you are coming from object oriented languages, or languages where you can associate methods with types like Go, you might expect methods in Elixir. There are no methods in Elixir, only functions. Methods are notorious for hiding mutability. That is, they mutate the object calling the method, sometimes in a surprising way. If you've worked with Rust you will know the complexity that can stem from tracking mutation throughout your code.

For example, consider the following Python class:

```python
class Person:
  first_name: str
  last_name: str
  age: int

  def increase_age(self):
    self.age += 1
```

The increase_age method mutates the calling object.

```python
p = Person("John", "Smith", 42)
assert p.age == 42 # passes
p.increase_age()
assert p.age == 43 # also passes
```

Elixir does not support mutability. Without mutability, there is little need for methods.

```
my_struct.mutate_some_field()
```

The above line is not materially shorter than the following line

```
new_struct = StructType.mutate_some_field(old_struct)
```

and the latter is far more clear as to which variable contains the mutated structure.

Instead, we associate functions to a struct by including them in the same module. Let's look at a similar example to the above Python example, but in Elixir.

```elixir
defmodule Person do
  defstruct first_name: "", last_name:"", age: 0

  def increase_age(%Person{
      first_name: first_name,
```

```
      last_name: last_name,
      age: age
  }) do
    %Person{
      first_name: first_name,
      last_name: last_name,
      age: age + 1
    }
  end
end
```

Using this function looks only slightly different in Elixir.

```
iex> p = %Person{
  first_name: "John",
  last_name: "Smith",
  age: 42
}
%Person{first_name: "John", last_name: "Smith", age: 42}
iex> import ExUnit.Assertions, only: [assert: 2]
Exunit.Assertions
iex> assert p.age == 42 # passes
true
iex> new_p = Person.increase_age(p)
%Person{first_name: "John", last_name: "Smith", age: 43}
iex> assert new_p.age == 43 # also passes
```

Similar to maps, you can create a new struct from an old struct using the same update syntax.

```
iex> p = %Person{
  first_name: "John",
  last_name: "Smith",
  age: 42
}
%Person{first_name: "John", last_name: "Smith", age: 42}
iex> p = %Person{ p | first_name: "Jane"}
%Person{first_name: "Jane", last_name: "Smith", age: 42}
```

Structs and Maps

Structs and maps are closely related data structures. They use similar syntax for isntantiation. And they both provide ways to work with key-value pairs. But there are important differences in terms of their behavior and use cases.

A struct is simply a map with some additional compile-time checks on its keys. That is, the underlying data structure of a struct is a map. The key difference is that structs have a fixed set of fields that are defined at compile-time, whereas maps are more flexible and can have arbitrary keys and values added at runtime.

When you define a struct using the `defstruct` macro, you specify the allowed keys and their default values. For example:

```
defmodule User do
  defstruct name: "", age: 0, email: ""
end
```

Under the hood this is defining a type that is backed by a map that has the keys `name`, `age`, and `email`

Structs provide compile-time checks and guarantees that only the defined fields are allowed. If you try to access a field that doesn't exist in the struct or if you pass an invalid field name when creating a struct instance, Elixir will raise a compile-time error. This helps catch mistakes early and ensures that the code is using the struct correctly.

On the other hand, maps are more flexible. They allow you to store key-value pairs without any predefined structure.

```
iex> user_map = %{
  name: "John Doe",
  age: 30,
  email: "john@example.com"
}
%{name: "John Doe", age: 30, email: "john@example.com"}
iex> user_map = %{
  user_map | name: "Jane Doe", email: "jane@example.com"
}
%{name: "Jane Doe", age: 30, email: "jane@example.com"}
```

Maps do not have any compile-time checks for keys, so you can freely add, access, or modify key-value pairs at runtime. This flexibility makes maps suitable for scenarios where the structure of the data may vary or when you need to dynamically add or remove fields.

Since a struct is a map under the hood, you can use map functions like `Map.get/2`, `Map.put/3`, and `Map.update/4` to access and manipulate struct fields. Keep in mind that using map functions on structs may bypass the compile-time checks and allow for modifications that violate the struct's defined structure.

```
iex> u = %User{
  name: "John",
  age: 42,
  email: "john@example.com"
}
%User{name: "John", age: 42, email: "john@example.com"}
iex> new_u = Map.update(u, :name, "Alice", fn _ -> "Alice"
↪   end)
%User{name: "Alice", age: 42, email: "john@example.com"}
```

Note the `Map.update/4` call worked, but now the `name` and `email` fields seem out of sync. Maybe that's fine or maybe it's a bug. The only way we can be certain is by using the functions from the `User` module to update the struct, rather than `Map`.

Another difference between structs and maps is their behavior when it comes to pattern matching. Structs provide more precise pattern matching because they match on both the struct type and the field values. When pattern matching on a struct, you can specify the expected values for specific fields, and the match will only succeed if the struct instance matches those values. Maps, on the other hand, only match on the key-value pairs present in the map, regardless of any additional keys that may exist. Let's look at an example

```
defmodule Dog do
  defstruct name: "", age: 0, bark_type: :loud
end

defmodule Cat do
  defstruct name: "", age: 0, fur_color: :black
end

defmodule PetOrganizer do
  def pets_name(pet) do
    case pet do
      %Dog{name: name} -> {:ok, "Dog name: #{name}"}
      %Cat{name: name} -> {:ok, "Cat name: #{name}"}
      _ -> {:error, "Unknown pet type"}
    end
  end
end
```

With this definition, we match based on the type of the pet (either a `Cat` or a `Dog`).

```
iex> d = %Dog{name: "Murph", age: 8}
%Dog{name: "Murph", age: 8, bark_type: :loud}
```

```
iex> c = %Cat{name: "Kat", age: 5}
%Cat{name: "Kat", age: 5, fur_color: :black}
iex> PetOrganizer.pets_name(d)
{:ok , "Dog name: Murph"}
iex> PetOrganizer.pets_name(c)
{:ok, "Cat name: Kat"}
```

We cannot do this with maps. Let's see what happens when we try.

```
defmodule PetOrganizer do
  def pets_name(pet) do
    case pet do
      %{name: name} -> {:ok, name} # what animal type?
    end
  end
end
```

To get this to work, we need to add extra fields we don't care about. It's not the end of the world, but adds unnecessary code and doesn't make things any clearer.

```
defmodule PetOrganizer do
  def pets_name(pet) do
    case pet do
      %{name: name, bark_type: _} -> {:ok, "Dog name:
      ↪ #{name}"}
      %{name: name, fur_color: _} -> {:ok, "Cat name:
      ↪ #{name}"}
      _ -> {:error, "Unknown pet type"}
    end
  end
end
```

Now we get the expected behavior, but our code is not particularly clear. The struct version is far clearer – the types indicate which branch is for which type.

```
iex> c = %{name: "Kat", age: 5, fur_color: :black}
%{name: "Kat", age: 5, fur_color: :black}
iex> PetOrganzier.pets_name(c)
{:ok, "Cat name: Kat"}
```

In terms of performance, structs and maps are generally very efficient in Elixir. Structs technically have a performance advantage over maps due to their fixed structure and compile-time checks. However, the performance difference is negligible. The driving factor when deciding between using a struct or a map should be based on the specific requirements and design of your application.

Building a Ring Buffer Module

Later in this book we will build a server that uses a ring buffer as
its backing data structure. This is the perfect chapter to build that
data structure and strengthen our familiarity and understand of
Elixir structs and modules.

A ring buffer is a data structure with a fixed amount of storage.
When a write exceeds the amount of storage, it overwrites the oldest
data currently stored. If you imagine the storage as a circle, every
write is written to the next spot in the circle (or "ring", hence *ring
buffer*). Ring buffers are common data structures for low-latency
systems, like in the kernel IO systems, as well as caches. These data
structures do not allocate memory and are often cache-optimized.
That is, sequential elements are on the same cacheline, which allows
the CPU to pre-fetch data.

```
defmodule CH4.RingBuffer do
  @enforce_keys [:capacity]
  defstruct [:data, :capacity, size: 0]

  def new(capacity) do
    %CH4.RingBuffer{
      size: 0,
      capacity: capacity,
      data: :queue.new()
    }
  end

  def put(%CH4.RingBuffer{} = buffer, elem)
      when buffer.size < buffer.capacity do
    new_buf = :queue.in(elem, buffer.data)
    %CH10.RingBuffer{
      buffer | data: new_buf, size: buffer.size + 1
    }
  end

  def put(%CH4.RingBuffer{} = buffer, elem)
      when buffer.size == buffer.capacity do
    {_, new_buf} = :queue.out(buffer.data)
    new_buf = :queue.in(elem, new_buf)
    %CH4.RingBuffer{
      buffer | data: new_buf
    }
  end

  def get(
```

```
  %CH4.RingBuffer{} = buffer
) when buffer.size > 0 do
  {elem, new_buf} = :queue.out(buffer.data)
  {elem, %CH4.RingBuffer{
    buffer | data: new_buf, size: buffer.size - 1
  }}
end

def get(
  %CH4.RingBuffer{} = buffer
) when buffer.size == 0 do
  {:empty_get_error, buffer}
end
end
```

5.4 Protocols and Polymorphism

Protocols provide a mechanism for achieving ad hoc polymorphism and abstraction in your code. Ad hoc polymorphism refers to the ability of functions to behave differently based on the type of the argument passed to the function. This is similar to interfaces in Go and Java. Protocols allow you to define a common interface that can be implemented by various structs and data types, enabling them to behave polymorphically.

A protocol is a behavior that can be adopted by different data types. It specifies a set of functions that the implementing data types must provide. By defining a protocol, you establish a contract that the conforming data types must adhere to. This allows you to write generic code that can work with any data type that implements the protocol, without needing to know the specific details of each type.

You define a protocol using the `defprotocol` macro . The protocol definition specifies the functions that the implementing data types must provide. For example, let's consider a protocol called Serializable that defines a function `serialize/1` and `deserializer/1`

```
defprotocol Serializable do
  def serialize(data)
  def deserialize(data)
end
```

This protocol declares that any data type implementing the Serializable protocol must provide a `serialize/1` function.

To implement a protocol for a specific data type, you use the

defimpl macro. The defimpl macro allows you to provide the
implementation of the protocol functions for a particular data type.
For example, let's implement the Serializable protocol for a User
struct:

```
defimpl Serializable, for: User do
  def serialize(user) do
    :erlang.term_to_binary(user)
  end

  def deserialize(bytes) do
    :erlang.binary_to_term(bytes)
  end
end
```

In this implementation, we define how the serialize/1 and dese-
rialize/1 functions should behave for the User struct.

Protocols are powerful because of their polymorphic behavior. Once
a protocol is defined and implemented for different data types, you
can write code that works with any data type that conforms to the
protocol. This allows for more generic and reusable code, as you
can operate on data types based on their behavior rather than their
specific implementation.

Elixir provides several built-in protocols that you can leverage in
your code. Some commonly used protocols include:

- Enumerable contains the count/1, member?/2, reduce/3, and
  slice/1 functions.
- String.Chars contains the function to_string/1.
- Inspect contains the function inspect/2.

You can integrate your custom types with Elixir's built-in functions
and libraries by implementing these protocols.

Of course, manually implementing a bunch of protocols for your
types can be tedious and time consuming. Luckily, Elixir provides
the ability to derive a protocol. A protocol that can be derived,
must have a protocol implementation for Any. That is, there must
exist a defimpl for Any. For example:

```
defimpl MyProtocol for: Any do
  # MyProtocol impl
end
```

If this exists, then other types may derive this protocol.

```
defmodule User do
  @derive [MyProtocol]
  defstruct [:name, :email]
end
```

Not every protocol will have an implementation for Any, which means not every protocol will be derivable. Consider the Enumerable protocol. There are types for which enumeration does not make sense (a person, for example, is not enumerable). As a result, we would expect that Enumerable is *not* derivable, which is indeed the case.

You can also specify default behavior for functions within your protocol by using @fallback_to_any. When you set @fallback_to_any true on your function (within a protocol), any type that hasn't implemented or derived your protocol will default the Any implementation. *Usually* you don't want to do this, but in some cases it may make sense.

Going back to our Serializable protocol, it may make sense to use :erlang.term_to_binary and :erlang.binary_to_term as the fallbacks. To do this, we would provide the following implementation.

```
defimpl Serializable, for: Any do
  @fallback_to_any true
  def serialize(o) do
    :erlang.term_to_binary o
  end

  @fallback_to_any true
  def deserialize(bytes) do
    :erlang.binary_to_term bytes
  end
end
```

Now any type that calls serialize/1 or deserialize/1 will fallback to our default implementatino.

5.5 What's Next

Now that we have a good handle on data structures, it is time to move on to functions. While a lot of the material we cover in the next chapter will feel familiar, there are some new concepts with Elixir's functions. This will particularly be the case if this is your first exposure to a functional language.

Chapter 6

Functions

As a functional language, functions sit at the core of Elixir. Functions can be passed as if they were data. They can be defined inline and assigned to variables (so-called lambdas or anonymous functions). Functions may have side-effects, such as writing to IO or writing to a file, or they may be pure, having no side-effect at all.

In this chapter we will learn how to use functions effectively. Starting with the basics and moving on to more advanced concepts. Nothing in this chapter is particularly *advanced* or complex. But if this is your first adventure in functional programming you will undoubtedly see some new ideas and idioms.

6.1   Defining and Calling Functions

Clearly inspired by Ruby, function signatures start with `def` followed by the function name and parameters, which are enclosed in parentheses. The the funciton body is defined using the `do-end` block syntax and there is no explicit return statement. Instead, the last expression is returned (similar to Rust).

Here's a simple function that takes two numbers and returns their sum:

```
def add(a, b) do
  a + b
```

```
end
```

In this example, the function is named add and takes two parameters, a and b. The function body consists of a single expression, a + b, which calculates the sum of the two numbers. Elixir automatically returns the value of the last expression in the function body, so there's no need for an explicit return statement.

Calling a function in Elixir is just as simple as defining one. You use the function name followed by a list of arguments enclosed in parentheses. For example, to call the add function defined above with the arguments 3 and 4, you would write:

```
result = add(3, 4)
```

The function call add(3, 4) invokes the add function with the arguments 3 and 4, and the returned value (in this case, 7) is assigned to the variable result. The parentheses are optional when calling a function; however, if there are multiple arguments you must still include the commas. Let's consider a new function, sum.

```
defmodule MathHelpers do
  def sum(a, b, c, d) do
    a + b + c + d
  end
end
```

Then the following calls are both valid:

```
iex> MathHelpers.sum(1, 2, 3, 4)
10
iex> MathHelpers.sum 1, 2, 3, 4
10
```

However, it's generally good practice to use parentheses as it leaves zero room for ambiguity. This is especially true when the function as 0 arity. In this case, omitting the parentheses makes it unclear if we are looking at a function evaluation or a variable.

Elixir uses eager evaluation. This means that functions are evaluated at their call-site, not when the value is needed. If you are coming from a language like Haskell, this may or may not surprise you.

Functions *must* be defined inside a module. *You cannot define functions outside of modules in Elixir.* This can be confusing to newcomers (though quite natural if you are deep in the world of Java). We will sometimes omit the `defmodule` in this book for the sake of brevity and reducing visual noise.

6.2 Function Arity

Elixir also supports defining multiple functions, each with different arity. Function arity refers to the number of arguments the function takes. Functions with the same name but different arity are considered distinct functions. This allows you to define multiple versions of a function that handle different numbers of arguments.

For example:

```
def greet() do
  "Hello, anonymous!"
end

def greet(name) do
  "Hello, #{name}!"
end
```

In this case, we have two versions of the greet function: one that takes no arguments and another that takes a single argument name. When calling the greet function, Elixir will dispatch to the appropriate version based on the number of arguments provided.

Elixir also supports default arguments for functions. You can specify default values for function parameters, which will be used if the corresponding argument is not provided when the function is called. This allows you to define functions with optional arguments and provides flexibility in how they can be invoked. Default arguments are specified by following the parameter name with `\\` `<default value`. For example:

```
def greet(name \\ "anonymous") do
  "Hello, #{name}!"
end
```

In this version of the greet function, the `name` parameter has a default value of `"anonymous"`. If the function is called without an argument, it will use the default value. Otherwise, it will use the provided argument.

6.3 Naming

Function names in Elixir generally use snake case. That is, prefer `this_function_name` over `thisFunctionName`. It's also a common idiom to end a function name with a question mark when the function returns a boolean result. For example, a function that checks whether a number is even might be called `even?/1`. You may see some functions in the standard library that start with the prefix `is_` rather than end with a `?`. These are macros that are safe to use in a guard clause. We will learn about guard clauses shortly.

Generally if a function fails it will return some type of error code. As we will learn later in the chapter, exceptions are reserved for exceptional circumstances. A more idiomatic approach in Elixir is to return some type of error code. However, there may be times where a function failure is exceptional and other times it isn't. In these circumstances, it is common to provide two versions of the function. The one that returns an exception will be suffixed with an exclamation point (`!`) .

For example, the Enum module, which we will cover in greater detail later in this book, has two functions for fetching an element from a list at a given index. One version, `Enum.fetch/2`, returns a tuple possibly containing the result. The alternative version, `Enum.fetch!/2`, will throw an exception if the given index is out of range.

```
iex> xs = [1, 2, 3]
[1, 2, 3]
iex> Enum.fetch(xs, 1)
{:ok, 2}
iex> Enum.fetch!(xs, 1)
2
iex> Enum.fetch(xs, 4)
:error
iex> Enum.fetch!(xs, 4)
** (Enum.OutOfBoundsError) out of bounds error
    (elixir 1.17.2) lib/enum.ex:1084: Enum.fetch!/2
    iex: (file)
```

The other nice characteristic of the bang-style function (i.e., the function suffixed with `!`), is that there is no data to unpack. You simply get the value you asked for. In situations where you know the value is in there, this results in much cleaner code.

6.4 Guards and Guard Clauses

Guards add constraints and checks to function clauses. They allow for more fine-grained control over pattern matching and function execution. A guard clause is a boolean expression evaluated alongside pattern matching to determine whether a particular clause should be executed. They provide a concise and expressive way to specify conditions that must be met for a function clause or case branch to be selected.

Guards are defined using the when keyword. The guard expression is placed after the function arguments and before the do or ->. If the guard predicate evaluates to true, the body of the function or matched case branch is executed, otherwise it is skipped.

Here's an example that demonstrates the usage of guards in a function definition:

```
defmodule GuardExample do

  def even?(n) when rem(n, 2) == 0 do
    true
  end

  def even?(_n) do
    false
  end

end
```

```
iex> GuardExample.even?(5)
false
iex> GuardExample.even?(4)
true
```

The first definition of GuardExample.even?/1 with the guard clause will only get called when n is even (i.e., the remainder when divided by 2 is 0). Otherwise, when n is not even, the other implementation of GuardExample.even?/1 is called, which returns false. Just as with case expressions, the pattern matching for function calls is evaluated in the order the functions are defined. This means you should always put the most specific pattern/guard first and the least specific at the end. Let's reverse the order of these functions and see what happens.

```elixir
defmodule GuardExample do

  def even?(_n)
    false
  end

  def even?(n) when rem(n, 2) == 0 do
    true
  end

end
```

```elixir
iex> GuardExample.even?(4)
false
```

In this second example, the first GuardExample.even?/1 definition matches every single call to GuardExample.even?/1. Even when we provide an argument that would also match the second pattern rem(n, 2) == 0, the first matching pattern takes precedence. Of course, this is a contrived example and a better implementation of GuardExample.even?/1 is

```elixir
defmodule GuardExample do
  def even?(n) do
    rem(n, 2) == 0
  end
end
```

Or, even better, just use the standard library version Integer.is_even.

Now let's look at using guard clauses with case expressions.

```elixir
defmodule GuardExample do
  def even?(n) do
    case n do
      n when rem(n, 2) == 0 -> true
      _ -> false
    end
  end
end
```

```elixir
iex> GuardExample.even?(4)
true
iex> GuardExample.even?(5)
false
```

Always keep guards as simple and focused as possible. They are generally easier to read than if-else expressions, but it's easy for things to get out of hand. Here are a few useful tips:

- Avoid complex logic or expensive operations, as they can impact performance.
- Guards cannot contain user-defined functions or macros.
- Guard expressions should be free of side effects. They should never modify program state.

6.5 Function Clauses and Pattern Matching

Elixir's pattern matching capabilities go beyond simple variable assignment. Function definitions also support pattern matching. If Elixir is your first exposure to functional programming, this may come as quite a surprise. Function clauses allow you to define multiple versions of a function, each with its own pattern to match against. When a function is called, Elixir will attempt to match the provided arguments against the patterns defined in the function clauses, executing the first clause that matches successfully. This powerful feature allows you to write concise and expressive code that handles different cases elegantly.

To define multiple function clauses, you simply define the function multiple times with different patterns for the arguments. Each clause is separated by the def keyword. When the function is called, Elixir will try to match the arguments against each clause in the order they are defined until it finds a match. If no clause matches, an error will be raised. Here's an example that demonstrates function clauses:

```
def greet(:morning, name) do
  "Good morning, #{name}!"
end
def greet(:afternoon, name) do
  "Good afternoon, #{name}!"}
end
def greet(:evening, name) do
  "Good evening, #{name}!"
end
```

In this example, we have three clauses for the greet function. Each clause matches a different pattern for the first argument, which is an atom representing the time of day. The second argument, name, is matched as is. When we call the greet function with an atom and a name, Elixir will dispatch to the appropriate clause based on the value of the first argument.

Function clauses can also use more complex patterns, such as tuples, lists, and maps. This allows you to match against the structure and content of the arguments. For example:

```elixir
def handle_result({:ok, result}) do
  "Success: #{result}"
end
def handle_result({:error, reason}) do
  "Error: #{reason}"
end
```

In this case, the `handle_result` function has two clauses that match against tuples. The first clause matches a tuple with the atom `:ok` as the first element and binds the second element to the variable `result`. The second clause matches a tuple with the atom `:error` as the first element and binds the second element to the variable `reason`. Depending on the tuple passed to the function, the appropriate clause will be executed.

6.6 Anonymous Functions

In addition to named functions, Elixir provides support for anonymous functions, also known as lambda functions or function literals. Anonymous functions are defined inline without being bound to a specific name. They are lightweight, first-class citizens in Elixir and can be assigned to variables, passed as arguments to other functions, or returned as values from functions. Anonymous functions are a powerful tool for writing concise and flexible code. They are essential when dealing with higher-order functions and functional programming concepts.

To define an anonymous function in Elixir, you use the `fn` keyword followed by the function parameters and the `->` symbol, which separates the parameters from the function body. The function body is then defined using the `do...end` block syntax or a single expression. For example, here's an anonymous function that takes two numbers and returns their sum:

```
sum = fn(a, b) -> a + b end
```

In this example, the anonymous function is assigned to the variable sum. The function takes two parameters, a and b, and its body consists of a single expression, a + b, which calculates the sum of the two numbers. To invoke an anonymous function, you use a dot followed by the function arguments enclosed in parentheses:

```
result = sum.(3, 4)
```

The function call sum.(3, 4) invokes the anonymous function assigned to the sum variable with the arguments 3 and 4, and the returned value (in this case, 7) is assigned to the variable result.

One of the key benefits of anonymous functions is their ability to capture variables from their surrounding scope, creating closures. A closure is a function that remembers the environment in which it was defined, including any variables that were in scope at the time of its creation. This allows anonymous functions to access and manipulate variables from the enclosing scope, even after the original scope has finished executing. Here's an example that demonstrates closures:

```
multiplier = fn(factor) ->
  fn(value) -> value * factor end
end
double = multiplier.(2)
triple = multiplier.(3)
result1 = double.(5)
result2 = triple.(5)
```

In this example, the multiplier function is an anonymous function that takes a factor parameter and returns another anonymous function that captures the value of factor. The returned function takes a value parameter and multiplies it by the factor captured from the outer function. We create two closures, double and triple, by invoking the multiplier function with different factors. Each closure remembers its own factor value, allowing us to multiply values by 2 or 3 respectively. We could have also written

```
result1 = multiplier.(2).(5)
result2 = multiplier.(3).(5)
```

Anonymous functions are particularly useful when working with higher-order functions, which are functions that take other functions as arguments or return functions as results. Elixir provides several built-in higher-order functions, such as `Enum.map/2`, `Enum.filter/2`, and `Enum.reduce/3`, which allow you to transform and manipulate collections using anonymous functions. For example, to double each element in a list using `Enum.map/2`:

```
iex> numbers = [1, 2, 3, 4, 5]
[1, 2, 3, 4]
iex> doubled = Enum.map(numbers, fn(x) -> x * 2 end)
[2, 4, 6, 8]
```

In this case, we pass an anonymous function to `Enum.map/2` that doubles each element of the numbers list, resulting in a new list `[2, 4, 6, 8, 10]` assigned to the doubled variable.

6.7   The Capture Operator

Elixir also provides a shorthand syntax for defining anonymous functions using the & operator, known as the capture operator. This might feel familiar if you are coming from a language like Scala. With the capture syntax, you can define anonymous functions more concisely by prefixing the function parameters with & and omitting the `fn` and `end` keywords. For example, the previous doubling example can be rewritten as:

```
iex> doubled = Enum.map(numbers, &(&1 * 2))
```

Here, `&1` represents the first parameter passed to the function. The capture syntax is particularly convenient when defining short, one-line anonymous functions.

Note that if you use the capture operator your function *must* use at least one argument. If you want an anonymous function that takes no arguments your only option is to use fn _ -> <body> end or fn(_) -> <body> end.

The other usecase for the capture operator is to capture a module public function. This capture allows you to use public module functions as if there were anonymous functions. Let's look at an example. Suppose we wanted to map a list of numbers to booleans based on whether they are odd or even. Naturally, we would reach for the library function `Integer.is_even/1` and `Enum.map/2`. Let's see what happens:

```
iex> require Integer
iex> xs = [1, 2, 3, 4, 5, 6]
[1, 2, 3, 4, 5, 6]
iex> Enum.map(xs, Integer.is_even/1)
** (UndefinedFunctionError) function Integer.is_even/0 is
↪   undefined or private. Did you mean:

      * is_even/1
```

The solution, as you might have guessed, is to use the capture operator.

```
iex> Enum.map(xs, &Integer.is_even/1)
[false, true, false, true, false, true]
```

The capture operator creates a new, anonymous function that wraps the captured function. You visualize it as:

```
captured_is_even = fn x -> Integer.is_even(x) end
```

Now `Integer.is_even/1` can be passed around like an anonymous function.

6.8 Higher-Order Functions

Functions are first-class citizens in functional programming. This means that functions can be assigned to variables, passed as arguments to other functions, and returned as values from functions. Functions that operate on other functions, either by taking them as arguments or returning them, are called higher-order functions. Higher-order functions are a powerful abstraction that allows for more expressive and composable code.

One common use case for higher-order functions is to transform data by applying a function to each element of a collection. Let's look at an example that combines `Enum.map/2`, `Enum.filter/2`, and `Enum.reduce/3`. Suppose we want to find the summed square of all even numbers in a given list.

```
iex> numbers = [1, 2, 3, 4, 5]
[1, 2, 3, 4, 5]
```

```
iex> squared = Enum.map(numbers, &(&1 * &1))
[1, 4, 9, 16, 25]
iex> filtered = Enum.filter(squared, &(rem(&1, 2) == 0))
[4, 16]
iex> result = Enum.reduce(filtered, 0, &(&1 + &2))
20
```

If it's not clear from the Enum.filter example, filter conditionally allows elements through, rather than filtering them out. That is, when the predicate is true elements are allowed through (kept). When the filter predicate is false, the element is filtered out. This is a common point of confusion with filter (not just in Elixir).

We could try nesting these functions, but that would quickly become a mess.

```
result = Enum.reduce(
  Enum.filter(
    Enum.map(numbers, &(&1 * &1)),
    &(rem(&1, 2) == 0)
  ),
  0,
  &(&1 + &2)
)
```

This is quite difficult to read and gets more difficult with each nested function evaluation.

Pipe Operator

Fortunately, Elixir provides the |> operator, known as the pipe operator, for just this problem. If you have spent any time working with OCaml this will feel very familiar. The pipe operator allows you to chain multiple functions together, passing the result of each function as the first argument to the next function. Let's rewrite that prior example with the pipe operator.

```
result = numbers
  |> Enum.map(&(&1 * &1))
  |> Enum.filter(&(rem(&1, 2) == 0))
  |> Enum.reduce(0, &(&1 + &2))
```

Notice how we are omitting the fist argument in each of these functions calls. The pipe operator takes the expression on the left-hand side and uses it as the first argument to the function on the right-hand side.

Function composition allows you to build complex transformations by combining smaller, reusable functions. The pipe operator makes function composition more readable by visually conveying the flow of data through the pipeline.

Another powerful aspect of higher-order functions is their ability to create specialized versions of functions by partially applying arguments. Partial application refers to the process of fixing some of the arguments of a function, creating a new function with fewer arguments. Elixir provides the `Kernel.partial/2` function to partially apply arguments to a function. For example:

```
multiply = fn(a, b) -> a * b end
double = Kernel.partial(multiply, [2])
result = double.(5)
```

In this example, we define a `multiply` function that takes two arguments and multiplies them. We then use `Kernel.partial/2` to partially apply the first argument as 2, creating a new function double that takes only one argument. When we call `double.(5)`, it multiplies 5 by the partially applied argument 2, resulting in 10.

Partial application allows you to create specialized versions of functions with some arguments preset, reducing the need to pass the same arguments repeatedly. It can make your code more concise and expressive by creating functions tailored to specific use cases.

6.9 Recursion

In functional programming, recursion is the primary method for iterating over data. Recursion is where a function calls itself repeatedly until a certain condition is met. It provides a powerful and elegant way to solve problems that can be broken down into smaller subproblems of the same structure. In Elixir, recursion is the primary mechanism for looping and iteration, as the language does not have built-in loop constructs like `for` or `while` loops found in imperative programming languages.

The basic idea behind recursion is to define a function that solves a problem by breaking it down into one or more simpler subproblems, and then calling itself to solve each subproblem. This process continues until the problem is reduced to a simple enough case that can be solved directly, known as the base case. The solutions to the subproblems are then combined to yield the solution to the original problem.

Let's illustrate recursion with a classic example: the factorial function. The factorial of a non-negative integer n, denoted as n!, is the product of all positive integers less than or equal to n. For example, $5! = 5 \times 4 \times 3 \times 2 \times 1 = 120$. Here's how we can define the factorial function recursively in Elixir:

```elixir
def factorial(0), do: {:ok, 1}
def factorial(n) when n > 0 do
  case factorial(n - 1) do
    {:ok, r} -> {:ok, r * n}
    {:error, msg} -
end
def factorial(n) when < 0 do
  {:error, "Factorial does not make sense for integers less
  ↪   than 0"}
end
```

In this implementation, we define three clauses for the factorial function. The first clause, `factorial(0)`, is the base case, which returns 1 when the input is 0. The second clause, `factorial(n)` when n > 0, is the recursive case. It multiplies n by the factorial of $n - 1$, effectively breaking down the problem into a smaller subproblem. The function keeps calling itself with smaller values of n until it reaches the base case, at which point the recursion stops and the results are combined to produce the final factorial value. The third clause, `factorial(n)` when n < 0, handles the error case when someone calls `factorial` for $n < 0$.

Tail-Call Optimization

They say with great power comes great responsibility. Recursion is a very powerful technique, but you must use great care when desigining a recursive function. One common issue is stack overflow, which occurs when a recursive function calls itself too many times, exhausting the available stack space. Each recursive call adds a new frame to the call stack, consuming memory. If the recursion depth is too large, it can lead to a stack overflow error.

Figure 6.1 illustrates the layout of process memory. The stack and heap are opposing allocations within the process memory. The stack space is pre-allocated when the process is created, and its pattern of allocation is last in, first out (LIFO). This is why stack memory

Figure 6.1: Process memory layout. Each process has its own heap and stack

is faster to access and clear. When you use up all of your stack, you get a stack overflow error.

To address this issue, Elixir uses a technique called tail call optimization (TCO). TCO is an optimization strategy that allows recursive calls in tail position (i.e., the last operation in a function) to be executed without consuming additional stack space.

When a function call is in tail position, the compiler can optimize it by reusing the current stack frame instead of creating a new one. This optimization effectively turns the recursive call into a loop, preventing stack overflow and enabling efficient recursive computations.

To take advantage of tail call optimization, it's crucial to structure recursive functions in a way that ensures the recursive call is the last operation performed. For simple recursive functions this is a rather simple task. However, as the function becomes more complex it is less clear how to do this.

The common strategy for implementing a tail-call optimized recursive function is to use a helper function in conjunction with an accumulator variable. The accumulator, often named `acc`, is used to accumulate the result value. The base case simply returns `acc`. All other calls modify `acc` in someway but using a modified version as the argument to the recursive call. The outer function, the one the user actually calls, simply returns the result from the call to the helper function.

Let's refactor our `factorial` implementation to make use of TCO.

```
def factorial(n), do: factorial_helper(n, 1)

defp factorial_helper(0, acc), do: {:ok, acc}

defp factorial_helper(n, acc) when n > 0 do
  factorial_helper(n - 1, n * acc)
end

defp factorial_helper(n, _) do
  {:error, "Factorial does not make sense for integers less
  ↪  than 0"}
end
```

In this version, we introduce a helper function `factorial_helper/2` that takes an additional accumulator parameter `acc`. The accumulator keeps track of the intermediate factorial value as the recursion progresses. The recursive call `factorial_helper(n - 1, n \* acc)` is in tail position, allowing the compiler to optimize it. When the base case is reached, the final accumulated value is returned.

Tail recursion can greatly imporve your recrusion efficiency. In just about every case you'll need to use a helper function to make the tail call feasiable, like we did above. The trade-off with TCO is an increase in code complexity. The example above, while slightly noisier, is still straightforward. It can be a balancing act keep your code clean and readable, but also efficient when using techniques such as tail recursion.

Wrapping Up

At this point we have a good feel for how to define functions. We know how to work with them, pass them around, and pattern match on them. What is noticably missing, however, is what to put *inside* the functions. How do we handle flow control? What should we do if we encounter an error? In the coming chapters we will look at branching, error handling, and pattern matching. After these chapters you will have the foundations you need to write Elixir code.

Chapter 7

Flow Control

7.1 Conditional Expressions

Conditional expressions are a fundamental concept in programming that allow you to control the flow of your program based on certain conditions. Elixir, as with most functional languages, there are a suite of options for managing the flow of your program. This chapter starts with the most basic flow control, the if-else expression, and quickly moves on to other forms of flow control.

Remember, always choose the tool that results in the simplest, easiest to follow code. Elixir gives you a lot of choice when it comes to flow control. Your responsibility as a software engineer is to write code that is correct, maintainable, and easily understood.

if-else

As with just about every programming language, Elixir offers if and else keywords for the most basic form of program flow control. These keywords allow you to execute a block of code only if a specified condition is true (or false).

```
iex> some_value = true
true
iex> if some_value do
  IO.puts "some_value was true"
else
  IO.puts "some_value was false"
```

```
end
some_value was true
:ok
```

If the condition is true, the code block immediately following the if is executed. If the condition is false, the code block following the else is executed. Notice that the value of the if-else expression was returned. This means we can do things like this:

```
iex> x = if true do
  2 * 3
else
  0
end
6
iex> x
6
```

As with other languages, an else branch is not required to come after an if block. That is, you can optionally do something or nothing.

```
iex> if false do
  "You will never see this"
end
```

unless

Elixir also has a conditional check called unless. When the predicate given to unless is false or nil, the body gets executed. This is intuitive. Imagine talking to your friend "Unless you hear from me, meet me at the park." You are telling your friend to *not* go to the park if they hear from you. If they *don't* hear from you, they should go to the park. Let's look at an example.

```
iex> unless false do
  "predicate evaluated false"
end
"predicate evaluated false"
```

cond

For situations where you have many if-else checks, Elixir also provides the cond expression. This will feel familiar if you have previously worked with a Lisp. The `cond` expression executes the code block associated with the first condition that evaluates to `true`.

Let's look at an example:

```
iex> x = 42
iex> cond do
  x >= 0 and x < 10 -> "less than 10"
  x >= 10 and x < 20 -> "greater than 10"
  x >= 20 and x < 30 -> "greater than 20"
  x >= 30 and x < 40 -> "greater than 30"
  x >= 40 -> "greater than 40"
  true -> "none of these were true"
end
"greater than 40"
```

Note the `true -> "greater than 40"` case at the end. This is the default arm of the `cond` expression. If none of the other conditions are true, this will get executed.

Elixir offers a lot of expression with respect to conditionals. Syntax like the `cond` expression can help us avoid deeply nested conditional expressions. This helps us write simpler, clearer, and ultimately less code. In the next secion we will explore case expressions and pattern matching. These are two common features of functional languages that offer lots of expressive power.

7.2 Pattern Matching

Pattern matching is one of the more powerful features of Elixir. It allows you to elegantly handle complex conditional logic and control flow. Pattern matching provides a concise and expressive way to match and destructure data. Used appropriately, pattern matching will make your code more readable and maintainable. One of the primary tools for pattern matching is the `case` expression.

case

A `case` expression in Elixir allows you to compare a value against multiple patterns. The corresponding code block for the first matching pattern gets executed. It consists of `case <input> do`, followed by patterns to match on. Patterns are generally variables or data constructors, followed by an arrow (`->`). If none of the patterns match, an error is raised. You can avoid this by using a default branch _ -> <brancy body>

Here's a simple example that demonstrates the usage of a case expression:

```
iex> check_status = fn status ->
...>    case status do
...>      :ok -> "Let's do some work"
...>      :error -> "Process failed"
...>    end
...> end
#Function<42.105768164/1 in :erl_eval.expr/6>
iex> check_status.(:ok)
"Let's do some work"
iex> check_status.(:error)
"Process failed"
iex> check_status.(42)
** (CaseClauseError) no case clause matching: 42
    (stdlib 5.2.3) erl_eval.erl:1106:
    ↳  :erl_eval.case_clauses/8
    iex:17: (file)
```

As we stated above, it is an error if there is no matching clause within the case expression. Let's modify our function to prevent this error.

```
iex> check_status = fn status ->
...>    case status do
...>      :ok -> "Let's do some work"
...>      :error -> "Something went wrong"
...>      _ -> "Unrecognized status code"
...>    end
...> end
#Function<42.105768164/1 in :erl_eval.expr/6>
iex> check_status.(42)
"Unrecognized status code"
```

Elixir supports pattern matching on various data types, including integers, atoms, strings, lists, tuples, and maps. You can also use variables within a pattern to bind values to the pattern. When a value matches a pattern, any variables in the pattern are bound to the corresponding values.

```
iex> check_status fn status ->
...>    case status, msg do
...>      {:ok, msg} -> "Success - #{msg}"
...>      {:error, msg} -> "Failed - #{msg}"
```

```
...>      {status_code, msg} -> "Unrecognized status code
↪   (#{status_code}) - #{msg}"
...>    end
...> end
#Function<42.105768164/1 in :erl_eval.expr/6>
iex> check_status.({:ok, "data processed"})
"Success - data processed"
iex> check_status.({:error, "data processing failed"})
"Failed - data processing failed"
iex> check_status.({42, "unknown state!"})
"Unrecognized status code - status code: 42 message: unknown
↪   state!"
```

Pinning

What if you want to match against the value of a variable? That is, suppose the value you want to match against is determined at runtime, rather than a constant like 42 or :some_atom? Elixir provides the pin operator for just this case. When matching on the value of a variable, you prefix it with ^. Let's look at an example (albeit, quite contrived).

```
iex> x = 3
3
iex> y = 3
3
iex> case y do
  ^x -> "val is 3"
  _ -> "val is not 3"
end
"val is 3"
```

We can repeat this with a different value of y to verify that x won't match any value.

```
iex> x = 3
3
iex> y = 4
4
iex> case y do
  ^x -> "val is 3"
  _ -> "val is not 3"
end
"val is not 3"
```

Matching on Data Structures

Pattern matching in case expressions is not limited to simple values
and tuples. You can also match against complex data structures
like lists and maps. This allows you to extract specific elements or
values from the data structure based on their positions or keys.

For example, suppose we define the following map:

```
iex> m = %{one: 1, two: 2}
{one: 1, two: 2}
```

The we could pattern match on the map as follows:

```
iex> case m do
...>   %{one: v} -> v
...> end
1
iex> case m do
...>   %{one: 1, two: v} -> v
...> end
2
iex> case m do
...>   %{one: 2, two: v} -> v
...> end
** (CaseClauseError) no case clause matching: %{one: 1, two:
↳   2}
    (stdlib 5.2.3) erl_eval.erl:1106:
    ↳   :erl_eval.case_clauses/8
    iex:6: (file)
```

Recall that it is an error in Elixir if a `case` expression fails to match
any of the patterns. The simplest way to avoid this is to include a
default case using a generic pattern or _.

```
iex> case m do
...>   %{one: two, two: v} -> v
...>   _ -> 42
...> end
42
```

One thing you *can't* do when pattern matching on maps is to match
against values, rather than keys. Let's see what happens when we
try to do just that.

```
iex> case m do
...> %{x: 1} -> x
...> end
```

```
** (CaseClauseError) no case clause matching: %{one: 1, two:
↪  2}
   (stdlib 5.2.3) erl_eval.erl:1106:
   ↪  :erl_eval.case_clauses/8
   iex:7: (file)
```

When pattern matching against maps, you must match on the keys. You can include the values as well, as we saw earlier, but the keys in your pattern must have specific values.

We can also do pattern matching on lists. Lists can match on the initial elements, the rest of the list, or every element in the list. Let's look at three cases demonstrating these different match scenarios.

```
iex> x = [1, 2, 3, 4]
[1, 2, 3, 4]
iex> case x do
...>    [head | tail] -> head # returns the first element of
↪  the list, 1
...>    [1, 2, third, 4 | tail] -> third # returns the third
↪  element, tail is the empty list
...>    [1, second, 3, 4] -> second # returns the second
↪  element of the list, not matching on the tail
...> end
1
```

Our case expression returns 1 because that is the first pattern that matched.

Depending on how you are experimenting with this code, you might encounter some unused variable warnings. For example, the following case expression would generate an unused variable warning:

```
iex> case x do
...>    [head | tail] -> head # tail is unused
...> end
```

You can silence these warning by prefixing the variable with an underscore. That is, if you are not using tail but want to keep it instead of a wildcard _, you can rename tail to _tail.

The other scenario we haven't covered is when we want to match a concrete value, but that value is stored in a variable. Consider the following example.

```
iex> first = 42
42
iex> second = 2
2
iex> l1 = [1, 2, 3, 4]
[1, 2, 3, 4]
iex> l2 = [42, 2, 5, 6]
[42, 2, 3, 4]
iex> case l1 do
...>    [first, second | tail ] -> "matches 1 and 2"
...>    _ -> "we were hoping for this one..."
...> end
"matches 1 and 2"
iex> case l1 do
...>    [^first, ^second | tail ] -> "matches 1 and 2"
...>    _ -> "we were hoping for this one..."
...> end
"we were hoping for this one..."
```

In the second example, the pin operator ^ prevents Elixir from binding the first two values of the list to first and second, shadowing
the original variables. Continuing this example

```
iex> case l2 do
...>    [^first, ^second | tail] -> tail
...> end
[5, 6]
```

Here the values of first and second, 42 and 2 respectively, match
on the first elements of the list, which is what we want (in this
specific exmaple).

Pattern matching in case expressions is a useful tool for handling
different scenarios based on the structure and content of your data.
It can be particularly useful in error scenarios. For example, consider
the two error handling scenarios

```
case result do
  {:ok, some_val} -> # success branch
  {:error, _} -> # error branch
end
```

```
{status, val} = result
if status == :ok do
  # success branch
else
  # failure branch
```

end

Recall that only :false, false, and nil will evaluate as false, which means :error will evaluate true. As a result, we must explicitly check for either :ok or :error.

7.3 Guards

We can also use guards in case expressions. Recall from the prior chapter that guards are defined using when <some predicate> syntax. We previously saw this used to refine which function version is selected during a function call. This same syntax works with case expressions as well.

```
iex> xs = [2, 4, 6, 8]
[2, 4, 6, 8]
iex> case xs do
...>    [head | _] when rem(head, 2) == 1 -> "the first
↪  element is odd"
...>    [head | _] when rem(head, 2) == 1 -> "the first
↪  element is even"
...>    _ -> "who can say what's going on?"
...> end
"the first element is even"
```

As always, just because you *can* put checks in the guard clause doesn't mean you *should*. Guard clauses are a powerful tool when they aid the clarity of your code. But putting too much control flow logic in your guard clauses and quickly have the opposite effect.

Case expressions help you write concise and expressive code that is easy to read and understand. We aren't trying to win any code golf competitions with our code, but concise and simple code is generaly easier to understand.

Here are a few tips to keep in mind when using a case expression:

- Keep case expressions focused. Avoid complex patterns.
- Use meaningful variable names in patterns
- Cover all possible cases

7.4   No Ternary Operator

If you are coming from a C-inspired language such as C++, Java, Javascript, etc. you may be wondering whether Elixir has a ternary operator. For better or worse, Elixir does *not* have a ternary operator. You can simulate a ternary operator the same way you do in Python: using an inline if-else expression. Let's take a look.

```
iex> is_even? = fn n -> if rem(n, 2) == 0, do: true, else:
↪   false end
#Function<42.105768164/1 in :erl_eval.expr/6>
iex> is_even?.(5)
false
iex> is_even?.(4)
true
```

7.5   try, catch, rescue, after

There three different ways in which Elixir signals something went wrong. The first is an error. For example, if a function received an invalid input it might return {:error, "bad input"}, otherwise the function would return {:ok, some_result}. However, if something truly exceptional occurs, say attempting to send a message to a non-existant PID, then an exception should be used. The guiding philosophy is "can I do something about this?" if the answer is "no," then an exception is the right call. Otherwise, use an error/status code.

Exceptions are created via raise/2 .

```
iex> raise "hello"
** (RuntimeError) hello
    iex:1: (file)
```

Note: Even though we are covering try, catch, and rescue, it is generally best to avoid using them if you can. As we will discussin in the following section, it's best to let the process crash and potentially be restarted with a fresh slate.

Errors you handle with pattern matching. Exceptions are either caught or you let them crash the process. This may feel wrong

when coming from other languages but letting a process fail is part
of Elixir's ethos. This is sometimes referred to as the "fail fast" or
"let it crash" philosophy. Elixir's supervisors (which we will learn
about later) can be used to start up failed processes. They are
highly configurable, giving you a lot of flexibility in how a process
should be restarted, how many times it can be restarted, if other
processes need to be restarted, etc. We will cover this in far greater
detail later in the book.

Back to exceptions. We just learned Elixir favors letting a process
crash. What if we don't want our process to crash (remember
though, we probably want to let it crash)? We can use `try` and
`rescue`.

```
iex> try do
...>   raise "hello"
...> rescue
...>   _ -> "all good!"
...> end
"all good!"
```

The `rescue` block uses pattern matching for different types of errors.
To see this in action, let's create some of our own exception types.
We create a module and use `defexception` to give the exception a
message.

```
# src/control_structures/exceptions.exs
defmodule ExampleError do
  defexception message: "something bad happened!"
end

defmodule AnotherExampleError do
  defexception message: "something REALLY bad happened!"
end

defmodule ExceptionExplorer do
  def try_exception(error) do
    try do
      raise error
    rescue
      e in ExampleError -> "ExampleError encountered
      ↪   #{e.message}"
      e in AnotherExampleError -> "AnotherExampleError
      ↪   encoutnered #{e.message}"
    end
  end
end
```

```
IO.puts(ExceptionExplorer.try_exception(ExampleError))
IO.puts(ExceptionExplorer.try_exception(AnotherExampleError))
```

We can also customize the message from these exceptions.

```
iex> raise ExampleError, message: "this is a different
↪  message"
** (ExampleError) this is another message
    src/control_structures/exceptions.exs:22: (file)
    (elixir 1.17.2) lib/code.ex:1491: Code.require_file/2
```

When you need to clean up a resource, regardless of whether an error occurred within your `try` block, you can use `after`.

More Pattern Matching

We covered a lot of pattern matching in this chapter. In the next chapter we will dive even deeper into pattern matching. Pattern matching is one of the hallmark features of functional programming, so it is only fitting that we develop a strong and intuitive understanding of its mechanics and patterns.

Chapter 8

Pattern Matching

We've already seen a brief overview of pattern matching in the prior chapter. This chapter will expand upon what we've already seen, exploring pattern matching on data, functions, and guards. By the end of this chapter you will have all the tools needed to make full use of pattern matching.

8.1 Overview

When most people are first introduced to functional programming there are two immediate observations: the learning curve for working with immutable data is steep and pattern matching is awesome. Pattern matching is one of those language features that is hard to live without. It simplifies control flow, data manipulation, and generally leads to cleaner and easier to read code.

In Elixir, the = operator is actually called the match operator, not an assignment operator. When you write an expression like x = 42, Elixir tries to match the left-hand side (the pattern) with the right-hand side (the value). If the match succeeds, any variables in the pattern are bound to the corresponding values, otherwise an error is raised. Notice that this definition implies that 42 = x should succeed, which it does.

```
iex> x = 42
42
```

```
iex> 42 = x
42
```

However, notice what happens if we try to use an unbound variable on the right side.

```
iex> 42 = z
error: undefined variable "z"
```

This implies that the reason the original `42 = x` match succeeded is because x was already bound.

Pattern matching goes beyond simple variable assignment. As we saw previously, you can pattern match match against literals, variables, tuples, lists, maps, and even complex nested data structures. This allows you to elegantly handle different cases and extract relevant data from complex structures in a single expression.

Pattern matching is not limited to simple assignments. It is used in function definitions to define multiple clauses with different patterns. When a function is called, Elixir tries to match the arguments against the patterns in each clause, and executes the body of the first matching clause. This allows you to define functions that handle different cases elegantly and concisely.

8.2   Basic Data Types

Pattern matching in Elixir extends to all the basic data types, allowing you to match against literals, bind variables, and destructure complex values. Let's explore how pattern matching works with integers, floats, booleans, atoms, and strings.

When matching against literals, the match succeeds if the value on the right-hand side is equal to the literal on the left-hand side. For example:

```
iex> y = :hello
:hello
iex> :hello = y
:hello
iex> 42 = 43
** (MatchError) no match of right hand side value: 43
```

Notice how the error isn't regarding equality or assignment, but rather about matching.

Strings can be matched against string literals or bound to variables.

```
iex> x = "forty two"
"forty two"
```

You can also match against parts of a string using the string concatenation operator

```
iex> "forty " ++ ones = "forty two"
"forty two"
iex> ones
"two"
```

8.3 Complex Data Structures

The prior examples aren't particularly illuminating. With the exception of the example showing pattern matching with the concatenation operator, most of the examples amount to variable assignment. Pattern matching really shines when working with complex data structures like tuples, lists, and maps. When working with these data structures, pattern matching provides a powerful way to extract and manipulate specific parts of these structures.

As we have seen with tuples, we can extract any and all values via pattern matching. This is often referred to as *destructuring* the tuple.

```
iex> {name, age} = {"Alice", 42}
{"Alice", 42}
iex> name
"Alice"
iex> age
42
```

Using and underscore (_) ignores the respective element in the match:

```
iex> {_, age} = {"Bob", 42}
{"Bob", 42}
iex> age
42
```

Pattern matching with lists starts with the individual elements of
the list, optionally followed by a match on the remaining elements
(the tail). You will most often see this as matching on the head of
the list and matching the remaining elements on the tail.

```
iex> [head | tail] = [1, 2, 3, 4]
[1, 2, 3, 4]
iex> head
1
iex> tail
[2, 3, 4]
```

With lists, the pipe operator (|) tells Elixir to match the remaining
elements (the tail) to the respective variable. Without this, Elixir
will try to match the entire list to the given variables, element by
element. This means you must have the same number of elements
on left-hand side as on the right, otherwise you get a MatchError.
Also note that only a single variable can follow the pipe operator.

```
iex> [x, y, z] = [1, 2, 3]
[1, 2, 3]
iex> x
1
iex> y
2
iex> z
3
iex> [x, y] = [1, 2, 3]
** (MatchError) no match of right hand side value: [1, 2, 3]
iex> [x, y | _] = [1, 2, 3]
[1, 2, 3]
iex> x
1
iex> y
2
```

Pattern matching with maps typically matches on the key and
extracts the value or extracts both key-value pairs simultaneously.
Only the key-value pairs in the pattern will be matched.

```
iex> %{name: name, age: age} = %{
...>     name: "Alice",
...>     age: 42,
...>     city: "New York"
...> }
%{name: "Alice", age: 42, city: "New York"}
```

If we want to require a key but aren't interested in the value, we use an underscore.

```
iex> %{name: _, age: age} = %{
...>    name: "Bob",
...>    age: 42,
...>    city: "London"
...> }
```

We can also specify the value for the given key.

```
iex> %{name: "Bob", age: age} = %{
...>    name: "Alice",
...>    age: 42,
...>    city: "New York"
...> }
** (MatchError) no match of right hand side value
iex> %{name: "Bob", age: age} = %{
...>    name: "Bob",
...>    age: 24,
...>    city: "San Francisco"
...> }
%{name: "Bob", age: 24}
```

In this example, we specify the value of the key :name on the left-hand side of the match expression. This has the effect of requiring the matching right-hand side map to contain the key-value pair name: "Bob". The first example has the key-value pair name: "Alice", so the match fails.

This particular example is contrived. It's rare you would specify the left-hand side like this in a single match expression. You typically see these patterns in a case expression.

Pattern matching with complex data structures becomes even more powerful when you combine them to match against nested structures. Each value on the left-hand side can be replaced with a valid pattern. You can define patterns that match against nested tuples, lists, and maps.

For example:

```
iex> %{name: name, friends: [best_friend | _]} = %{
...> name: "Alice",
...> friends: ["Bob", "Christina", "Dave"]
}
%{name: "Alice", friends: ["Bob", "Christina", "Dave"]}
```

```
iex> best_friend
"Bob"
```

Here we match the first element of the `friends` list, ignoring the tail of the list.

Pattern matching to extract nested data can be quite useful at times. However, it is important to remember: with great power comes great responsibility. Nested pattern matching can both make your code cleaner and easier to read as well as more complex and harder to follow. It's generally a good idea to avoid overly nested patterns. Just because you can technically do something in a single line of code, doesn't always mean you should.

8.4   The Pin Operator

So far we have seen binding values to variables via pattern matching. We saw above that we can also use values on the left-hand side of the pattern matching expression to filter on a specific values.

Referring back to a prior example:

```
iex> %{name: "Bob", age: age} = %{
...>   name: "Alice",
...>   age: 42,
...>   city: "New York"
...> }
** (MatchError) no match of right hand side value
iex> %{name: "Bob", age: age} = %{
...>   name: "Bob",
...>   age: 24,
...>   city: "San Francisco"
...> }
%{name: "Bob", age: 24}
```

What happens if `"Bob"` is stored in a variable?

```
iex> name = "Bob"
"Bob"
iex> %{name: name, age: age} = %{name: "Alice", age: 32}
%{name: "Alice", age: 32}
iex> name
"Alice"
```

The original variable `name` was shadowed by a new variable `name` with the value of `"Alice"`. This might be what we want in *some* cases, but not this case. How do we tell Elixir to use the *value* of name, rather than rebind it? As we saw in the prior chapter, we can fix this with the pin operator.

Let's try this again.

```
iex> name = "Bob"
"Bob"
iex> %{name: ^name, age: age} = %{name: "Alice", age: 32}
** (MatchError) no match of right hand side value: %{name:
↪  "Alice", age: 32}
iex> %{name: ^name, age: age} = %{name: "Bob", age: 42}
%{name: "Bob", age: 42}
```

Now we get the desired behavior. The pin operator tells Elixir "don't rebind this variable but instead treat it as if it were a value."

8.5 Function Definitions

Pattern matching is not limited to simple assignments and data destructuring; it also plays a crucial role in function definitions in Elixir. But before we dive into pattern matching on function definitions, let's discuss some terminology. A *function clause* is made up of a function signature and body. That is, a function clause is made up of the def .... do .... end triple. A *funciton definition* consists of all function clauses with the same name.

You can define multiple function clauses for different scenarios and Elixir will pattern match to the most appropriate function clause at runtime. Elixir pattern matches the first function clause that matches the call site. That is, if you define two function clauses that match a given call to your function, Elixir will choose the one defined higher up in the file (i.e., smaller line number). This means you should put your most specific patterns first and least specific patterns last.

```
defmodule Calculator do
  def calculate(:add, x, y) do
    {:ok, x + y}
  end

  def calculate(:subtract, x, y) do
    {:ok, x - y}
  end

  def calculate(:multiply, x, y) do
```

```
    {:ok, x * y}
  end

  def calculate(:divide, _, 0) do
    {:error, "Cannot divide by 0"}
  end

  def calculate(:divide, x, y) do
    {:ok, x / y}
  end

  def calculate(op, _, _) do
    {:error, "Unrecognized operation (#{op})"}
  end
end
```

Let's try this out.

```
iex> Calculator.calculate(:add, 2, 3)
{:ok, 5}
iex> Calculator.calculate(:multiply, 2, 3)
{:ok, 6}
iex> Calculator.calculate(:divide, 4, 2)
{:ok, 2}
iex> Calculator.calculate(:divide, 4, 0)
{:error, "Cannot divide by 0"}
iex> Calculator.calculate(:rem, 5, 2)
{:error, "Unrecognized operation (rem)"}
```

Notice that calculate(:divide, _, 0) is a more specific pattern
when compared to its counterpart, calculate(:divide, x, y).
When a user calls calculate(:divide, some_val, some_other_val),
Elixir first checks if some_other_val is zero.   In the event
some_other_val is not equal to zero, the other implementation of
calculate(:divide, x, y) is called. Let's see what happens if we
reorder these functions.

```
defmodule Calculator do
  # Other code omitted

  def calculate(:divide, x, y) do
    {:ok, x / y}
  end

  def calculate(:divide, _, 0) do
    {:error, "Cannot divide by 0"}
  end
```

end

Now the less specific version is first. Since y can match anything, including zero, we will never hit the error case.

```
iex> Calculator.calculate(:divide, 4, 0)
** (ArithmeticError) bad argument in arithmetic expression:
↪   4 / 0
```

We can also use function clauses with anonymous functions. Let's see what happens if we rewrite our example using an anonymous function.

```
iex> calculate = fn
...>   :add, x, y -> {:ok, x + y}
...>   :subtract, x, y -> {:ok, x - y}
...>   :multiply, x, y -> {:ok, x * y}
...>   :divide, _, 0 -> {:error, "Cannot divide by 0"}
...>   :divide, x, y -> {:ok, x / y}
...> end
#Function<40.105768164/3 in :erl_eval.expr/6>
iex> calculate.(:divide, 6, 3)
{:ok, 2}
iex> calculate.(:divide, 5, 0)
{:error, "Cannot divide by 0"}
```

There's a catch with this example. The our calculate function *always* takes the same number of arguments. What if we expect a different number of arguments depending on the function? Let's take a look by adding a `:square` branch.

```
iex> calculate = fn
...>   :add, x, y -> {:ok, x + y}
...>   :subtract, x, y -> {:ok, x - y}
...>   :multiply, x, y -> {:ok, x * y}
...>   :divide, _, 0 -> {:error, "Cannot divide by 0"}
...>   :divide, x, y -> {:ok, x / y}
...>   :square, x -> {:ok, x * x}
...> end
error: cannot mix clauses with different arities in
↪   anonymous functions
```

This has a very simple solution – wrap the parameters in a tuple.

```
iex> calculate = fn
...>   {:add, x, y} -> {:ok, x + y}
...>   {:subtract, x, y} -> {:ok, x - y}
```

```
...>   {:multiply, x, y} -> {:ok, x * y}
...>   {:divide, _, 0} -> {:error, "Cannot divide by 0"}
...>   {:divide, x, y} -> {:ok, x / y}
...>   {:square, x} -> {:ok, x * x}
...> end
#Function<42.105768164/1 in :erl_eval.expr/6>
iex> calculate.({:square, 5})
{:ok, 25}
```

This technique (wrapping parameters in a tuple), is quite common in Elixir.

As a reminder, the order of function clauses matters. Elixir evaluates the clauses from top to bottom, and the first matching clause is executed. This implies we must always put the most specific function clauses first and the least specific function clauses last.

Another thing to be careful with here is overly complex function bodies when pattern matching. Overly complex or large function bodies obscure the patterns, making the code harder to understand. Breaking out the complex body into a helper function is a useful technique to reduce the visual complexity in this case.

8.6   Guards

Guards are a useful complement to pattern matching. They allow you to refine the conditions under which a pattern match succeeds. In some sense, you can think of them as an assertion that is always true if the function body is being executed.

Guards are boolean expressions, specified with the when keyword as we saw earlier. They can be used in various contexts where pattern matching occurs, such as function clauses, case expressions, and conditional statements. When a pattern match is attempted, Elixir first checks if the pattern matches the given value. If the match succeeds, the guard expressions are then evaluated.

We can rewrite our caclulate function from above with a guard to avoid division by zero.

```
defmodule Calculator do
  # Other code omitted

  def calculate(:divide, _, y) when y == 0 do
    {:error, "Cannot divide by 0"}
  end
```

```
  def calculate(:divide, x, y) do
    {:ok, x / y}
  end
end
```

Here, rather than specifying the arg y = 0 we use a guard on y ==
0. The guards ensure that only the appropriate clause is executed
based on the value of the guard.

So what can go in a guard? Comparison, arithmetic, binary, and
unary operators are all safe. Elixir also provides a number of guard-
safe functions for inspecting data. Macros constructed from guard-
safe functions are also safe. The primary concern with functions in
a guard clause is mutation. Functions used in a guard clause *must*
be pure (that is, they don't modify their input).

Chapter 9

Enum and Stream

9.1   The Enum Module

The Enum module is a powerful and versatile tool in Elixir for working with enumerables, which are data structures that can be iterated over, such as lists, maps, and ranges. It provides a wide range of functions for manipulating, transforming, and querying collections of data. The Enum module is one of the most frequently used libraries in Elixir, as it offers a concise and expressive way to perform common operations on collections.

One of the core concepts in the Enum module is the idea of enumeration. Enumeration is the process of iterating over each element in a collection and performing some operation on it. The Enum module provides a variety of functions for enumeration, such as `Enum.each/2` and `Enum.map/2`. The difference between these two is that `Enum.each/2` simply applies a function to each element while `Enum.map/2` uses the given function to transform the element (i.e., it's expected the function returns a value).

Another important aspect of the Enum module is its ability to filter and search collections. Functions like `Enum.filter/2` allow you to create a new collection containing only the elements that satisfy a given condition. `Enum.find/3` helps you locate the first element in a collection that matches the given predicate. `Enum.any?/2` and `Enum.all?/2` let you check if any or all elements in a collection satisfy a condition, respectively. These functions are invaluable

113

when working with large datasets or complex conditions.

The Enum module also provides functions for sorting and ordering collections. `Enum.sort/1` and `Enum.sort/2` allow you to sort elements in ascending order, either using the default comparison operator or a custom comparison function. `Enum.sort_by/2` lets you sort elements based on a derived value, which is useful when sorting complex structures or objects. Additionally, `Enum.min/1`, `Enum.max/1`, and `Enum.sum/1` help you find the minimum, maximum, and sum of elements in a collection, respectively.

The Enum module works with anything that implements the `Enumerable` protocol. One of the major strengths of the Enum module is that it provides a consistent and unified interface for manipulating and querying a large number of data structures. This promotes code reuse and allows you to write more generic and flexible functions that can handle various types of input.

Note

A quick note about the examples in this chapter. In most pipeline examples in this chapter, I will omit the IEx prefix (e.g., `iex>`) and instead just show the pipeline. However, I will start new lines with `|>`, rather than end lines with `|>`. This is typically how you will see pipelines formatted in projects. The one exception is in IEx, where your lines must *end* with `|>`.

9.2   The Stream Module

In Elixir, streams provide a powerful abstraction for working with collections of data in a lazy and composable manner. Functions in the Enum module eagerly evaluate and process entire collections at once. Streams, on the other hand, consist of a series of transformations and computations that are only executed when the result is actually needed. This lazy evaluation makes streams particularly useful for handling large or infinite datasets. It also makes them an excellent choice for building efficient and memory-friendly data processing pipelines.

At its core, a stream is a composable enumerable that represents a sequence of computations to be performed on a collection. Instead of immediately applying these computations and generating intermediate results, streams build up a series of operations that can be chained together using the pipe operator |>. This allows you to express complex data transformations in a clear and readable manner, without the overhead of creating intermediate collections at each step.

One surprisingly useful feature of streams is their ability to handle infinite sequences. With the Enum module, working with infinite collections is not possible. The Enum module's eager evaluation means the entire collection needs to fit in memory, so an infinite collection would require an infinite amount of memory. Streams, on the other hand, can efficiently process infinite sequences by generating values on-demand, only when they are needed. This makes streams a powerful tool for tasks such as processing real-time data feeds, or implementing complex algorithms that operate on unbounded input.

The careful reader might notice that up to this point we have typically used lists in our examples, and lists are not lazy. If streams are lazy, how do we create the input to the stream? The simplest stream is a Range. We create a range using the syntax first..last//step where first, last, and step are integers.

```
iex> x = 1..5
1..5
```

Let's try creating a simple stream.

```
iex> 1..5 |> Stream.map(&(&1 * 2))
#Stream<[enum: 1..5, funs: [#Function<50.105594673/1 in
↳   Stream.map/2>]]>
```

This creates a stream that, when evaluated, will apply the doubling function to each element in the list. Notice how a stream is returned, not a collection. No actual computation is performed until the stream is consumed using functions like Enum.to_list/1 or Enum.each/2. Let's conver this to a list using Enum.to_list/1.

```
iex> 1..5 |> Stream.map(&(&1 * 2)) |> Enum.to_list
[2, 4, 6, 8, 10]
```

The Stream module also provides a number of useful functions for creating streams:

- `Stream.cycle/1` - infinitely cycles through the given `Enumer-able`.
- `Stream.unfold/2` - the opposite of `Enum.fold/2`. Starting at the first argument, `acc`, it generates successive values until the `next_fun` returns `nil`. `next_fun` takes the current `acc` and returns the next `acc`.
- `Stream.resource/3` - converts the given resource (for example, a file, network connection, etc.) into a stream. This resource is created with `start_fun` (the first parameter). The second parameter, `next_fun`, is called each time a new element is requested from the stream. Once `next_fun` returns `{:halt, acc}`, `after_fun` (the last parameter) is called. This is typically used for resource cleanup (e.g., closing the file, network connection, etc.).

Let's build a function that determines whether a given number is prime our not. We will use it to look at the difference between streaming values through it using `Stream.map/2` (i.e., computing primes lazily) versus using `Enum.map/2` (i.e., computing the primes eagerly). As a reminder, a prime number is a number that is only divisible by itself and 1. We showed a function earlier that does this probabilistically. Why primes? Because finding primes is a computationally expensive problem.

Here's our function:

```
def probably_prime(n, k \\ 50) do
  is_fermat_probable_prime = fn a -> rem(pow(a, n - 1), n)
  ↪  == 1 end
  cond do
    n == 2 -> true
    rem(n, 2) == 0 -> false
    true -> Enum.find(
      1..k,
      :prime,
      fn _ -> not is_fermat_probable_prime.(:rand.uniform(n
      ↪  - 1)) end
    ) == :prime
  end
end
```

As a quick aside, for those curious about this function, it probabilistically determines whether a number is prime or not. That is, it doesn't say for certain a number is prime. It tells you a number is prime with a probability $1/2^k$ of being wrong. Let's give it a try.

```
20000..20500
|> Stream.map(fn x ->  {x, Primes.probably_prime(x)} end)
|> Stream.map(&IO.inspect/1)
|> Enum.to_list
# Output omitted
```

We pick a range of large numbers to make the computation somewhat more challenging/interesting. You'll notice the numbers are printed to the screen one by one. Let's see what happens when we change the `Stream.map` to an `Enum.map`

```
20000..20500
|> Enum.map(fn x ->  {x, Primes.probably_prime(x)} end)
|> Enum.map(&IO.inspect/1)
|> Enum.to_list
# Output omitted
```

Now you should see a pause, and then all numbers printed out at once. This is the difference between lazy and eager. Streams process their input one by one, where each input travels through the processing pipe before the next input is processed. The eager way, using `Enum.map`, processes the entire input at each stage of the pipeline.

What if we moved the call to `IO.inspect/1` to inside the anonymous function executed by `Stream.map`?

```
20000..20500
|> Stream.map(fn x ->
  IO.inspect({x, Primes.probably_prime(x)})
end)
|> Enum.to_list
# Output omitted
```

Ok, not too interesting. The behavior is the same as before. What happens when we change `Stream.map/1` to `Enum.map/1` though?

```
20000..20500
|> Enum.map(fn x ->  IO.inspect({x,
↪  Primes.probably_prime(x)}) end)
|> Enum.to_list
# Output omitted
```

Now we see the same behavior as a stream! What's happening here? When we moved the `IO.inspect/1` call inside the anonymous

function, the function composition had the same effect as pipelining.
However, it's important to note that the Enum.map/1 version is still
eager. Even though we are seeing the numbers "stream" on the
screen, we are really just seeing that stage of the pipeline being
computed. The effect is more clear if we add a second Enum.map/1
and nested IO.inspect/1 call.

```
20000..20500
|> Enum.map(fn x -> IO.inspect({x,
↪    Primes.probably_prime(x)}) end)
|> Enum.map(fn x -> IO.inspect(elem(x, 0)))
|> Enum.to_list
# Output omitted
```

Although the output appears to be streaming, it is very clear that
we are computing each stage in its entirety before moving on to the
next stage. First we create a collection of tuples {<number>, <is
prime>}, and then map them to a collection of numbers {<number>}.

We've focused on creating streams from a range. In the next section,
we will look at a few other useful functions for creating streams.

9.3   Creating, Composing, and Manipulating Streams

The Stream module provides a number of useful functions that
make it easy to create streams. The simplest way to create a stream
is by using Stream.map/2 function on an enumerable data structure.
Let's create a stream of squares:

```
iex> [1, 2, 3, 4, 5] |> Stream.map(&(&1 * &1))
#Stream<[
  enum: [1, 2, 3, 4, 5],
  funs: [#Function<50.105594673/1 in Stream.map/2>]
]>
```

This creates a new stream that will return a stream of squares. We
can evaluate part of the stream with Stream.take/1.

```
[1, 2, 3, 4, 5]
|> Stream.map(&(&1 * &1))
|> Stream.take(3)
|> Enum.to_list
# [1, 4, 9]
```

We can check that we never square the numbers 4 and 5 by adding an IO.inspect/1 call

```
[1, 2, 3, 4, 5]
|> Stream.map(&(&1 * &1))
|> Stream.map(&IO.inspect/1)
|> Stream.take(3)
# 1
# 4
# 9
# [1, 4, 9]
```

Recall that the pipe operator (|>) passes the value on the left as the first argument to the function on the right. The pipe oeprator is used extensively in enumerable and stream composition.

Composing streams is as simple as piping the output of one stream function into the input of another. This creates a flow of data through the pipeline. Each function in the pipeline receives the stream from the previous operation, applies its transformation, and passes the resulting stream to the next function. The process continues until the final result is computed or the stream is exhausted. Consider the following pipeline that filters out odd numbers, squares each remaining number, and takes the first five results:

```
[1, 2, 3, 4, 5, 6, 7, 8, 9, 10]
|> Stream.filter(&(rem(&1, 2) == 0))
|> Stream.map(&(&1 * &1))
|> Enum.take(5)
# [4, 16, 36, 64, 100]
```

The list is piped into Stream.filter/2, which removes all odd numbers. Each value output from Stream.filter/2 is even and is then squared by the folowing Stream.map/2. We then pipe the result into Enum.take/2, which collects the first 5 elements and returns them as a list.

Another useful function for creating streams is Stream.iterate/2. Stream.iterate/2 generates an infinite stream by repeatedly applying a function to the initial value. The function tells iterate/2 how to generate the next value in the sequence. This next value will then be fed back to the function and so on. The resulting stream will consist of the starting value, followed by the result of applying the function to the starting value, then the result of applying the function to that result, and so on. Let's look at a toy example, streaming powers of 2.

```
Stream.iterate(1, &(&1 * 2))
|> Stream.take(5)
|> Enum.to_list
[1, 2, 4, 8, 16]
```

How about something a little more complex, like the Fibonacci numbers?

```
Stream.iterate({0, 1}, fn {x, y} -> {y, x + y} end)
|> Stream.map(&(elem(&1, 0)))
|> Stream.map(&IO.puts/1)
|> Stream.take(10)
|> Stream.run
# 0
# 1
# 1
# 2
# 3
# 5
# 8
# 13
# 21
# 34
# :ok
```

This example uses a new function we have not yet seen: Stream.run/1. We use Stream.run/1 to consume a stream without needing its output. For example, maybe the stream is deleting or moving files.

Another useful function from the Stream module is Stream.resource/3. Stream.resource/3 takes three different functions. The first function is called to kick off the stream. The second function is used to iterate through the stream. The final function is used to cleanup resources after iteration has completed.

Let's look at an example of streaming the lines of a file.

```
Stream.resource(
  fn -> File.open!(filename) end,
  fn file ->
    case IO.read(file, :line) do
      data when is_binary(data) ->
          {[String.trim(data)], file}
      _ -> {:halt, file}
    end
```

```
  end,
  &File.close/1
)
|> Stream.map(&IO.puts/1)
|> Stream.run
```

In addition to the functions mentioned above, the Stream module provides many other useful functions for manipulating streams, such as `Stream.concat/2` for concatenating two streams, `Stream.uniq/1` for removing duplicates, and `Stream.scan/3` for accumulating values over a stream. These functions, along with the ability to compose operations using the pipe operator, make streams an indispensable tool for processing large or complex datasets in Elixir.

Creating and manipulating streams in Elixir is a powerful and flexible way to process data in a lazy and efficient manner. By compose functions together you can build sophisticated data processing pipelines that are both expressive and performant. Whether you're working with large datasets, infinite sequences, or complex transformations, streams provide a valuable abstraction for handling data in a functional and composable way.

9.4   Building Pipelines

One of the most powerful features of streams in Elixir is the ability to compose multiple operations together to build efficient data processing pipelines. By chaining stream functions using the pipe operator (`|>`), you can create a sequence of transformations that are executed in a lazy and memory-efficient manner. This allows you to express complex data manipulations in a clear, readable, and concise way, without the overhead of creating intermediate collections at each step.

Let's extend our previous example of finding prime numbers to filter out numbers that aren't prime.

```
20000..20500
|> Stream.map(fn x ->  {x, Primes.probably_prime(x)} end)
|> Stream.filter(&(elem(&1, 1)))
|> Stream.map(&IO.inspect/1)
|> Enum.to_list
```

The real power of stream composition lies in its ability to handle large or infinite datasets without consuming excessive memory.

Because streams are lazy, each operation in the pipeline is only executed when its result is actually needed, and intermediate results are discarded as soon as they are no longer required. This allows you to process data incrementally, in small chunks, rather than loading the entire dataset into memory at once. For instance, you can use streams to efficiently process large files:

```
File.stream!("large_file.txt")
|> Stream.map(&String.trim/1)
|> Stream.filter(&(String.length(&1) > 0))
|> Stream.map(&String.to_integer/1)
|> Enum.sum()
```

This pipeline reads the file line by line, trimming whitespace, filtering out empty lines, converting each line to an integer, and computing the sum of all numbers in the file, without ever loading the entire file into memory.

Another benefit of stream composition is the ability to reuse and combine pipelines to create more complex data processing workflows. You can build a library of transformation functions that can be composed and applied to different inputs. Let's take a look at how this is done.

```
defmodule Enumerate do
  def enumerate(enum) do
    enumerator = fn i, acc -> {[{acc, i}], acc + 1} end
    enum |> Stream.trasnform(0, enumerator)
  end
end
```

This function provides functionality similar to Python's `enumerate` function.

```
iex> ["a", "b", "c"] |> Enumerate.enumerate |> Enum.to_list
[{0, "a"}, {1, "b"}, {2, "c"}]
```

This functionality is so useful, the Stream module already provides it via the `Stream.with_index/2` function (though the index is the second element, not the first).

In addition to common functions like `map`, `filter`, and `take`, the Stream module provides a wide range of useful functions.

- `Stream.flat_map/2`: Applies the given function to each element of the stream, and flattens the resulting streams into a single stream.

- Stream.scan/2: Performs a cumulative operation over the stream, similar to Enum.reduce/3, but emits the intermediate results as a stream.
- Stream.chunk_every/2: Splits the stream into chunks of a specified size, emitting each chunk as a separate stream.
- Stream.zip/2: Combines two streams, emitting a stream of tuples containing the corresponding elements from each stream.

- Stream.concat/2: Concatenates two streams, emitting the elements of the first stream followed by the elements of the second stream.

Let's look at a few quick examples

```
iex> [1, 2, 3] |>
...> Stream.flat_map(fn x -> 0..x) |>
...> Enum.to_list
[0, 1, 0, 1, 2, 0, 1, 2, 3] # 0..n for each element
iex> [1, 2, 3, 4] |>
...> Stream.scan(&(&1 * &2)) |>
...> Enum.to_list
[1, 2, 6, 24] # n! for each element
iex> [1, 2, 3] |>
...> Stream.chunk_every(1) |>
...> Enum.to_list
[[1], [2], [3]]
iex>
#Stream<[enum: [1, 2, 3, 4], funs: [#Function<56.105594673/1
↪   in Stream.scan/2>]]>
iex> Stream.zip([1, 2, 3, 4], factorials) |> Enum.to_list
[{1, 1}, {2, 2}, {3, 6}, {4, 24}] # (n, n!) for each n
iex> Stream.concat(1..4, 4..1//-1) |> Enum.to_list
[1, 2, 3, 4, 4, 3, 2, 1]
```

Let's take a look at using Stream.scan/3 to implement Python's enumerate function, like we did with Stream.transform/3.

```
defmodule Enumerate do
  def enumerate(enum) do
    enum |> Stream.scan(
      {-1, nil},
      fn x, {i, _} -> {i + 1, x} end
    )
  end
end
```

9.5   Infinite Streams

One of the more interesting effects of streams being lazy is their ability to represent infinite sequences of data. Traditional collections like lists, maps, and sets have a finite size and are stored in memory Streams on the other hand can generate values on-demand, producing an endless supply of data without consuming excessive resources. This makes streams an ideal tool for working with unbounded datasets, generating complex sequences, and implementing algorithms that operate on infinite inputs.

Functions like `Stream.iterate/2`, `Stream.cycle/1`, or `Stream.repeatedly/1` are some of the more useful stream functions for creating infinite streams. `Stream.iterate/2` generates an infinite stream by repeatedly applying a function to a starting value, producing a sequence of values where each element is derived from the previous one. For example, to create an infinite stream of natural numbers starting from 1, you can use:

```
iex> Stream.iterate(1, &(&1 + 1)) |> Stream.take(10) |>
↪   Enum.to_list
[1, 2, 3, 4, 5, 6, 7, 8, 9, 10]
```

This stream will generate the sequence of natural numbers 1, 2, 3, 4, and so on.

`Stream.cycle/1` creates an infinite stream by repeatedly cycling through the elements of an enumerable. This is useful when you need to generate a repeating pattern or process a sequence of values indefinitely. For instance, to create an infinite stream of alternating 0s and 1s, you can use:

```
Stream.cycle([0, 1])
```

This stream will produce the sequence 0, 1, 0, 1, 0, 1, and so on, forever.

`Stream.repeatedly/1` generates an infinite stream by repeatedly invoking a given function and returning the value returned by the function. This is useful when you need to generate a constant stream of values or randomized data. For example, to create an infinite stream of of values from the distribution $U(0, 1)$ with two digits of precision, you can use:

```
random_numbers = Stream.repeatedly(fn -> Enum.random(0..100)
↪    / 100 end)
```

Of course we don't really need *infinite* here. Infinite streams are useful for handling sequences of data that never end. For example, we can model continuous flows of data in real-time data processing and event-driven systems as infinite streams. This allows us build pipelines that process and analyze the data incrementally, responding to new events as they arrive.

Infinite streams may feel a bit like lazy evaluation with an infinite while-loop in other languages. They share a lot of similarity, which means they also share the same risks. Although the memory overhead of infinite streams is minimal, they do require quite a bit of care. Infinite streams can very easily lead to infinite loops and excessive resource consumption (e.g., CPU, network requests, etc.). As with all tools, use when and where appropriate, and make sure to carefully consider what might go wrong.

9.6 Conclusion

At this point in the book you have most of the Elixir knowledge you will need to write just about any program you can imagine. You should know how to write idiomatic Elixir code, define your own modules and functions, pipeline operations, and work with streams of data. So what's left? Concurrency.

The rest of this book will teach how to take your Elixir code and run it concurrently. It will teach you how to think about fault-tolerance within the world of OTP and how to realize those ideas in code. This work will culminate in a chapter where we walk through building a multi-service system that leverages gRPC, Kafka, and Postgres.

Chapter 10

Processes and Concurrency

Processes (and the BEAM) are one of the primary reasons people come to Erlang and Elixir. They are the fundamental building blocks for concurrent programming and form the foundation for building scalable and fault-tolerant systems. Elixir processes are lightweight and isolated. A single machine can run tens of thousands of processes without issue. Each process has its own memory space and communicates with other processes through message passing, ensuring no shared mutable state between them.

Exlir processes are more efficient than OS threads in terms of memory usage and context switching. A context switch of an Elixir process is done by a BEAM scheduler thread. This is generally more efficient than a kernel context switch and is what allows Elixir to spawn and manage a large number of processes without significant overhead. You can read more about BEAM internals in Appendix A.

One of the key benefits of Elixir's processes is fault isolation. Processes are isolated from each other so a failure in one process does not directly impact other processes. Crashed or failed processes can be independently restarted without affecting other processes within the system.

Processes in Elixir communicate with each other through message passing. Each process has a unique process identifier (PID). This PID is used as an address when sending messages between processes. Message passing is asynchronous, which allows processes to work concurrently. Each process has its own small heap. The heap grows as needed and it's memory is automatically reclaimed when the process terminates.

10.1   Creating and Managing Processes

The `spawn/1` function creates a process. [1] It takes a function as an argument and creates a new process to execute that function. The spawned process runs independently and concurrently with the parent process that created it. The spawn function returns a process identifier (PID) that uniquely identifies the process. This PID can also be used communicate with the process and monitor its lifecycle.

Here's a simple example of spawning a new process:

```
pid = spawn(
  fn -> IO.puts("Hello from #{inspect(self())}!") end
)
```

Here we spawn a process that immediately prints `"Hello from #PID<some pid>!"`. The function `self/0` returns the PID of the process from which the function was called. `spawn/1` also returns the PID of the created process, which we can use to send messages (covered in the next section). We use the `inspect/2` function to print the PID. We would get an error about `String.Chars` not being implemented for `#PID<...>` if we had omitted that.

You might wonder if we can create a process from within a process. In fact, we can. Elixir provides the `spawn_link/1` function, for just this puprose and links created process to the parent process. If one of the linked processes terminates abnormally (e.g., due to an error), the other process also terminates. This linking mechanism is useful for establishing a relationship between processes and propagating failures. If the linked process terminates normally, the parent process is unaffected.

---

[1]Recall, functions that aren't prefixed with a module are from the Kernel module . The Kernel module contains a number of functions that are commonly used, including many of the Elixir keywords.

Before we get too deep into creating and managing processes, I should point out that generally you won't create processes with `spawn/1` or `spawn_link/1`. There are other techniques leveraging Tasks, Agents, and GenServer which are simpler and offer better abstractions. However, these are built on top of the functionality offered by `spawn/1` and `spawn_link/1`, so it's important we understand the basics first. We will cover these other techniques later in the book. Elixir provides several built-in functions to simplify managing processes. The Process module offers functions for interacting with processes, such as sending messages (`Process.send/3`[2] or `send/2`), checking process information (`Process.info/1`), and monitoring process termination (`Process.monitor/1`). These functions allow you to communicate with processes, retrieve process metadata, and handle process lifecycle events.

The challenge with using PIDs for communication is you don't know the PID until after the process has been created. Elixir allows you to assign a unique name to a process to solve this issue. Once a process is registred via `Process.register/2`, it can be referenced by its name instead of its PID.

When a process terminates, regardless of how, it sends an exit signal to its linked processes. By default, the exit signal causes the linked processes to terminate as well. However, processes can trap exit signals using `Process.flag(:trap_exit, true)` function, allowing them to handle the termination gracefully and perform any necessary cleanup or recovery actions.

In addition to the low-level process management functions, Elixir provides higher-level abstractions and libraries for building concurrent and distributed systems. The `Task` module simplifies the creation and management of short-lived processes that perform a specific task. The `Agent` module provides a simple way to manage shared state across processes. The GenServer behavior encapsulates the common patterns for building generic server processes that maintain state and handle client requests. These abstractions build on top of the basic process primitives and offer a more structured and convenient approach to concurrent programming.

---

[2]As we just saw, there are actually two different ways to send a message. One, `Process.send/3`, from the Process module, allows you to specify whether a connection to an external node. The other version, `send/2` (from the Kernel module), also sends a message, but will establish a connection with a remote node if necessary. Generally prefer the `send/2` over `Process.send/3`, unless you have a good reason not to.

10.2   Message Passing

In Elixir, processes communicate with each other through message passing. Message passing allows processes to exchange data and coordinate their activities without sharing memory or resources directly. When a process sends a message to another process, the message is put in the receiving processes mailbox. When the receiving process is ready to read its message, it fetches it from the mailbox. This avoids blocking on message send/receive.

Messages are sent using send/2. The first argument is the PID of the receiving process and the second argument is the message itself. The message can be just about any Elixir datatype.

```
send(pid, "Hello")
```

A pattern you will see far more often is sending a tuple, where the first element of the tuple is an atom that indicates the intent of the message. This makes the receiving code a bit more clear, as the atom indicates what kind of message is being processed.

The send operation is asynchronous, meaning that the sending process does not wait for the receiving process to acknowledge or process the message. The message is simply placed in the mailbox of the receiving process, and the sending process continues its execution immediately. This asynchronous nature of message passing allows processes to work independently and concurrently, without blocking each other.

A process uses the receive do block to retrieve messages from its mailbox. The receive block consists of a series of pattern matching clauses that specify how to handle different types of messages. When a message arrives in the process's mailbox, Elixir tries to match it against the patterns in the receive block, executing the corresponding code block for the first matching pattern. If no pattern matches the message, the process blocks until a matching message arrives or a timeout occurs.

To get a better feel for processes, let's create function that listens to messages forever and takes action based on the received message.

```
defmodule MyProcess do

  def pid do
    inspect(self())
```

```
    end

  defp listen do
    IO.puts(
      "#{pid()} commands: {:stop, reason}, {:echo, msg}"
    )

    receive do
      {:stop, reason} ->
        IO.puts("#{pid()} is exiting: #{reason}")
        :stop_listening

      {:echo, msg} ->
        IO.puts("#{pid()} received message: #{msg}")
        :keep_listening

      _ ->
        IO.puts("#{pid()} received unrecognized msg")
        :stop_listening
    end
  end

  def listen_forever() do
    case listen() do
      :stop_listening -> IO.puts("exiting")
      :keep_listening -> listen_forever()
    end
  end
end
```

The private function `MyProcess.listen/0` blocks and waits for a message. Depending on the message received, `MyProcess.listen_forever/0` will either recursively call itself (listening again) or exit. Notice for this functionality we need something that repeats over and over until we receive a `:stop` message. The most natural way to implement this is through recursion. Putting most of the logic in `MyProcess.listen/0` makes it easier and cleaner to make the recursion tail-call optimized.

Let's try this out in IEx.

```
iex> p1 = spawn(fn -> MyProcess.listen_forever() end)
#PID<p1 pid>
"#PID<p1 pid> commands: {:stop, reason}, {:echo, msg}"
iex> send(p1, {:echo, "Hello there from
↪    #{inspect(self())}"})
"#PID<p1 pid> received message: Hello there from #PID<parent
↪    pid>"
```

An important note to point out is you can also use registered process names or a tuple of registered process name and node name. So far we have only considered processes on a local machine, but Elixir can easily scale across many machines. Communicating with a process on another machine only requires the name of the machine and the process identifier (registered name or PID).

It's worth repeating, the PIDs in this example are simplified. You will see different, and longer, numbers (e.g., `#PID<0.127.0>`). Here we create a reference to the parent PID of the shell (`my_pid`). We then spawn a new process (`#PID<2>`) and send a message to the parent process (`#PID<1>`). The parent process receives this message with the `receive do` block.

Message passing in Elixir is not limited to simple data types. You can send complex data structures, such as lists, maps, or even functions, as messages between processes. This flexibility allows processes to exchange rich data and collaborate on more intricate tasks. However, it's important to keep in mind that message passing involves copying the data, so sending large data structures can impact performance.

One of the benefits of message passing is that it enables location transparency. Processes can communicate with each other regardless of whether they are running on the same node or distributed across multiple nodes in a cluster. Elixir's distributed programming capabilities, built on top of the Erlang VM, allow processes to send messages transparently across network boundaries, making it easy to build scalable and fault-tolerant distributed systems.

In addition to the basic send and receive primitives, Elixir provides higher-level abstractions and libraries that build upon message passing. The GenServer module, for example, encapsulates a common pattern of building server processes that receive requests, process them, and send a reply. The Agent module provides a simple way to manage shared state across processes using message passing behind the scenes. These abstractions make it easier to work with processes and message passing in a more structured and maintainable way.

10.3   Process Registration

Using PIDs for communication poses a problem. How do you know what the PID is? In the prior example, we are spawning a process and sending a message to the spawned process all from the same root process. In this context, we have the PID of the spawned process. What should we do if we want to send a message from another process?

Fortunately, Elixir provides functionality to assign a name to a spawned process. We can use this name to send messages, rather than relying on the PID. Let's try this in IEx. First let's define a simple echo process. It will loop forever, waiting for a message. When it receives an :echo message, it echoes the given message. Upon receiving a :exit message, it exits.

```
# process/my_process.ex
defmodule MyProcess do
  def start() do
    loop()
  end

  defp loop() do
    receive do
      {:echo, msg} ->
        IO.puts("Echoing: #{msg}")
        loop()
      {:exit} ->
        IO.puts("Exiting")
    end
  end
end
```

Let's spawn this and send a message using the process's PID.

```
iex> c "my_process.ex"
[MyProcess]
iex> pid = spawn(&MyProcess.start/0)
#PID<0.1.0>
iex> send(pid, {:echo, "Hello with a pid"})
"Hello with a pid"
```

Now let's register the process and try again.

```
iex> Process.register(pid, :my_process)
true
iex> send(:my_process, {:echo, "Hello world using a name!"})
"Hello world using a name!"
iex> Process.registered()
[..., :my_process, ...] # Some output omitted
```

10.4   Process Linking and Monitoring

In Elixir, process linking and monitoring are two essential techniques for building fault-tolerant and resilient systems. They allow processes to establish relationships and react to the termination or failure of other processes, enabling effective error handling and recovery strategies. By linking and monitoring processes, developers can create systems that gracefully handle failures and maintain a consistent state even in the presence of errors or crashes.

Process linking is a mechanism that creates a bidirectional relationship between two processes. When a process links to another process, it establishes a connection that allows both processes to receive notifications about each other's termination. If one of the linked processes terminates abnormally (i.e., crashes or raises an unhandled exception), the other process also terminates. This behavior ensures that related processes fail together, preventing inconsistencies and maintaining a coherent system state.

To link two processes in Elixir, you can use the `spawn_link/1` or `spawn_link/3` functions instead of the regular `spawn/1` or `spawn/3` functions. These functions create a new process and automatically link it to the calling process. For example:

```
pid = spawn_link(fn -> IO.puts("Linked process") end)
```

In this case, the newly spawned process is linked to the parent process that called `spawn_link`. If either the parent process or the linked process terminates abnormally, the other process will also terminate.

Process monitoring, on the other hand, is a unidirectional relationship between processes. When a process monitors another process, it receives notifications about the monitored process's termination, regardless of the reason for termination (normal or abnormal). Unlike linking, monitoring does not cause the monitoring process to terminate when the monitored process terminates. Instead, the monitoring process receives a message indicating the termination reason, allowing it to handle the situation gracefully.

To monitor a process in Elixir, you can use the `Process.monitor/1` function. This function takes a process identifier (PID) as an argument and returns a unique reference that identifies the monitoring relationship. For example:

```
ref = Process.monitor(pid)
```

After calling `Process.monitor/1`, the monitoring process will receive a message of the form `{:DOWN, ref, :process, pid, reason}` when the monitored process terminates. The `ref` is the monitoring reference returned by `Process.monitor/1`, `pid` is the identifier of the terminated process, and reason indicates the termination reason (e.g., `:normal`, `:shutdown`, `{:exit, error}`).

Process linking and monitoring are particularly useful when building supervisor hierarchies. Supervisors are processes that are responsible for starting, monitoring, and restarting child processes in case of failures. By linking or monitoring child processes, supervisors can detect and handle process terminations, ensuring that the system remains in a consistent state. Supervisors can implement various restart strategies, such as one-for-one (restarting only the failed process), one-for-all (restarting all child processes), or rest-for-one (restarting the failed process and the ones started after it).

Elixir's OTP (Open Telecom Platform) framework provides a set of tools and abstractions for building fault-tolerant systems using process linking and monitoring. The `Supervisor` and `GenServer` behaviours, both of which are part of OTP, provide common patterns for process supervision and server-client interactions. They allow developers to focus on writing the business logic of their applications while relying on the proven fault-tolerance mechanisms provided by OTP.

10.5 Tasks

Tasks provide a convenient interface for concurrent execution of work. They simplify spawning and managing concurrent units of work. Think of them as a way to convert a blocking task (no pun intended) into a concurrent, asynchronously running process.

A task in Elixir represents a concurrent operation that can be spawned and executed independently of other tasks. Tasks are typically used for short-lived, one-off operations that don't require complex state management or long-running computations. Examples of tasks include making HTTP requests, querying databases, or writing to a file. Tasks are implemented using the `Task` module, which provides a set of functions for creating, starting, and managing tasks.

You create tasks using the `Task.async/1` function, passing an anonymous function or a named function as an argument. The `Task.async/1` function spawns a new process to execute the given function asynchronously. The function is non-blocking and returns a task struct representing the spawned task. You can monitor task progress, wait for its completion, and retrieve its result from the tast struct.

```
iex> task = Task.async(fn ->
...>    Process.sleep(5000) # sleep 5s
...>    IO.puts("Hi from #{inspect(self())}")
...> end)
%Task{
  mfa: {:erlang, :apply, 2},
  owner: #PID<0.109.0>,
  pid: #PID<0.110.0>,
  ref: #Reference<0...>
}
iex> IO.puts("hi")
hi
:ok
Hi from #PID<1>
```

Notice how the task spawns, returns the task struct, and then we are returned to the IEx prompt. If you type fast enough (or increase the sleep interval), you can write to std out (e.g., `IO.puts("hi")`) before the spawned task executes its `IO.puts/1`.

You can `await` task completion using `Task.await/2` function, which also returns the task result. The `Task.await/2` function takes the task struct and an optional timeout value as arguments. It blocks the calling process until the task completes or the specified timeout is reached. If the task completes successfully, the result of the task is returned. If the task fails or raises an exception, the error is propagated to the calling process. Here's an example of awaiting a task:

```
iex> Task.await(
...>    Task.async(fn ->
...>    Process.sleep(3000)
...>    IO.puts("Hi from task")
...>    end)
...> )
Hi from task
```

Notice we changed the sleep interval to 3 seconds. This is because the default timeout for `Task.await/2` is 5 seconds. `Task.await/2` also accepts `:infinity` as a second arugment, in which case it blocks until the task completes.

`Task.yield/2` is another useful function from the `Task` module. It is a non-blocking function that returns the status of the task. `Task.yield/2` returns {:ok, result} if the task has completed, otherwise it returns `nil`.

The `Task` module also provides the `Task.async_stream/3` function, which allows you to create a stream of tasks and process them concurrently. It takes an enumerable, a function to apply to each element, and options for configuring the concurrency and timeout. The `Task.async_stream/3` function returns a stream that can be used to retrieve the results of the tasks as they complete. Let's try it out.

In the first example, we are going to set an optional paramter `:ordered` to `false` so that results are returned as they are ready, rather than in the order in which their owning task was created.

```
iex> Task.async_stream(
...>    1..5,
...>    fn i ->
...>      Process.sleep((5 - i) * 1000)
...>      "i = #{i}"
...>    end,
...>    max_concurrency: 5,
...>    ordered: false)
...>    |> Stream.map(fn {_, res} -> IO.puts(res))
...>    |> Stream.run
...> )
i = 5
i = 4
i = 3
i = 2
i = 1
:ok
```

Here we are creating five tasks. For each task i, we sleep for $5 - i$ seconds. So the first task sleeps for 5 seconds, the second 4 seconds, and the last task sleeps for 1 second. Notice that the last task we create, $i = 5$, is the first task to finish and, also, the first task to return its result. This illustrates that, with `:ordered` set to `false`, `Task.async_stream/3` processes tasks as they complete, rather than as they are created. Let's try it again, but this time with `:ordered` set to true.

```
iex> Task.async_stream(
...>     1..5,
...>     fn i ->
...>         Process.sleep((5 - i) * 1000)
...>         "i = #{i}"
...>     end,
...>     max_concurrency: 5,
...>     ordered: false)
...>     |> Stream.map(fn {_, res} -> IO.puts(res))
...>     |> Stream.run
...> )
i = 1
i = 2
i = 3
i = 4
i = 5
:ok
```

Here, even though task $i = 5$ is the first to finish, its result is buffered until the remaining tasks complete. The results are then returned in the order in which their tasks were created.

As with many of the other techniques we ahve learned, always choose the right tool for the job. Tasks are lightweight and ideal for short-lived operations, like network requests, disk IO, etc. There are better tools for long-running, CPU-intensive tasks such as GenServer and the Flow framework. These tools provide additional functionality for things like managing state, fault tolerance, and back-pressure.

Conclusion

Now we have seen the low-level mechanics of concurrency in Elixir. As I mentioned earlier, you will generally *not* use the spawn functions mentioned throughout this chapter. Instead, you will design your applications using behvaiours like GenServer and Supervisor (maybe Agent). These help you focus on core application logic and high-level fault-tolerance ideas rather than dealing with the lower-level pieces of actually spawning and linking processes.

Chapter 11

OTP

11.1 Introduction

The Open Telecom Platform (OTP) is a set of libraries and design principles for building concurrent, fault-tolerant applications. It was developed at Ericsson in the 1980s, initially for telephony applications (unsurprisingly). The OTP provides useful abstractions for complex concurrency and fault-tolerance mechanisms. These abstractions come in the form of middleware, tools, and libraries for building reliable distributed systems. Despite being initially designed for telecom systems, the OTP is generally useful for distributed systems of all kinds.

One of the core focuses of the OTP initially was addressing the challenges of building highly available systems that leverage a massive amount of concurrency. Availability, in the distributed systems world, is when a system is reachable by its clients. A system that is highly available is one that rarely goes down.

There are four major pieces of the OTP:

- **Behaviours** – we will see a number of these throughout the book, such as `GenServer`, `Supervisor`, `Application`, and `Task`
- **Supervision Trees** – as we will see in the chapter on Supervisors, supervision trees are a powerful tool for building reliable, self-healing systems.
- **Release Handling** – the OTP provides a number of tools for packaging and deploying your code.

- **Middleware** – the less glamorous modules for handling essential functionality for any system, such as logging, configuration, and event handling.

In addition to the major components of the OTP, there are several guiding philosophies and idioms put forward to simplify buildling reliable distributed systems. These include

- **BEAM VM** - this provides Erlang (and by extension, Elixir) the ability to handle massive concurrency
- **Message Passing** - state is shared via asynchronous messages, rather than a shared memory location.
- **Fault Isolation** - process crashes are contained. Unless an exit signal propogates all the way to the root process, a crashed process will not bring down the entire system.
- **Supervision Strategies** - these are how you customize the response of the system in the face of failure.

One of the core ideas underlying the OTP is the idea of abstracting away concurrency. Sequential programs are much simpler to understand an reason about than their concurrent counterparts. One way in which the OTP encourages abstracting

At its core, OTP is based on the actor model[1], a concurrency model that treats computation as the exchange of messages between independent entities called actors. In Elixir, these actors are represented by processes, which are lightweight and isolated units of computation that communicate with each other through message passing. OTP provides a set of abstractions and behaviors that help manage these processes, making it easier to build and reason about concurrent systems.

11.2   Let it Crash

One of the more unique aspects of the OTP is its approach to error handling. In most languages, the focus is on preventing as many errors as possible. If you've ever worked on a production system you've likely encountered at least one code base littered with try-catch statements. The OTP, and by association, Elixir, takes a different approach. As we saw in chapter 8, Elixir prefers working with error atoms and pattern matching.

---

[1]This is commonly repeated but sometimes questioned and probably not true. This is discussed in greater detail in a later footnote in this chapter.

If you spend any time around Elixir or Erlang you will hear the idea of "let it crash." It's not always clear what is meant by this. Let's start with what it *doesn't* mean. "Let it crash" does not mean you can stop worry about errors and error handling.

You should still check a file exists before trying to write to it. If you create a network connection, you should check that the connection was successfully created before using it. These are all common error scenarios we need to worry about in any language and any setting. *How* we handle those checks in Elixir may be different (i.e., error codes and pattern matching), but we still need to worry about errors.

So what does "Let it crash" mean? It means we don't need to go through herculean efforts to make sure no exception or error *ever* bubbles up through our program. If a process crashes, no sweat. Since processes are isolated, a failure in one wont affect another. This is *not* the case in other languages like Go, Java, C++, or Python.

Let's take a look at a common scenario in Go where a crash in one goroutine (conceptually very similar to an Elixir process) will bring down the entire program.

```go
import (
    "http"
    "log"
)

type Data struct {
    Person *Person `json:"person,omitempty"`
}

type Person struct {
    Name  string `json:"name"`
    Email string `json:"email"`
}

func handleRequest(req) {
    var data Data

    if err := json.Unmarshl(req.data, &person); err != nil {
        log.Errorf("encountered an error - %s", err)
        return
    }

    person := data.Person
```

```
    // This line will bring down the whole server
    // if person is nil
    saveDataToDb(person.Name, person.Email)
}

func RequestHandler(req http.Request) {
    // Creates a "goroutine", similar to a process
    go handleRequest(req)
}
```

Go is an easy language to read, but it's worth walking through the code. (If you do know Go, I've intentionally omitted some stuff to keep this example as simple as possible.) The function RequestHandler is getting called by some other function to handle the http.Request. It offloads this work to the function handleRequest. The call to handleRequest does not happen sequentially. Instead, it is executed in a goroutine (this is indicated by go preceding the function call). Goroutines are Go's equivalent of processes, but they are *not* isolated. Otherwise, they work largely the same. They are scheduled and executed by the Go runtime just like Elixir processes are scheduled by the BEAM VM.

Where things get a little different with Go is the call to saveDataToDb. Note that we are dereferencing the field Data.Person, which is a pointer. If the request payload doesn't contain JSON for a Person, then person will be nil and the accesses to its fields, person.Name and person.Email will result in goroutine panics due to a nil pointer dereference.

In Go, when you are using goroutines like this, you generally need to write some additional code to catch the panic from the goroutine. Ironically, this code *also* needs to be in a goroutine. It's not particularly difficult, but is easy to miss.

Elixir's isolated processes mean we don't need to worry about situations like this. That is the "let it crash" philosophy.

11.3   Concurrency and Parallelism

Erlang and Elixir's concurrency model will feel quite new if you are coming from a more typical language like Python or Java. Erlang, and by extension, Elixir, follow the actor model [2]. With

---

[2]You will get different answers to this depending on who you ask. Generally, the Elixir and Erlang communities refer to these languages using the actor

the actor model, processes do not share mutable state. Instead, they communicate using message passing. In this way, there is no mutable state that needs to be protected by a mutex or that creates a race condition. Although race conditions can still happen in Elixir, they are not as common as other languages.

To understand why race conditions are less common in Elixir when compared to other non-actor model languages, consider the mechanism of communication. In *most* of these languages, communication between threads, processes, etc. happens via some shared state. This means there is a thread writing to the shared state and another thread (or threads) reading from the same state. A race condition can occur if a thread reads (or writes) before the other consuming thread expects it to. This is harder to do with message passing.

In the message passing setting, the writing thread sends a message to the reading thread. The reading thread doesn't have to proactively look for data. Instead, its processing is triggered by the receipt of a message in its mailbox.

Another aspect of Elixir's concurrency model is that the processes are lightweight. As we have mentioned before, the BEAM VM can handle 10s of thousands of processes simlutaneously. One of the reasons this is possible is because the BEAM VM handles the preemptive scheduling of the processes. That is, it assure fair execution of these processes.

This is quite different from multi-threading, where the user must manually manage threads, resources, and shared memory accesses. Because this is so difficult to get right, most languages that rely on OS threads for concurrency recommend using a library to manage the execution of concurrent work. For example, the best practice in Java is to avoid manual thread management and instead reach for something like a `ThreadPool` or `ForkJoinPool`.

Just because the recommended practice in Java is to use `ThreadPool` or `ForkJoinPool` for your concurrent tasks doesn't mean you have

---

model of concurrency. However, in the talk *BEAM Concurrency in Action* at YOW! 2022, Sasa Juric mentions two counter points to this conventional wisdom. He states that the creators of Erlang were not aware of the actor model when creating Erlang. He also mentions one of the authors of the original Actor Model paper, *A Universal Modular Actor Formalism for Artificial Intelligence*, has stated that Erlang (and Elixir) is not an actor implementation. That being said, they are similar models so I'm not sure the distinction is all that important.

to actually do that. It also relies on you *knowing* that's the best practice. This problem isn't unique to Java. The same is true with C++, C#, Go[3] (to some extent), and many other languages. In Elixir, there is one way to manage concurrency, and it is the correct way.

11.4 Design Patterns and Behaviours

The OTP encourages liberal use of concurrency. Processes are very lighweight and the BEAM VM is cable of managing tens of thousands of them or more, depending on the system. However, there are a few things the OTP architectural and design principles encourage. These principles were created to help engineers maange the complexity of their systems.

The more concurrency in a system, the harder it becomes to reason about. You lose event ordering (that is, you don't know which event happened first). When it comes to concurrency, as much as you can, limit concurrency primitives to as few modules as possible. I want to make it clear that this *does not* imply you shouldn't use concurrency. If concurrency makes sense for what you are trying to accomplish, absolutely leverage it. The OTP encourages engineers to be thoughtful about *where* the concurrency primitives occur.

The other pattern you should always follow is that of leveraging the behaviours provided by the OTP. These include GenServer, Application, Task, and Supervisor. Leveraging these behaviours promotes consistency across modules and code bases. A GenServer in one codebase will work in a very similar manner to a GenServer in another codebase.

- `GenServer` - use this behaviour when you need to build a server that interacts with client. The most important callbacks to implement are:

    - `init/1` - used for initializing the server

---

[3]Go's concurrency model is based on the work of Tony Hoare on Communicating Sequential Processes (CSP). Go's concurrency model is more similar to Elixir's concurrency model in many aspects. Go supports tens of thousands of processes referred to as *goroutines*. These processes are managed by the Go runtime. The primary difference is Go relies on shared memory and channels (essentially thread-safe queues) to communicate between processes. As we saw earlier, goroutines are not isolated like processes are in Elixir and Erlang.

  - handle_call/3 - this callback is invoked by clients interacting with the server and expecting a response (synchronous communication).
  - handle_cast/3 - like handle_call/3 but asynchronous
  - handle_info/2 - this callback is called when a message is received by the server that was handled by the other message handling callbacks.
  - terminate/2 - gets called when the server is exiting, unless the server is killed with the :brutal_kill signal

- Supervisor - use this behaviour when you need a process that monitors other processes. Supervisor only has one callback: init/1, which is called when ther supervisor is created. If you have GenServer processes running, you should probably have a Supervisor process watching them and keeping them healthy.

- Task - tasks are short-lived, temporary processes that encapsulate a unit of work. This might be something like making an HTTP request and processing the response or it might be some kind of startup task like warming a cache or testing connections to other services. The primary functions are:

  - async/1 and async/3 - these start the task. Tasks started with either of these functions must be awaited with await/1. Howevever, if you spawn a task inside a GenServer, it will be awaited automatically and its message will be handled by the GenServer's handle_info/2 callback.

- Task.Supervisor - similar to Supervisor, but this module is for supervisors that monitor tasks. Similar to Task, the usual functions of async/1 and async/3 exists, along with a few other more relevant to monitored tasks. In general you should prefer to create monitored tasks rather than non-monitored tasks. That is, prefer Task.Supervisor.async/1 over Task.async/1.

- Application - applications are the OTP's way of packaging libraries. They contain functionality for configuring the application's environment (which, in this context, refers to a specific set of atoms and strings). Applications can be started and stopped. This is a key distinction to them just being a collection of code. Some of the main callbacks to be aware of are

- `start/2` - this is called when the application has completed its startup routine. Generally this function should start the root supervisor process of the supervision tree for the application. The expectation is this function will return one of {`:ok`, `pid`} or {`:ok`, `pid`, `state`} if startup was successful.
- `stop/1` - this is called after the application has been stopped (usually propagated up from the supervision tree).

- `Agent` - this module provides basic functionality for managing shared state. Agents manage this shared state on a server. Clients interact with the agent to fetch or update the state. You can think of them as trimmed down GenServers. They lack the functionality of GenServers like the message handling callbacks standard with GenServer. There are no callbacks for agents, only functions.

  - `get/3` - a somewhat unique API for fetching a value. Rather than pass in a key or lookup value, you pass in a single arity anonymous function. This function will be passed the agent's `state` and returns some value. The third and optional parameter is the timeout.
  - `update/3` - similar to `get/3`, `update/3` uses a single arity anonymous function to update the state. However, this function returns the state, rather than some value derived from the state.

11.5   Putting it all together

As engineers, it is tempting for us to dive in and start writing code. In the context of Elixir, though, you are best-suited spending some time reading through all the different behaviours (if you aren't familiar with them) and map them to the different pieces of your application.

The way I like to plan out my projects looks something like this:

1. Think through the different functionality the application will perform. This functionality will for the leaf nodes of my supervision tree. I like to put each distinct piece of functionality in its own module. These modules are pure in the sense that they don't use any OTP behaviours, just application logic.

2. Map out the runtime dependencies of my application. What processes are long-lived? If so, they should be encapsulated in a `GenServer`. Do they rely on any ephemeral logic? If so, this logic can be encapsulated in a `Task`. Do I need to consider startup order? What about runtime name lookups? This is where I start to group my functionality in terms of sibling processes (that is, processes that are somewhat independent of eachother) and child processes (processes spawned or required by another process). You can think of this step as doing a topological sort on the processes where the edges are defined by process dependence.

3. Now that the processes are grouped, I add a supervisor to each group. Some groups will get an additional process added to them - this is the supervisor for the child processes of that group. At this point, we have our supervision tree.

4. Finally, I have a root supervisor, and I encapsulate this into an `Application`, along with any application and/or environment specific state. For example, I may have a `dev` configuration and a `prod` configuration (at least for personal projects, enterprise projects probably have at least twice as many configurations).

11.6 Conclusion

In the coming chapters we will cover a number of these behaviours. Starting with GenServer, then moving on to Supervisor and Application. These chapters will culminate in a chapter where we put it all together and build a distributed system of servers, a database, gRPC, and Kafka.

Chapter 12

GenServer

As we learned in chapter 11, behaviours are similar to interfaces or protocols from languags like Go or Rust. The GenServer behaviour directs us in how to build a server in a manner that aligns with the OTP. Being part of the OTP, GenServer seamlessly integrates into OTP's fault-tolerant supervision strategies. As we will see in this chapter, GenServer helps us abstract the complexities of process management and message-passing by providing a high-level interface for managing state, handling requests, and ensuring robustness in distributed environments.

The GenServer behaviour provides an standard server interface. The interface consists of state initialization and functions for responding to client requests. Its usefulness comes from this standardization. Throughout the chapter we will discuss various functions from GenServer. Even though we will prefix these functions with `GenServer`, we are almost always referring to your module's implementation of these functions. That is, if you are writing `MyServer` that implements the `GenServer` behaviour, when we refer to `GenServer.handle_call/3` you should read this as `MyServer.handle_call/3`.

The following sections explore the ideas behind GenServer. We will start with the basics of starting a server to more advanced topics like distributed state and error handling.

12.1   GenServer Basics

A GenServer is a process that handles state and responds to requests. Just about every GenServer consists of:

- **State** – the internal memory (state) that the GenServer updates and maintains over the course of its lifetime. The GenServers state is initialized in `GenServer.init/1`, where you defined starting conditions. For example, if your server relies on any kind of data structure (e.g., a buffer), this is where you would create that data structure (i.e., allocate the memory).
- **Callbacks** – the functions that dictate how the GenServer responds to incoming requests.

GenServer Lifecycle

The GenServer lifecycle starts with `GenServer.start_link/3`. This function instantiates a GenServer via `GenServer.init/1`. The `GenServer.init/1` function is responsible for setting the initial state, connections with external services and so on. Once the server is up and running, it simply sits and waits for a message. If it receives a message via `GenServer.call/3`, it synchronous handles the request and sends a response. If, instead, it receives a message via `GenServer.cast/2`, it asynchronously processes the message, typically with no response. Upon unexpected terminations, the GenServer sends either the error or the error message (depending on whether the parent process is trapping exits) causing the termination to its parent process.

Anatomy of a GenServer

The `GenServer` behaviour consist of a number of callbacks. You don't *have* to implement all of them, but there are a handful you should generally implement (or at least think about).

init/1

You will want to create a `GenServer.init/1` function in just about every scenario. The only time you don't need to implement `GenServer.init/1` is when your server doesn't handle any kind of internal state. In my experience, it is rare for a backend server to not maintain any state or connections (clients) to external services or resources.

handle_call/3

This handles all synchronous messages, which are sent when clients use `call/3` to send a message to the GenServer. Messages sent with `call/3` have an associated `from` tuple (the second argument passed to `handle_call/3`). The `from` tuple consists of the PID of the sender and a unique call ID. Most of the time your responses from `handle_call/3` will start with `:reply`. As we will see, there are a couple of cases where you can return `:noreply` and send the reply later (using `reply/2`). Most of the time though, your messages will consist of a some kind of response, which we denote `reply_msg`, and a new internal state for the GenServer (which may be the same as the old state). Here are the possible response tuple:

- `{:reply, reply_msg, new_state}` – probably the most common response. No timeout, no hibernation, just sending a reply to the received message and (possibly) updating the GenServer's internal state.

- `{:reply, reply_msg, new_state, timeout}` – same as above, but sets a timeout to wait for the next message. If a message isn't received within `timeout` milliseconds, a `:timeout` message is processed by the GenServer's `handle_info/2` function.

- `{:reply, reply_msg, new_state, :hibernate}` – sends a response and then puts the GenServer into a low memory utilization state. This should only be used when you expect long intervals (say on the order of minutes or hours) between messages. It can be less efficient when the server is constantly waking up from hibernation and going back into hibernation. The server will wake up upon receipt of a new message in its queue.

- `{:reply, reply_msg, new_state, {:continue, continue_arg}}` – responds to the caller with `reply_msg` and then invokes `handle_continue/2` with the given `continue_arg` and newly updated state. This is useful when there is additional processing that needs to be done after a response is sent to the client.

- `{:noreply, new_state}` – you can also return with `:noreply`, which updates the internal state but does not send a response to the client. This is typically done if you need to reply from a separate process. For example, you may have one process ingesting requests, fanning them out to separate processes that handle the actual processing and response. The response is then sent using `GenServer.reply/2`.

handle_cast/2

This is the asynchronous version of `handle_call/3`. It is invoked when clients call `cast/2`. Note that because this is asynchronous, the client is not waiting for, nor are they expecting a response. Similar to `handle_call/3`, `handle_cast/2` can return the following tuples.

- `{:noreply, new_state}` – updates the GenServer state to `new_state`

- `{:stop, stop_reason, new_state}` – signals to the GenServer it is time to start shutdown preparations. This starts by the GenServer invoking `terminate/2` with the given `stop_reason` and new state.

- `{:no_reply, new_state, timeout}` – this timeout is a timeout on received messages. If a message isn't received within `timeout` milliseconds, a `:timeout` message is processed by the GenServer's `handle_info/2` function.

- `{:no_reply, new_state, :hibernate}` – updates the GenServer's internal state and puts it into hibernate mode, a low-memory state that is used to conserver system resources.

- `{:no_reply, new_state, {:continue, continue_arg}}` – updates the state and signals to the GenServer that it should invoke `handle_continue/2` with the giving `continue_arg` as the first argument (the GenServer's internal state is the second argument).

handle_info/2

This is invoked for all message types not handled by `handle_call/3` or `handle_case/2`. This is typically messages sent using `send/2`. This is optional, as the default beahvior is to log the received message. This may also be invoked when there is a timeout, in which case the first argument is `:timeout` instead of a message from another process.

`handle_info/2` returns `{:noreply, new_state}` and like the other message handling functions, can specify a `:timeout`, `:hibernate`, or a continuation `{:continue, continue_arg}`.

handle_continue/2

This is an optional callback with no default implementation. handle_continue/2 is useful for times when you need to call some additional logic after committing updates (or initialization) to the GenServer's state. This function is invokable from handle_call/3, handle_cast/2, and handle_info/2. For each of these, the invokation mechanism is the same: the returned tuple should have {:continue, continue_arg} as the last element in the returned tuple. Note that the returned tuples for the respective functions vary in size and format (slightly).

terminate/2

This is generally invoked before the server exits. The arguments are the current state as well as the reason the server is exiting. However, there is *no guarantee* this callback will be called. For example, if the GenServer is being terminated because it received a :brutal_kill message, this function will *not* be called. The GenServer will also not call this function if it receives a :kill message and still has messages to process *unless* the server is trapping exits. This is all to say that this function is not meant for resource cleanup.

reply/2

Sends a response to a client that made a request with either call/3 or multi_call/4. This function takes two arguments. The first is the from argument received in the corresponding handle_call/3 callback. The second is the actual response.

Table 12.1: Comparison of message processing callbacks (excluding handle_info/2).

Callback	Invoked by	async/sync	reply/noreply
handle_call/3	call/3	sync	:reply
handle_cast/2	cast/2	async	:noreply
handle_info/2	send/2	sync	:noreply

Implementing a GenServer

Now that we have a general idea of the type of functionality a GenServer has, let's get our hands dirty by actually building one.

We will use the ring buffer we made in the prior chapter and expose it as a service via our GenServer.

Let's look at a sample server.

```elixir
# lib/ch10/ring_buffer_server.ex
defmodule CH11.RingBufferServer do
  use GenServer
  alias CH10.RingBuffer, as: RingBuffer

  def start_link(buffer_size) do
    GenServer.start_link(
      __MODULE__,
      buffer_size,
      name: __MODULE__
    )
  end


  # Callbacks
  @impl true
  def init(buffer_size) do
    buffer = RingBuffer.new(buffer_size)
    {:ok, buffer}
  end

  @impl true
  def handle_call(
    {:put, elem},
    _from, %RingBuffer{} = state
  ) do
    new_state = RingBuffer.put(state, elem)
    {:reply, :ok, new_state}
  end

  @impl true
  def handle_call(:get, _from, state) do
    case RingBuffer.get(state) do
      {:empty_get_error, buffer} ->
        {
          :reply,
          {:error, "Called 'get' on empty buffer"},
          buffer,
        }
      {elem, new_buffer} ->
        {:reply, elem, new_buffer}
    end
  end
end
```

One thing that probably stands out immediately is the use of

__MODULE__. This is just a reference to the name of the module. Rather than typing the module name everywhere you can simply reference it via __MODULE__.

You might notice in GenServer.start_link/3 we are setting the name of the created process to __MODULE__, which has the effect of setting it to RingBufferServer. Customizing the name in this manner allows us to refer to the process by its name, rather than its PID. PIDs change each time the process is created but the name does not. By setting a name to our server we can write code that communicates with the server without needing to know the PID ahead of time. This is a common pattern and is useful as long as you only plan on starting a single instance of this service. If you intend to start more than one instance, you will need to leverage a Registry, which we cover later in this chapter.

An idiom that is common with GenServers is providing a set of client functions that wrap the calls to the GenServer functions. Notice how we have a function get/0 that returns the element at the front of the buffer by calling GenServer.call(__MODULE__, :get). We also provide a function put/1 that is a wrapper around GenServer.call(__MODULE__, {:put, value}). This makes interacting with our GenServer far more ergonomic.

We provide two implementations of GenServer.handle_call/3, one for each operation of our RingBuffer. The first argument determines which operation we are performing. This is a common pattern with GenServers. The second argument is a tuple containing the PID of the calling process along with an unique call identifier. The last argument is the current state of the GenServer. That state is initialized in the GenServer.init/1 function as the second element of the returned 2-tuple.

Each time GenServer.handle_call/3 is called, it returns a tuple that, at a minimum, specifies how to respond (if at all), and the new state. The first element of the tuple can be one of the following:

- :reply - send the specified response data as a reply to the caller
- :noreply - do not send a response to the caller
- :stop - terminates the server

For each of these response scenarios, there are different tuples that can be returned.

There are two interesting return values that can be included with both :reply and :noreply, namely :hibernate and :timeout. Returning :hibernate puts the server's process into a low-memory state. It will be awakened when a client sends new messages. This is useful when you want to conserver server resources, but use it judiciously. *Always* returning :hibernate will negatively impact server performance in situations where there is no lull in incoming messages. This is becuase the server will constantly be alternating between going to sleep and waking up.

At first glance, returning :timeout from a callback might seem counter-intuitive, but it is useful for kicking off async actions if no messages arrive within a certain perio. However, it is quite useful. When you specify :timeout in your response, the server waits the specified timeout and then calls GenServer.handle_info/2, passing the specified timeout as the first argument. If a new message is received while waiting for the timeout to elapse, the reply will reset the timeout and the wait will begin again. There is no guarantee GenServer.handle_info/2 will be called from an elapsed timeout. If you need to guarnatee logic is executed after GenServer.handle_call/3 (as well as GenServer.handle_cast/2), you should use :continue and GenServer.handle_continue/2.

If you need to sequence work, GenServer.handle_continue/2 is quite useful. When either of GenServer.handle_call/3 or GenServer.handle_cast/2 returns a tuple with {:continue, continue_arg}, GenServer.handle_continue/2 is called. This can handle cleanup, complete longer running tasks, or kick-off additional work you didn't want to initiate during GenServer.handle_call/3 or GenServer.handle_cast/2.

In general, a caller using GenServer.call/3 (which invokes GenServer.handle_call/3) will expect a response, so you will typically use :reply in GenServer.handle_call/3. This is because the GenServer.handle_call/3/GenServer.call/3 pair is blocking (synchronous). We block when we expect a response.

The GenServer module provides a non-blocking version of GenServer.handle_call/3 called GenServer.handle_cast/2. As you might have guessed, the client-side invoking function is called GenServer.cast/2. The main scenarios you would provide a non-blocking API for are situations where the client wants to trigger a side-effect (i.e., change state without a response) or long-running computations that the client doesn't want to wait for.

There are a couple of ways a client can interact with the our Ring-
BufferServer. They can call GenServer.call/3. This is a function
defined in the GenServer module. Calling this function will invoke
RingBufferServer.handle_call/3 defined above. The implementation will pattern match on the first arg being :put or :get.

Let's take a look using IEx.

```
# iex -S mix
iex> alias CH10.RingBufferServer, as: RBS
CH10.RingBufferServer
iex> {_, pid} = RBS.start_link(5)
{:ok, #PID<0.1.0> }
iex> GenServer.call(pid, {:put, 1})
:ok
iex> GenServer.call(pid, {:put, 2})
:ok
iex> GenServer.call(pid, :get)
{:value, 1}
iex> GenServer.call(pid, :get)
{:value, 2}
iex> GenServer.call(pid, :get)
{:error, "Called 'get' on an empty buffer"}
```

Though this works, there is a problem. When you come back to
this code in three months how will you know what GenServer is
calling? What is the implementation that is accepting {:put, 1}?

The solution to this problem is to implement the client interface within the same module. This is done above with the functions RingBufferServer.put/2 and RingBufferServer.get/1. These
functions provide a simpler, more ergonomic interface. This is
a contrived example, but even in this contrived example Ring-
BufferServer.put(pid, some_val) is easier to read and clearer than
GenServer.call(pid, {:put, some_val}). Let's add that to our implementation.

```
defmodule CH10.RingBufferServer do
  # Client functions
  def put(element) do
    GenServer.call(__MODULE__, {:put, element})
  end

  def get() do
    GenServer.call(__MODULE__, :get)
  end

  // Other code omitted
```

end

Now we can make the same calls but using the new client-side helper functions instead.

```
# iex -S mix
iex> alias CH10.RingBufferServer, as: RBS
CH10.RingBufferServer
iex> RBS.start(5)
{:ok, #PID<0.1.0> }
iex> RBS.put(1)
:ok
iex> RBS.put(2)
:ok
iex> RBS.get()
{:value, 1}
iex> RBS.get()
{:value, 2}
iex> RBS.get()
{:error, "Called 'get' on an empty buffer"}
```

This is much cleaner than our initial attempt.

GenServers are generally single-threaded. Each message that is sent to them (via GenServer.call/3 or GenServer.cast/2) is processed one at a time. The advantage of this is that we don't have to worry about race conditions. The disadvantage is that slow operations on a message will block the processing of other messages.

There is another useful function that can handle unknown incoming messages: GenServer.handle_info/2 . This function gets called when a message is sent to the server from something *other than* GenServer.call/3 and GenServer.cast/2. Let's try it out.

```
defmodule CH10.RingBufferServer do
  # Prior code omitted

  def handle_info(msg, state) do
    IO.puts("Received unknown message: #{msg}")
    {:noreply, state}
  end
end
```

We can trigger this behaviour by sending a message using send/2.

```
iex> alias CH10.RingBufferServer, as: RBS
CH10.RingBufferServer
iex> RBS.start(5)
```

```
{:ok, #PID<0.1.0>}
iex> send(RBS, {:hello})
Received unknown message: {:hello}
{:hello}
```

The last function you should always think about, if not always implement, is GenServer.terminate/2 . This function gets called when the server is about to exit. Use this function to cleanup any resources, existing connections, etc. There are several situations in which this function will not get called. The first is when the server receives a :brutal_kill signal. The second is when the server receives an exit seignal from a process that isn't trapping exits.

12.2 Fault Tolerance

GenServer isn't just about requests and state. It plays a key role in making sure your application can recover from errors without crashing your entire system.

The last line of defense, which we will learn about in the next chapter, is the Supervisor. A Supervisor watches over a process or multiple processes and restarts them if/when they fail. Supervisors are like a safety net for your system. They aren't the only safety mechanism we have at our disposal though.

There are two primary techniques we rely on for building fault-tolerant servers: pattern matching and try-catch blocks. Let's take a look at the pattern matching using pattern matching for fault-tolerance.

Just before this section we looked at the function handle_info/2. I was very specific about testing this functionality using send/2 and *not* GenServer.call/3. Let's see why that was

```
iex> alias CH10.RingBufferServer, as: RBS
CH10.RingBufferServer
iex> RBS.start(5)
{:ok, #PID<0.1.0>}
iex> GenServer.call(RBS, {:hello}) # using call now
19:41:38.416 [error] GenServer CH10.RingBufferServer
↪   terminating
** (FunctionClauseError) no function clause matching in
↪   CH10.RingBufferServer.handle_call/3
(other omitted text)
```

Notice how `GenServer.handle_info/2` wasn't called? Remember, `handle_info/2` is called for messages that are sent using `send/2`, *not* the GenServer message sending functions. How can we remedy this? It's quite simple – we simply implement another `GenServer.handle_call/3` as a sort of catchall function. We can gracefully handle unexpected requests by implementing a catchall clause. Let's add another `GenServer.handle_call/3` to match any unknown message type. This allows us to return a clean error response, rather than crashing.

```elixir
defmodule CH10.RingBufferServer do
  # Previous code omitted

  def handle_call(request, _from, state) do
    IO.puts("Received invalid call: #{request}). Prefer
    ↪  put/1 and get/0")
    {
      :reply,
      {:error, "invalid request - use put/1 or get/0"},
      state
    }
  end
end
```

Let's try it again, now with our catchall function.

```elixir
iex> alias CH10.RingBufferServer, as: RBS
CH10.RingBufferServer
iex> RBS.start(5)
{:ok, #PID<0.1.0>}
iex> GenServer.call(RBS, {:hello}) # using call now
Received unknown request: {:hello} - use :put or :get
{:error, "invalid request - use :put or :get"}
```

Much better! Now our server remains healthy and notifies the client there was an error.

As for try-catch blocks, we covered that in detail in chapter 7.

Error Handling

One phrase you will hear often within the Elixir community is "let it crash." Newcomers to the language might take this to mean you let errors propagate and never worry about error handling. This an unfortunate misinterpretation. "Let it crash" is more about not worrying when a process crashes. Processes are isolated, so one process crashing won't necessarily impact a sibling process. You should *always* strive to write correct, robust code. If you are writing to a file, you should handle the obvious case where the file doesn't exist.

Where Elixir diverges from languages like Java or Python is the proliferation of try-catch blocks. Instead of relying on exceptions, we favor tuples returning :ok or :error attoms. For example, in Python you might write something like

```python
class MyServer:
  def handle_request(self, req):
    try:
      conn = self.establish_conneciton(req.data)
      resp = self.make_req(conn)
      do_something(resp)
    except ConnectionFailureException as e:
      logger.error(f"failed to establish connection - {e}")
    except RequestFailureException as e:
      logger.error(f"request failed - {e}")
```

In Elixir, this would look more like

```elixir
defmodule MyServer do
  def handle_request(req) do
    with {:ok, conn} <- establish_connection(req.data),
         {:ok, resp} <- make_request(conn) do
      do_something(resp)
    else
      {:error, :conn_error} ->
        logger.error("connection error")
      {:error, :request_error} ->
        logger.error("request error")
    end
  end
end
```

The main point I want to hammer in here is that we still need to think about errors and how to handle them. Elixir's approach is far more functional in its structure and syntax. Where Java, C++, and Python rely on more traditional try-catch constructs, we rely on pattern matching. I personally prefer the pattern matching approach. I find the code more readable and generally easier to reduce the amount of indentation.[1]

---

[1] I use the amount of indentation in a section of code as a rough metric for its complexity. I always strive for the simplest, easiest to understand code and reducing the amount of indentation is one of my core strategies. Using tools

12.3   State Management

Our GenServer examples up to this point have been relatively simple, so we haven't had to worry about state management too much. There are a few rules to keep in mind when thinking about state management

1. Keep state small and simple – as size and complexity increase, so does the cognitive load.
2. Use maps – `Map` is very flexible, allowing you to easily evolve your state management needs over time.
3. Avoid storing large amounts of data in memory – if you have a lot of data to manage in your state, you should offload it to an external data store.

For offloading data, you could of course always use a database. We will kick that can down the road. In a later chapter we will discuss databases and ORMs. For now, we will focus on Erlang Term Storage (ETS) and Mnesia. Both of these come from Erlang.

Erlang Term Storage

Erlang Term Storage (ETS) is an in-memory key-value store. Any process is able to read and write to ETS. This makes it a great option for a central cache or short-term storage. Since it is in-memory, it is fast. However, in-memory also means it is not persistent. You should never store data in ETS you cannot lose.

ETS provides an interface to storing data inside an Erlang runtime system. Data is stored in tables within ETS. These tables are created by processes. When the creating process terminates, its table is deleted. This has two implications. If a process crashes, its table (and respective data) is deleted. Conversely, if a process lives for a very long time, the data will stick around for just as long (unless manually deleted).

Access rights to the tables are assigned when the table is created by the creating process. There are three rights availble:

- `:private` - only the owning process can read and write
- `:protected` (default) – only the owning process and write, any process can read.
- `:public` – every process can both read and write

---

like Elixir's `with/1` makes for low-indentation, elegant code in my opinion.

In addition to specifying access rights, you can also specify the backing data structure for an ETS table. There are four options:

- `set` – guarnatees all keys are unique, $O(1)$ lookups
- `bag` – guarantees all records are unique, $O(1)$ lookups
- `ordered_set`– guarantees uniqueness of keys and keys are ordered, $O(\lg_2 n)$ access.
- `duplicate_bag` – allows duplicate records, $O(n)$ inserts, $O(1)$ lookups

We insert data into an ETS table via `:ets.insert/2` or `:ets.insert_new/2` . These take a tuple where the first value of the tuple is considered the key.

If you haven't worked with bags before, it can be a little difficult to develop intuition around them. I find in these cases the best approach is to play around with some code. Let's fire up IEx.

```
iex> b = :ets.new(:bag1, [:bag])
#Reference<...>
iex> :ets.insert(b, {:a, "hello"})
true
iex> :ets.insert(b, {:a, "hello"})
true
iex> :ets.tab2list(b)
[a: "hello"] # key-value pair is unique
iex> :ets.insert(b, {:a, "world"})
true
iex> :ets.tab2list(b)
# key-value pairs are still unique, duplicate keys
[a: "hello", a: "world"]
iex> :ets.insert(b, {:a, "hello", "world"})
true
iex> :ets.tab2list(b)
# Note the tuples can be different sizes
[{:a, "hello"}, {:a, "world"}, {:a, "hello", "world"}]
```

That is pretty instructive. The key aspect of the bag is that the objects (i.e., values) of the tuples must be unique. The keys may be repeated. This is not the case with sets. Let's take a look.

```
iex> s = :ets.new(:set1, [:set])
#Reference<...>
iex> :ets.insert(s, {:a, "hello"})
true
iex> :ets.insert(s, {:a, "world"})
true
iex> :ets.insert(s, {:a, "hello", "world"})
```

```
true
iex> :ets.tab2list(s)
[{:a, "hello", "world"}]
```

With the set we are simply replacing the respective tuple with the new value each time. Let's try out the duplicate bag.

```
iex> b = :ets.new(:dupe_set, [:duplicate_set])
#Reference<...>
iex> :ets.insert(b, {:a, "hello"})
true
iex> :ets.insert(b, {:a, "hello"})
true
iex> :ets.tab2list(b)
[a: "hello", a: "hello"] # key-value pairs are not unique
```

So which one should you choose? Pick ordered_set if you care about processing data in the order determined by the keys. Otherwise, pick the data structure that provides the behavior you need. If you need to handle duplicates, choose duplicate_bag. If you need duplicate keys but not objects, choose bag, otherwise you are left with set.

Erlang also provides a module for more persistant storage called Mnesia.

Mnesia

Mnesia provided a distributed key-value database. Tables can be stored both on disk and in memory. Mnesia can replicate tables across nodes and also provides location transparency. This means processes can access data without needing to know where the data is located. Most importantly, transaction are atomic, meaning they either succeed or fail. Data is never left in an inconsistent state.

Mnesia is incredibly feature rich. It even includes its own query language. It is a major part of the Erlang ecosystem, but is out of scope for this book. I could probably write a completely separate book just on the topic of Mnesia. We will leave the discussion of Mnesia for another day. If you are curious, check out the documention on erlang.org.

Conclusion

At this point you should have a pretty good feel for building your own server. The main piece we are missing at the moment is how to supervise our servers. In the next chapter we will learn about the Supervisor behaviour. Supervisors are GenServers whose sole responsibility is to watch over their children processes (e.g., other GenServers) and make sure they are healthy. If a child process fails, the supervisor may decide to restart the process. Understanding and using supervisors (and so-called, supervision trees) is core to building resilient, self-healing systems in Elixir.

Chapter 13

Supervisor

13.1 Introduction to Supervisors

Supervisors are processes that monitor and manage other processes, making sure they are in a consistent and healthy state. They play a crucial role in building fault-tolerant and resilient systems. They form the core of Elixir's "let it crash" philosophy, allowing the system to recover gracefully from failures. We generally refer to the supervised process as the child process.

A supervisor manages one or more children. It has a singular responsibility: make sure the child are up and running. This leads to a natural question: can a supervisor supervise another supervisor?

It turns out they can! In fact, this is a very popular pattern in Elixir. This pattern creates what is referred to as a supervision tree . Supervision trees allow you to create complex hierarchies of fault-tolerant workers and supervisors. Each level knows how to respond to failures. The level's response varies depending on where in the hierarchy the failure occurred. You can use this hierarchical tree structure of supervisors to create a fault-tolerant system capable of recovering from a number of different types of failures.

Supervisors give you the ability to isolate failures. This prevents cascading failures within your system. The supervisor can restart a crashed process in isolation without affecting other parts of the system. Or it can restart every process it supervises. There is immense flexibility on how supervisors respond to failure.

Supervisors also provide a way to manage the lifecycle of processes. They can start processes in a specific order to ensure that dependencies are satisfied and the system is initialized correctly. Supervisors are also able to gracefully terminate processes in a specific order, providing a clean and controlled shutdown.

13.2   Creating Supervisors

Creating a supervisor in Elixir involves defining a module that implements the `Supervisor` behaviour . This module encapsulates the supervisor's configuration and child specifications. The Supervisor behaviour requires the implementation of the `Supervisor.init/1` callback function, which is invoked when the supervisor is started. In the `Supervisor.init/1` function, you specify the supervision strategy and the list of child processes to be supervised.

Supervisors are processes, so they have `init/1` and `start_link/2` functions. However, their behaviour is a little less customized when compared to their GenServer counterparts. In fact, where GenServer has eight callbacks that can be customized, Supervisor has only 1, namely `Supervisor.init/1`

Because there is so little to customize with a Supervisor, you can create them via the Supervisor module or be defining your own module. To create a supervisor, you start by using the Supervisor module and invoking the `Supervisor.start_link/2` or `Superviser.start_link/3` function.   These functions are responsible for starting the supervisor process and linking it to the calling process. The `Supervisor.start_link/2` function takes a list of children process specs and their initial arguments as parameters, while `Supervisor.start_link/3` allows you to provide additional options.

Let's look at an example. Suppose we have already defined a GenServer module `MyChildServer`. It's not important what that module does, though we will also assume it takes a single string for its initialization (via `init/1`). Creating a supervisor for this process looks something like this:

```
child_spec = %{
  id: MyChildServer,
  start: {MyChildServer, ["hello world"]},
  type: :worker
}
```

```
supervisor = Supervisor.start_link([child_spec], strategy:
↪   :one_for_one)
```

Supervisor takes care of the rest. It will create a new instance of MyChildServer, start it, and then link it to itself. If and when the MyChildServer process goes down, the supervisor will start it back up. We are not completely out of the woods though. Non-normal exits in the child process (MyChildServer here) can still bring down the supervisor. We will learn more about how to deal with this later in the chapter. We will also discuss what is meant by strategy: :one_for_one later in this chapter. In this case it doesn't do anything since our supervisor is only supervising a single process.

Restart Strategies

Inside the supervisor module, you define the Supervisor.init/1 callback function. This function initializes the supervisor and returns a tuple specifying the supervision strategy and the list of child specifications. The supervision strategy determines how the supervisor should handle child process failures. Elixir provides several built-in strategies, such as :one_for_one, :one_for_all, and :rest_for_one.

- :one_for_one – only the child process is restarted. This strategy is suitable when child processes are independent and do not have any direct dependencies on each other. It allows for isolated restarts and minimizes the impact of a single child process failure on the overall system.

- :one_for_all – if one child terminates, terminate all other children and then restart them (including the originally failed process). This strategy is useful when child processes have dependencies on the processes that were started before them. It allows for a partial restart of the system, affecting only the necessary processes while leaving the independent ones untouched.

- :rest_for_one – if one child terminates, terminate all children that started *after* the failed child and restart them.

Child Specifications

Child specifications define how each child process should be started and supervised. They are represented as maps or structs that contain information such as the child module, function to start the child process, and any additional options. The `Supervisor.child_spec/2` function is commonly used to create child specifications, taking the child module and its initial arguments as parameters. The child spec allows you to define how the child should be restarted (if at al), how the process should be terminated, and whether the child process is a worker (`:worker`) or a supervisor (`:supervisor`).

The `:restart` atom specifies how the child process should be restarted. It can be one of three values.

- `:permanent` (default) – always restart the process
- `:temporary` – never restart the process
- `:transient` – only restart the process if it terminates abnormally. That is, don't restart it if exits with `:normal`, `:shutdown`, or `{:shutdown, reason}`. Otherwise, restart the process.

You can also specify how the child process should be terminated by its supervisor via the `:shutdown` atom. The `:shutdown` option specifies how the supervisor should treat the child while it is terminating. This option supports several different values:

- `:brutal_kill` – the process is terminated via `Process.exit(pid, :kill)`
- `:infinity` – the supervisor will not unconditionally `Process.exit(pid, :kill)` the child process. This is useful if the child process may take a long time to shutdown (e.g., it is also a supervisor and terminating other children).
- Non-negative integer (default: $5,000$) – this is the amount of time the process as to terminate before it is unconditionally terminated via `Process.exit(pid, :kill)`.

13.3   Supervisor Strategies

The best way to get a feel for all of this is with an example. Our example will create a few processes that will randomly terminate themselves. This will let us get a feel for what happens when a child process crashes.

We will tackle this in a few iterations. Our first iteration will be naive and incorrect. After understanding the issues with the naive approach we will make improvements to a more idiomatic, robust solution.

Our example will consist of workers that generate random numbers and send them to the PID of a process known at worker intialization. The catch is that the workers will occasionally exit with signal :kill.

Separately we will have a listener process that receives the random numbers from the worker processes. This process will simply track the received values and log the average. Similar to the worker process, this process will also occasionally exit with signal :kill.

To keep this simple, we will put the entire implementation in a single script file, supervisor.exs. I will leave out most of the file in each code block to keep things easier to read and follow. Please keep in mind that just because some code is omitted from the block *doesn't* mean it has been removed from the file.

We will need a way to run a function at a set interval. Luckily we can use Erlang's :timer.apply_interval/4 function to handle this for us.

Let's start with the listener process. This process simply waits to be sent a message and, upon receiving that message, logs the average of the numbers it has received. Every second the listener checks if it should exit.

```elixir
# supervisor.exs
defmodule Listener do
  use GenServer

  defp exit_prob, do: 0.05

  def maybe_exit(pid) do
    if :rand.uniform() > 1 - exit_prob() do
      IO.puts("EXIT: Listener #{inspect(self())}")
      Process.exit(pid, :kill)
    end
  end

  def send(n), do: GenServer.call(__MODULE__, n)

  def start_link() do
    GenServer.start_link(
      __MODULE__,
      [],
      name: __MODULE__
    )
```

```elixir
  end

  @impl true
  def init(_) do
    :timer.apply_interval(
      1000,
      __MODULE__,
      :maybe_exit,
      [self()]
    )
    IO.puts("INIT: Listener #{inspect(self())}")
    {:ok, {0, 0}}
  end

  @impl true
  def handle_call(n, _, {count, sum}) when is_integer(n) do
    if count > 0 do
      IO.puts("AVG(#{sum}, #{count}): #{sum / count}")
    end

    {:reply, :ok, {count + 1, sum + n}}
  end

  @impl true
  def handle_call(_, _, _) do
    IO.puts("Invalid request")
    {:reply, :error, nil}
  end
end
```

Now that we have the Listener module, let's build the worker process. We will continue in the same file, below the Listener module. There are three pieces of functionality we need to handle.

1. Randomly exit with some probability (say, $P(x < X_{exit}) \leq .1$).
2. Generate a random number every second.
3. Send the randomly generated number to the given PID.

```elixir
# src/supervisor/supervisor.exs
# Listener module omitted above
defmodule Worker do
  use GenServer

  defp exit_prob, do: 0.1

  defp maybe_exit(pid) do
    if :rand.uniform() > 1 - exit_prob() do
      IO.puts("EXIT: Worker #{inspect(self())}")
      Process.exit(pid, :kill)
```

```elixir
    end
  end

  @impl true
  def init(_) do
    IO.puts("INIT: Worker #{inspect(self())}")
    :timer.apply_interval(1000, __MODULE__, :send_msg,
    ↪  [self()])
    {:ok, nil}
  end

  def start_link() do
    GenServer.start_link(__MODULE__, nil)
  end

  def send_msg(pid) do
    maybe_exit(pid)

    IO.puts("MSG_SEND: Worker #{inspect(self())}")
    Listener.send(:rand.uniform(100))
  end
end
```

Finally, we need to start the processes and see what happens. Let's create five workers and a single listener.

```elixir
workers =
  for i <- 1..5 do
    %{
      id: "worker-#{i}",
      start: {Worker, :start_link, []},
      type: :worker
    }
  end

listener = %{
  id: Listener,
  start: {Listener, :start_link, [5]},
  type: :supervisor
}

Supervisor.start_link([listener | workers], strategy:
↪  :one_for_one)

receive do
end
```

There are three pieces here. The Worker module defines the logic of the workers. All they do is send a random number every second. Every time the worker tries to send a message to the Listener, it has a 10% chance of exiting (`Worker.exit_prob/0`).

Note the last few lines:

```
receive do
end
```

This is required to keep the script running. Without these lines the entire tree of `Listener` and `Workers` will exit. I encourage you to play around with removing these lines and observing the output to the terminal.

Restart Strategies

You likely noticed that if you run the above code it will eventually exit. You will see a message like

---
```
** (EXIT from #PID<0.98.0>) shutdown
```

Why does it exit if the processes are being supervised? The issue is with our `Supervisor` config. We only specified the restart strategy. But there are many other things we can specify. For example, we can specify the `:max_restarts` the supervisor will allow in a given timeframe. The default for this parameters is 5.

You may wonder "what is the timeframe?" Well, it turns out that is also a parameter we can specify via `:max_seconds`. The default for `:max_seconds` is 5. This means a default supervisor will exit if it hits five restarts in five seconds.

Our `Workers` have a 10% chance of exiting every second. The `Listener` has a 5% chance of exiting every second. Since we are running five `Workers` and a single `Listener`, we should expect, on average, $5 \times 0.1 + 0.05 = 0.55$ exits per second, or 2.75 exits every five seconds. Put another way, there is about a 5% chance we exit in any given five second interval. In the first 10 seconds there are 10 of these five second intervals (they are overlapping). This means we have about a 50% chance of exiting within 10 seconds.

This strategy doesn't feel quite right. `Worker` failures are counting against `Listener` failures. We should probably separate them. We can do this by creating a supervision tree.

13.4 Supervision Trees

We are going to create two new modules: `WorkerSupervisor` and `ListenerSupervisor`. Each of these modules will implement the `Supervisor` behaviour. We will omit the initial GenServer code and just show the new Supervisor modules.

Let's start with the supervisor for the workers. Add the following module. Note that we are still using the same `supervisor.exs` file.

```elixir
# src/supervisor/supervisor_2.exs
# Worker and Listener modules included in source
# but omitted here for brevity.

defmodule WorkerSupervisor do
  use Supervisor

  def start_link do
    IO.puts("WorkerSupervisor starting up")
    Supervisor.start_link(__MODULE__, :ok)
  end

  def init(_) do
    IO.puts("WorkerSupervisor initializing")

    children = for _ <- 1..5, do: %{
        id: Worker,
        start: {Worker, :start_link, []},
        type: :worker
      }

    Supervisor.init(children, strategy: :one_for_one)
  end
end
```

All we've done here is move the children spec and supervisor creation logic into its own module. Let's do the same for the listener module.

```elixir
# supervisor.exs
# Other modules omitted

defmodule ListenerSupervisor do
  use Supervisor

  def start_link do
    IO.puts("ListenerSupervisor starting up")
    Supervisor.start_link(__MODULE__, :ok)
  end

  def init(_) do
```

```
IO.puts("ListenerSupervisor initializing")

children = [
  %{
    id: Listener,
    start: {Listener, :start_link, []},
    type: :worker
  }
]

Supervisor.init(children, strategy: :one_for_one)
end
end
```

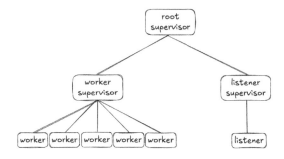

Figure 13.1: Supervision tree for the workers and listeners

At this point we have two supervisors, each supervising a piece of our system. The WorkerSupervisor has five children to supervise. The ListenerSupervisor just makes sure the listener is up and running at all times. The last step is to create a root supervisor that makes sure these two supervisors are always up and running as well. This is illustrated by figure 13.1.

```
supervisors = [
  %{
    id: WorkerSupervisor,
    start: {WorkerSupervisor, :start_link, []},
    type: :supervisor
  },
  %{
    id: ListenerSupervisor,
    start: {ListenerSupervisor, :start_link, []},
    type: :supervisor
  }
]

Supervisor.start_link(supervisors, strategy: :one_for_one)
```

```
receive do
end
```

If you run this example, you will notice the processes may fail, but on the whole our root process doesn't exit. That's because the root supervisor is supervising two other supervisors. These supervisors may occasionally exit, but it is *impossible* for them to exit five times in five seconds.[1].

Transient Processes

What if you want to monitor a process to make sure it completes its work, but *don't* want it restarted when it exits successfully? This is a usecase for the :transient restart strategy.

Let's look at another example. In this example, we will create a server that waits 1 second and then exits. Here's our server.

```
defmodule TransientServer do
  use GenServer

  def start_link do
    IO.puts("Server starting up from pid:
    ↪  #{inspect(self())}")
    GenServer.start_link(__MODULE__, [], name: __MODULE__)
  end

  def init(_) do
    IO.puts("Server initializing with #{inspect(self())}")
    :timer.apply_after(1000, __MODULE__, :exit, [])
    {:ok, []}
  end

  @impl true
  def handle_call(:exit, _from, state) do
    IO.puts("Cancelling timer and exiting
    ↪  #{inspect(self())}")
```

---

[1]For the root process to exit, it needs to initiate five restarts in five seconds. If we look at the ListenerSupervisor, the only way it will restart is if the Listener exits every second. The likelihood of that happening is $(.05)^5 = 0.00003\%$. So the best we can do with ListenerSupervisor is one failure every five seconds. Our best chance is with the WorkerSupervisor. If all our Workers fail every seconds, we will get five failures in five seconds. The probability of this happening is $5 \times (.1)^5 = 0.005\%$. And remember, this is just to get the WorkerSupervisor to exit *once* in five seconds. Thus, the best we can do is two exits in five seconds at the root supervisor, making it impossible for this process to exit.

```
    Process.exit(self(), :normal)
    {:reply, :ok, state}
  end

  def exit() do
    GenServer.call(__MODULE__, :exit)
  end
end
```

Notice in TransientServer.handle_call/3 we call Process.exit/2 with a :normal exit. This tells the supervising process that the exit is expected and normal (for lack of a better word). If the supervisor uses the :transient restart policy, it will not restart the worker when it exits under normal conditions.

Let's also define an observer of our process as well as a supervisor.

```
defmodule SupeObserver do
  def observe(pid) do
    %{active: active} = Supervisor.count_children(pid)
    IO.puts("Supervisor has active #{active} worker(s)")
  end
end

{_, pid} =
  Supervisor.start_link(
    [
      %{
        id: TransientServer,
        start: {TransientServer, :start_link, []},
        type: :worker,
        restart: :transient
      }
    ],
    strategy: :one_for_one
  )

IO.puts("Supervisor started (pid: #{inspect(pid)})")

:timer.apply_repeatedly(
  500,
  SupeObserver,
  :observe,
  [pid]
)

receive do
end
```

The SupeObserver will run in a separate process, occasionally checking how many active workers the supervisor has. Each time it checks the number of workers it prints them to standard out.

Let's see what happens when we run this.

```
$ elixir src/supervisor/transient.exs
Server starting up from pid: #PID<0.109.0>
Server initializing with #PID<0.110.0>
Supervisor started (pid: #PID<0.109.0>)
Supervisor has active 1 worker(s)
Supervisor has active 1 worker(s)
Cancelling timer and exiting #PID<0.110.0>
Supervisor has active 0 worker(s)
```

We can see after the TransientServer process exits normally it is not restarted by the supervisor. This is the behaviour we expected.

If we change the argument to Process.exit/2 from :normal to :kill, the supervisor will see the exit was not expected. Even with a :transient restart policy, the worker server will be restarted.

```
$ elixir src/supervisor/transient.exs
Server starting up from pid: #PID<0.109.0>
Server initializing with #PID<0.110.0>
Supervisor started (pid: #PID<0.109.0>)
Supervisor has active 1 worker(s)
Supervisor has active 1 worker(s)
Cancelling timer and exiting #PID<0.110.0>
Server starting up from pid: #PID<0.109.0>
Server initializing with #PID<0.116.0>
Supervisor has active 1 worker(s)
Supervisor has active 1 worker(s)
Cancelling timer and exiting #PID<0.116.0>
Server starting up from pid: #PID<0.109.0>
Server initializing with #PID<0.120.0>
Supervisor has active 1 worker(s)
```

Now we can see the TransientServer exiting and the supervisor restarting it, yielding a new PID.

You may have noticed we used two different types of child specifications in this example. They primarily differ in their type. The Worker processes are assigned the type :worker (actually, we don't explicitly assign that, it's the default). The Listener process is created as a :supervisor.

Child specifications also play an important role in defining how child processes should be started and managed by the supervisor. Child specifications are maps or structs that contain information about each child process. This includes the module name, function to start the process, and any additional options. The Supervisor.child_spec/2 function is commonly used to create child specifications, taking the child module and its arguments as parameters.

Here's an example of a child specification:

```
%{
  id: SomeProcess,
  start: {SomeProcess, :start_link, [arg1, arg2]},
  restart: :permanent,
  shutdown: 5000
  type: :worker
}
```

In this example, we are defining a child process named SomeProcess. The start field specifies the module that will be run in this process, the function that should be called to start the process (:start_link), and the args to be passed to the startup function. The restart field indicates the restart strategy for the child process, which, as we discussed above, can be :permanent, :temporary, or :transient. The shutdown field specifies the maximum time allowed for the child process to terminate gracefully, and the type field denotes whether the child process is a :worker or a :supervisor.

Choosing the right supervision strategy and defining the necessary child specifications is important to creating a robust supervision tree. You should always spend some time thinking carefully about what makes sense for your application.

13.5   Process Monitoring

In the prior example we spawned a process to monitor the number of children in our supervisor. It turns out that monitoring other processes is a rather common pattern. To that end, Elixir provides a function for exactly this usecase: Process.monitor/1.

When a monitor is created within a given process, that process will receive a message upon termination of the process it is monitoring. The received message is a tuple containing the atom :DOWN, a reference to the monitor, the PID or {name, node} tuple of the monitored process, and the reason the process terminated.

```
{:DOWN, <monitor reference>, :process, <monitored
 ↪   pid/name-node tuple>, <exit reason>}
```

We can do some interesting things with this pattern. The return value from `Process.monitor/1` is a monitor reference. This is the same reference we get when the process exits. Let's look at an example where we store this reference inside the state of a GenServer.

```
# /src/supervisor/monitor.exs
defmodule CountAndExit do
  def count_and_exit(0) do
    IO.puts("Done counting!")
  end

  def count_and_exit(n) do
    IO.puts("Counting down: #{n}")
    :timer.sleep(1000)
    count_and_exit(n - 1)
  end
end
```

Here we have defined a function that counts from n down to 0 and exits, waiting 1 second in between counts.

Now let's define the monitor GenServer that will track this process. The idea here is to create monitors on each `CountAndExit` process we create. Once the process exits, our `CounterMonitor` GenServer should be notified of the exit, along with the status.

```
# src/supervisor/monitor.exs
defmodule CounterMonitor do
  use GenServer

  def start_link(pid_map) do
    GenServer.start_link(__MODULE__, pid_map, name:
    ↪   __MODULE__)
  end

  def init(pid_map) do
    state =
      List.foldl(Map.to_list(pid_map), %{}, fn {pid, name},
      ↪   acc ->
        ref = Process.monitor(pid)
        Map.put(acc, ref, name)
      end)

    IO.puts("Using state: #{inspect(state)}")
    {:ok, state}
```

```
    end

    def handle_info({:DOWN, ref, :process, _obj, reason},
    ↪   state) do
      with {:ok, val} <- Map.fetch(state, ref) do
        IO.puts("Counter #{val} has excited with reason
        ↪   #{inspect(reason)}")
      end

      {:noreply, Map.delete(state, ref)}
    end
end
```

As you can see, we track the monitor reference within the state of the GenServer.

```
# src/supervisor/monitor.exs
pid_a =
  spawn(fn ->
    IO.puts("Spawning counter A!")
    CountAndExit.count_and_exit(5)
  end)

pid_b =
  spawn(fn ->
    IO.puts("Spawning counter B!")
    CountAndExit.count_and_exit(5)
  end)

pid_map = %{pid_a => "counter A", pid_b => "counter B"}
CounterMonitor.start_link(pid_map)

receive do
end
```

Finally, we spawn of two processes and launch our monitoring GenServer. Let's run this and look at the output.

```
Spawning counter A!
Spawning counter B!
Counting down: 5
Counting down: 5
Using state: %{#Reference<0.0.0> => "counter A",
↪   #Reference<1.1.1> => "counter B"}
Counting down: 4
Counting down: 4
Counting down: 3
Counting down: 3
Counting down: 2
Counting down: 2
```

```
Counting down: 1
Counting down: 1
Done counting!
Done counting!
Counter counter A has execited with reason :normal
Counter counter B has execited with reason :norma
```

13.6   Designing Fault-Tolerant Systems

The key to designing fault-tolerant systems is considering the potential failure mechanisms. As engineers, we tend to enjoy focusing more on the beauty and elegance of our code than we do thinking about how things might go wrong. Yet, considering the failure states will often lead to more stable systems than finding the perfect abstraction.

The first step to thinking through failure modes of your system is identifying the core functionality and state of the system. That is, the functionality that, if unavailable, leads to a system that doesn't function correctly, if at all. Essential state is the state maintained by the system that is required by the core functionality.

For example, consider a failed monitoring process that provides observability metrics. The system can still run, we have just lost some of our visibility into the system. On the other hand, a lost connection to a database that handles authentication will result in an outage. It's also important to consider whether a process might exit abruptly and unexpectedly or degrade slowly over time.

Correctly handling failures is often less about your code and more about your configuration. How should parent processes respond to a failing child? Should you arbitrarily restart your child process? Should you wait a while? If so, how long should you wait? How do you know? How many child processes are there? What if they all fail at the same time? These are the kinds of things you not only need to consider, but appropriately handle in your supervisor configurations and child specs.

A pattern will start to emerge as you think through the failure modes and process dependencies within your system. Some pieces may be tightly coupled, such that a failure of one means the other should be restarted. In other cases, you'll notice failures in one set of processes really have no impact (or shouldn't have any impact) on another set of processes. These types of observations will guide you in building a supervisor tree.

Recall the example earlier in the chapter of the worker processes sending messages of random numbers to an aggregating process. In the original design, the failures of the worker processes would sometimes impact the aggregating process. This lead to a natural evolution of our system. Instead of spawning these processes side-by-side on the same supervisor, we split them off into two groups. Each group had its own supervisor, and the two new supervisors were supervised by the original supervisor. This is how you slowly tease out the overall structure of your supervision tree.

One other consideration is the startup order of your application. In the ideal setting, the startup order does not matter. Every process that has a dependency is able to understand if it is able to connect or communicate with its dependency, rather than requiring the depdnency starts first. When you have startup orders coupled, you will eventually run into race conditions and hard to debug issues. It's generally better to communicate via some external state, whether that's ETS, a database, or some other system.

13.7 Conclusion

Now that we've studied supervisors and GenServers, we have the core pillars of creating robust and self-healing applications. These behaviours will form the foundation of just about all of your future systems. However, our servers are still rather unpolished. We don't have any configuration and we are running them by manually calling start_link/3. In the next chapter we will cover the Application behaviour. With this behaviour you will have the last piece of the puzzle. You will learn how to structure your Mix project to start your application and configure it based on the deployment environment.

Chapter 14

Application

Applications are how libraries are packaged and deployed in Elixir. You can think about Elixir applications similar to libraries from other languages. The similarity is mostly conceptual. Elixir applications can be loaded, started, and stopped. The application developer can specify what happens when the package is started and stopped through the Application behaviour.

Applications also have their own environment. The term environment does not refer to the OS environment but rather both a compile-time and runtime configuration that can be referenced by the application.

The application environment is simply a map of atom to value. These values are fetched with either `Application.fetch_env/2` or `Application.compile_env/3` and their bang equivalents. As a reminder, this environment is *not* the same as the OS environment, though it's possible (and often common) that the values defined in the application environment are pulled from the OS environment.

The two primary callbacks in the `Appication` behaviour are `start/2` and `stop/1`. Unsurprisingly, these are called when the function is started and stopped, respectively.

In the rest of this chapter we are going to build a toy project with an imported application. We will see how to leverage `Application.start/2` and `Application.stop/1` for resource creation and cleanup. This chapter will be somewhat unique in that part of the code will be in a separate GitHub repo. This is done to demonstrate

how to package an application up and how it can then be imported
by other Mix projects.

One important note before we dive into the code. The example we
use in this chapter is creating an application, and then importing
it from GitHub into another project, where it is used. This is
done purely to illustrate the mechanics of the process. In reality,
the dependency we pull in is really an internal dependency and
should not be imported this way. It is an anti-pattern to manage
internal dependencies externally via git, Hex, or some other pub-
lication method. Umbrella projects are designed to solve exactly
this problem. We will cover these in a subsequent chapter.

14.1   Application Basics

To start, let's create a new Mix project.

```
$ mix new brdcst
```

In this project we will create a GenServer that maintains an internal
state containing a single value and a list of subscribers. When the
value is updated, the server should broadcast this info to all of its
subscribers. Let's build get started.

First we will create a file lib/brdcst_server.ex, where we will put
the module BrdcstServer.

```
# lib/brdcst_server.ex
defmodule BrdcstServer do
  use GenServer

  def start_link do
    GenServer.start_link(__MODULE__, [], name: __MODULE__)
  end

  def init(_) do
    IO.puts("Initializing BrdcstServer")
    {:ok, %{value: nil, listeners: []}}
  end

  def handle_cast(
    {
      :update,
      update_fn
    }, %{
      value: value,
```

```
    listeners: listeners
  } = state) do
  new_value = update_fn.(value)
  IO.puts("Updating value to #{inspect(new_value)}")
  Enum.each(
    listeners,
    fn pid ->
      GenServer.call(pid, {:update, new_value})
    end)
  {:noreply, %{state | value: new_value}}
  end

  def handle_call(:register, {pid, _}, %{listeners:
  ↪ listeners} = state) do
    IO.puts("Registering #{inspect(pid)}")
    {:reply, :ok, %{state | listeners: [pid | listeners]}}
  end

  def handle_info(msg, state) do
    IO.puts("Received unknown message: #{inspect(msg)}")
    {:noreply, state}
  end
end
```

Let's add the client functions as well. In the same module (`Brdcst-Server`) add the following functions.

```
# lib/brdcst_server.ex
defmodule BrdcstServer do
  # Other code omitted

  def update(update_fn) do
    GenServer.cast(__MODULE__, {:update, update_fn})
  end

  def register(pid) do
    IO.puts("Attempting to register #{inspect(pid)}")
    GenServer.call(__MODULE__, :register)
  end
end
```

There are two message types we handle in `BrdcstServer`: `:update` and `:register`. Registering with the `BrdcstServer` simply updates the internal `listeners` state with a new pid. There are a few problems with this that we will acknowledge but ignore.

First, there is nothing preventing the registration of duplicate PIDs. We could use a set instead of a list to store the PIDs to resolve that problem. Secondly, we don't have a way to unregister or remove

PIDs. This could happen if a client doesn't want to receive updates anymore. Perhaps more likely, the client may have crashed and the PID is no longer valid.

Neither of these issues are relevant to this example. The focus here is to keep the example as small and focused as possible. We could make our code more robust, but that may come at the expense of clarity of what we are trying to achieve this chapter.

Adding the Application Behaviour

Now we are ready to setup the application. When the application starts we want to create a supervisor that monitors the BrdcstServer process. Similarly, we want to tear down the BrdcstServer when the application stops. Let's do that now.

```elixir
# lib/brdcst.ex
defmodule Brdcst do
  use Application
  require Logger

  @impl true
  def start(_type, _args) do
    children = [
      %{
        id: "brdcst_server",
        start: {BrdcstServer, :start_link, []}
      }
    ]

    opts = [strategy: :one_for_one, name: Brdcst.Supervisor]
    IO.puts("Starting Brdcst.Supervisor")
    {:ok, pid} = Supervisor.start_link(children, opts)
    IO.puts("Started Brdcst.Supervisor")
    {:ok, pid, pid}
  end

  @impl true
  def stop(pid) do
    IO.puts("Stopping Brdcst.Supervisor")
    Supervisor.stop(pid)
    :ok
  end
end
```

If you haven't already, this is a good point to commit and push this code to a GitHub repository. For convenience, name the repository the same as the package, brdcst.

Running the application

Before we pull this application into another application, let's make sure it works. If we run this with the standard command we learned earlier, mix run, the application will start up and then exit. This happens because the main server gets spawned in a process.

We previously got around this by adding

```
receive do
end
```

This works, but is a bit of a hack (though it is certainly useful at times). Instead of this, we can use the --no-halt flag.

From the root directory, run the following command

```
$ mix run --no-halt
```

The --no-halt flag tells Mix to keep running after starting the application. This has the same effect as the receive-do block, without actually requiring it.

We should see the following output:

```
$ mix run --no-halt
Compiling 1 file (.ex)

Starting Brdcst.Supervisor
Initializing BrdcstServer
Started Brdcst.Supervisor
```

From the output we can see that Brdcst.start/2 gets called first. From there, it creates the BrdcstServer, which results in BrdcstServer.init/1 getting called. Once the server is intialized, Brdcst.start/2 finishes up. If we want to interact with it, we can run the application for IEx. This can be useful for debugging.

```
$ iex -S mix
Erlang/OTP 26 [erts-14.2.5] [source] [64-bit] [smp:24:24]
↪  [ds:24:24:10] [async-threads:1] [dtrace]

Starting Brdcst.Supervisor
Initializing BrdcstServer
Started Brdcst.Supervisor
```

```
Interactive Elixir (1.17.2) - press Ctrl+C to exit (type h()
↪  ENTER for help)
iex>
```

Let's see if we can register with the server.

```
iex> BrdcstServer.register(self())
Attempting to register #PID<0.138.0>
Registering #PID<0.138.0>
:ok
```

It looks like that worked!

Let's see what happens if we send an :update message.

```
iex(2)> BrdcstServer.update(fn _ -> 42 end)
:ok
Updating value to 42
GenServer BrdcstServer terminating
** (stop) exited in: GenServer.call(#PID<0.138.0>, {:update,
↪  42}, 5000)
    ** (EXIT) time out
    (elixir 1.17.2) lib/gen_server.ex:1128: GenServer.call/3
    (elixir 1.17.2) lib/enum.ex:987:
↪  Enum."-each/2-lists^foreach/1-0-"/2
    (brdcst 0.1.0) lib/brdcst_server.ex:30:
↪  BrdcstServer.handle_cast/2
    (stdlib 5.2.3) gen_server.erl:1121:
↪  :gen_server.try_handle_cast/3
    (stdlib 5.2.3) gen_server.erl:1183:
↪  :gen_server.handle_msg/6
    (stdlib 5.2.3) proc_lib.erl:241:
↪  :proc_lib.init_p_do_apply/3
Last message: {:"$gen_cast", {:update,
↪  #Function<42.105768164/1 in :erl_eval.expr/6>}}
State: %{value: nil, listeners: [#PID<0.138.0>]}

Initializing BrdcstServer
```

A fantastic result! We see the update succeeded and then for some reason the BrdcstServer crashed. Let's read through the stacktrace to better understand what happened.

The first line tells us GenServer.call/3 timed out. The message it was trying to send was the message we sent, {:update, 42}. We can check our pid in IEx via

```
iex> self()
```

```
#PID<0.138.0>
```

It looks like it was trying to send us this message. Two lines down we can see this is happening inside the Enum.each/2 function. Remember from our implementation, once the BrdcstServer receives an :update message, it iterates through all registered PIDs and makes a GenServer.call/3 to each pid. In our case, we didn't have anything to read the message. GenServer.call/3 is a synchronous call. It blocks until we read the message and respond.

There is another nice result here. After the server process crashes, its supervisor restarts the process. I suppose this isn't too surprising after what we learned in the chapter about the Supervisor behaviour. Then again, it's always a pleasant surprise when things work the way they are supposed to!

Let's see what happens if we modify the implementation to use GenServer.cast/2, instead. That is, we update Brdcst-Server.handle_cast/2 to the following implementation

```
def handle_cast({:update, update_fn}, %{value: value,
↪   listeners: listeners} = state) do
  new_value = update_fn.(value)
  Logger.info("Updating value to #{inspect(new_value)}")
  # This is the updated line
  Enum.each(listeners, fn pid -> GenServer.cast(pid,
  ↪   {:update, new_value}) end)
  {:noreply, %{state | value: new_value}}
end
```

Let's try it again...

```
iex -S mix
Erlang/OTP 26 [erts-14.2.5] [source] [64-bit] [smp:24:24]
↪   [ds:24:24:10] [async-threads:1] [dtrace]

Compiling 1 file (.ex)

Starting Brdcst.Supervisor
Initializing BrdcstServer
Started Brdcst.Supervisor

Interactive Elixir (1.17.2) - press Ctrl+C to exit (type h()
↪   ENTER for help)
iex(1)> BrdcstServer.register(self())
Attempting to register #PID<0.153.0>
Registering #PID<0.153.0>
:ok
```

```
iex> BrdcstServer.update(fn _ -> 42 end)
:ok
Updating value to 42

iex(3)> receive do
...(3)> msg -> IO.puts(inspect(msg))
...(3)> end
{:"$gen_cast", {:update, 42}}
:ok
```

This time the `BrdcstServer` isn't waiting for acknowledgement that the message was received. The message is delivered to our process's mailbox, and we are able to read it using `receive-do`.

Let's move on to pulling this application into another application.

14.2   Publishing a Package

We need a way to publish this application before we can pull it into another application. The two simplest ways of publishing your application are through Hex and git. Publishing on Hex is as simple as registering an account, preparing your package by updating the metadata (in `mix.exs`) and documentation, and pushing your package to Hex.

Using git (with GitHub in our case) is even simpler - just push your repo to GitHub! The repo can be private or public. If it is private, any machine running code that depends on your package will need to be able to pull the repo. Adding the dependency is as easy as adding any dependency from Hex, you just point the the GitHub repo.

For this example, let's use GitHub. Create a private repo called `brdcst` and push your local Mix project to the repo. Since Mix initializes a git repo automatically you will need to set the `origin` repo.

```
$ git remote add origin <your git@github.com:<your
↪  username>/brdcst.git
$ git push origin main # assuming main branch name
```

That's it!

If you are going to publish a package publicly, Hex is the way to go. If you are publishing a package internally, you should probably use an umbrella project . Using a GitHub repo to publish a project is OK. However, it is best to keep the total number of internal packages published via GitHub low. Remember, you cannot make atomic updates across GitHub repos. So the more repos you have the harder global updates can become.

14.3   Using Internal Dependencies

Now that we have published our package, let's create a new project and pull in our application as a dependency. Let's create a project called `brdcst_listener`.

```
$ mix new brdcst_listener
```

Open up `mix.exs` and add the application we just published (privately or publicly) on GitHub.

```
# mix.exs
defmodule BrdcstListener.MixProject do
  use Mix.Project

  # other code omitted for brevity

  defp deps do
    [
      # Add the following line
      {:brdcst, git: "git@github.com:<your git
      ↪ user>/brdcst.git"}
    ]
  end
end
```

Now run

```
$ mix deps.get
```

And you should see Mix fetch and build your project. If we need to update a specific dependency, we can do so with the following command `mix deps.update <dep name>`. For example, we can update the `brdcst` package via

```
$ mix deps.update brdcst
```

The Mix Lockfile

You may have already noticed a file called `mix.lock`. This file contains information that specifies the exact versions of each of your dependencies. This makes the development environment consisting of your dependencies reproducible. Unless Elixir is your first programming language, you are likely familiar with the concept of a lock file. The `mix.lock` file tells you the *exact* versions of everything you depend on.

One thing that will inevitably happen to you is instead of running

```
mix deps.update <dep>
```

You will run

```
mix deps update <dep>
```

This will list your dependencies. You *might* think you've updated some or all of your dependencies (I've made this mistake!) when in fact you haven't. You can *always* rely on the `mix.lock` file to show you what is going on.

Specifically for us, the `mix.lock` file·will contain the commit hashes of our dependency. This will point at the specific version of our `brdcst` application we are pulling in. Also note that when you update a git-based dependency you will see the repo get pulled in.

Creating a Listener

We will need some processes that will update the `BrdcstServer` value. They will also listen for the update notifications. Let's create a new module, `BrdcstListener`. Similar to what we did in chapter 13, we will call a function at some set interval using Erlang's `apply_interval/4`.

```elixir
# /lib/brdcst_listener.ex
defmodule BrdcstListener do

  use GenServer
  require BrdcstServer

  def send_update() do
    BrdcstServer.update(fn _ -> :rand.uniform(100) end)
    IO.puts("#{inspect(self())} Sent updated value to
    ↪  BrdcstServer")
```

```elixir
  end

  def init(_) do
    IO.puts("Setting up periodic interval")
    BrdcstServer.register(self())

    :timer.apply_interval(
      1000,
      __MODULE__,
      :send_update,
      []
    )

    {:ok, %{}}
  end

  def start_link(name) do
    IO.puts("got name #{name}")
    GenServer.start_link(__MODULE__, [], name: name)
  end

  def handle_cast({:update, value}, state) do
    IO.puts("Received updated valued #{value} from
    ↪  #{inspect(self())}")
    {:noreply, state}
  end
end
```

Let's review what's going on here. The function BrdcstLis-tener.send_update/0 sends a random integer sampled from the half-open interval $U[0, 100)$ and sends it to the BrdcstServer. Remember that BrdcstServer.update/1 takes an update function as its input, rather than a value. This is a common pattern for performing atomic updates on a value where the updated value may depend on the prior value.

The BrdcstListener.init/1 function registers the process' PID with the BrdcstServer. Once it is registered, it creates a repeating process that calls BrdcstListener.send_update/0 every second. This will help us visualize the broadcast updates.

The last piece worth pointing out is the BrdcstListener.handle_cast/2 function. We simply log that we received an :update message along with the received value.

Creating the application

At this point we have some code in place to both send `:update` messages to the `BrdcstServer` as well as receive update notifications from the `BrdcstServer`. Now we need to create a separate application that will run our example. We will call our `Application` module `Runner`. Create a file `lib/runner.ex` and implement it as follows.

```
# lib/runner.ex
defmodule Runner do
  use Application

  require BrdcstServer

  def start(_type, _args) do
    {self()}
  end
end
```

Rather than implement this all in one go, let's take it one piece at a time. We've added in our dependency. Let's update our `mix.exs` file to run `Runner` as the primary application. Make the following changes to `mix.exs`

```
defmodule BrdcstListener.MixProject do
  use Mix.Project
  # other lines omitted for brevity

  def application do
    [
      mod: {Runner, []}, # <-- add this
      extra_applications: [:logger]
    ]
  end
end
```

Now let's run `mix run --no-halt`. You shoud see something like the following

```
Compiling 1 file (.ex)
Starting Brdcst.Supervisor
Initializing BrdcstServer
Started Brdcst.Supervisor
```

Notice we didn't do anything in our `Application.start/2` function. Just by including `Brdcst` as a dependency, the `Brdcst` application was started and running in its own process. Now let's add in the listener logic.

```
# lib/runner.ex
defmodule Runner do
  use Application

  require BrdcstServer

  def start(_type, _args) do
    children = [
      %{
        id: "brdcst_listener_1",
        start: {
          BrdcstListener,
          :start_link,
          [:brdcst_listener_1]
        }
      },
      %{
        id: "brdcst_listener_2",
        start: {
          BrdcstListener,
          :start_link,
          [:brdcst_listener_2]
        }
      }
    ]

    IO.puts("Starting BrdcstServer and BrdcstListeners")
    pids = Supervisor.start_link(
      children,
      strategy: :one_for_one
    )

    pids
  end
end
```

This pattern should feel pretty familiar by now. It's the same pattern we used in the Brdcst application. We launch our BrdcstListeners as children of a supervisor. When the application starts up, it creates our two listener processes as children of a parent supervisor. Let's see wha happens when we run the application.

```
mix run --no-halt
Compiling 1 file (.ex)
Starting Brdcst.Supervisor
Initializing BrdcstServer
Started Brdcst.Supervisor
```

```
got name brdcst_listener_1
Setting up periodic interval
Attempting to register #PID<0.151.0>
Registering #PID<0.151.0>
Registered with BrdcstServer: :ok
got name brdcst_listener_2
Setting up periodic interval
Attempting to register #PID<0.154.0>
Registering #PID<0.154.0>
Registered with BrdcstServer: :ok
#PID<0.156.0> Sent updated value to BrdcstServer
#PID<0.157.0> Sent updated value to BrdcstServer
Updating value to 8
Received updated valued 8 from #PID<0.154.0>
Received updated valued 8 from #PID<0.151.0>
Updating value to 99
Received updated valued 99 from #PID<0.154.0>
Received updated valued 99 from #PID<0.151.0>
```

14.4   Configuration

Right now we are hardcoding the number of listeners. That's
fine for our toy application. In the real world we would want to
pull this from our configuration. Luckily, Elixir provides built-in
facilities to help us with application configuration. Specifically,
Elixir provides the Config module. By convention, configs live in
the config directory and the root config file is config/config.exs.

Let's create the file config/config.exs (you will likely need to create
the directory too). You should have the following layout

- README.md
- config/
  - config.exs
- lib/
  - brdcst_listener.ex
  - runner.ex
- mix.exs
- mix.lock

Add the :brdcst_listener configuration to the application

```
# config/config.exs
import Config

config: :brdcst_listener
```

```
import_config "#{config_env()}.exs"
```

There are a few pieces here. Let's start with the last line. Con-fig.import_config/1 imports additional config files into config.exs. The idea behind this line is you have some global configuration that is shared across all environments. This belongs in config.exs. The remaining, environment-specific, configuration goes into config files like config/dev.exs, config/test.exs, or config/prod.exs.

Just because a value changes across environments doesn't always imply that it doesn't belong in config/config.exs. It can sometimes be useful to use config/config.exs to provide sensible defaults for the other environments. In this case, if a value is left out of one of the environment-specific configurations, the application can still run using the default value.

Now let's add configuration to specify the number of child listeners we create.

```
# config/config.exs
import Config

config :brdcst_listener
  n_children: 2

import_config "#{config_env()}.exs"
```

Note

Depending on your editor, you may get an error message at the import_config line stating something like

```
** (File.Error) could not read file
  "<your path>/brdcst_listener/config/test.exs": no such
  ↪   file or directory
```

This is coming from your editor checking your code using a test en-vironment. There are two fixes. If you plan on having environment-specific configuration, add the env-specific files like config/test.exs, config/dev.exs, and config/prod.exs. Otherwise, if you won't have environment-specific configuration, remove the import_config line.

We now need to update `lib/runner.ex` to use this value from our application environment. There are a few functions we can use to fetch values from the application environemnt.

- `Application.fetch_env/2` – takes the application name and key, returing `{:ok, <value>}` or `:error`.

- `Application.fetch_env!/2` – same as above, but returns the value or raises `ArgumentError` if the key doesn't exist.

- `Application.get_env/3` – following the pattern above, it takes the application name, the key name, and optionally a default value (which defaults to `nil`) to use if the key doesn't exist. This function returns the value or the given default value.

You might be wondering, if these functions take the application name as the first argument, maybe we can use these functions to read the application environment of our dependencies. This is not something you should do, as it can lead to unexpected behavior.

```elixir
# lib/runner.ex
defmodule Runner do
  use Application

  require BrdcstServer

  def start(_type, _args) do
    n_children = Application.get_env(
      :brdcst_listener,
      :n_children
    )
    children =
      for i <- 1..n_children, do: %{
        id: "brdcst_listener_#{i}",
        start: {
          BrdcstListener,
          :start_link,
          [:"brdcst_listener_#{i}"]
        }
      }

    IO.puts("Starting BrdcstServer and BrdcstListeners")
    pids = Supervisor.start_link(
      children,
      strategy: :one_for_one
    )

    pids
  end
```

```
end
```

Running this gives us the following output (omitting some log lines for brevity):

```
Starting Brdcst.Supervisor
Initializing BrdcstServer
Started Brdcst.Supervisor
got name brdcst_listener_1
Registered with BrdcstServer: :ok
got name brdcst_listener_2
Registered with BrdcstServer: :ok
got name brdcst_listener_3
Registered with BrdcstServer: :ok
```

As you can see, we spawned three processes this time, instead of two. This maps to our application config key :n_children, which has a value of 3.

What if you need to pull in a value from the system environment? This belongs in config/runtime.exs. These values are fetched from the system environment using the function System.get_env/2 . This function takes the name of the environment variable, as well as a default to use if the variable doesn't exist.

For example, the DB host is frequently configured at runtime from the environment. Your config/runtime.exs file might look something like

```
import Config

config :my_app,
  host: System.get_env("DB_HOST")
```

It is important you keep all your System.get_env/2 (and related) calls inside the config/runtime.exs file. If you are curious why, continue to the following sub-section. Otherwise, you can skip to the Logging section.

Runtime vs Compile-time

The reason you should only use System.get_env/2 in config/runtime.exs has to do with when this function gets evaluated. Let's create a small toy project to illustrate the differences.

```
$ mix new config_test
```

Now creat the following files

- config/config.exs

- config/runtime.exs

Update lib/config_test.ex to the following:

```
# lib/config_test.ex
defmodule ConfigTest do
  def start(_, _) do
    api_token = Application.get_env("API_TOKEN")
    IO.puts("Hello world!")
    IO.puts("Application environment API token:
    ↪ #{api_token}")
    {:ok, self()}
  end
end
```

Let's update config/config.exs to the following:

```
# config/config.exs
import Config

config :config_test,
  api_token: System.get_env("API_TOKEN")
```

Now, if all we ever do is run our application with one of mix run or iex -S mix, then we will always be ok because these two commands compile the application and then run it. This is what can make this behavior so confusing when first encountered. Until you actually deploy an Elixir application, you may never encounter a difference between the compile-time and runtime environments. Without diving into the exact details, let's build a release of our application.

```
$ mix release
* assembling config_test-0.1.0 on MIX_ENV=dev
* using config/runtime.exs to configure the release at
↪ runtime
```

You should see a new directory _build/dev/rel/. Use the following command to run the release:

```
_build/dev/rel/config_test/bin/config_test start
```

You should see the following output

```
Hello world!
Application environment API token:
```

So far, so good. We haven't set the API token environment variable so this isn't too surprising. Let's build a new release, this time altering the command for our release slightly.

```
API_TOKEN="my-local-token" mix release
```

Ok, realistically we would never build something in this manner. This is just to similuate your environment. In reality, you may have something like

```
# .bashrc
export API_TOKEN="my-local-token"
```

in your .bashrc file. This makes the following behavior even more devious as it can happen without you knowing. Anyways, back to the example at hand.

Now let's re-run our release again.

```
Hello world!
Application environment API token: my-local-token
```

Ok, not too surprising. Now let's see what happens if we override this environment variable at runtime.

```
$ API_TOKEN="my-dev-token"
↪   _build/dev/rel/config_test/bin/config_test start
Hello world!
Application environment API token: my-local-token
```

So what happened? The System.get_env/2 function was evaluated when the application was compiled, not when it was released. That is, System.get_env("API_TOKEN") pulled in the value of API_TOKEN when the application was built. The System.get_env/2 is, in essence, replaced by this value in the built artifact. At runtime, there is nothing to pull in because the `System.get_env/2` function doesn't get evaluated.

We can fix this by using `config/runtime.exs`. Update your config/runtime.exs file to the following

```
# config/runtime.exs
import Config

config :config_test,
  api_token: System.get_env("API_TOKEN")
```

and let's change `config/config.exs` to the following

```
# config/config.exs
import Config
  build_version: System.get_env("BUILD_VERSION")
```

Now let's rebuild our application

```
$ BUILD_VERSION="my-version" mix release
```

And run it with the following

```
$ API_TOKEN="runtime-api-token"
↪ _build/dev/rel/config_test/bin/config_test start
Hello world!
Application environment API token: runtime-token
```

We can add the `BUILD_VERSION` to our application as well.

```
# lib/config_test.ex
defmodule ConfigTest do
  require Application

  def start(_, _) do
    api_token = Application.get_env(:config_test,
    ↪ :api_token)
    build_version = Application.get_env(:config_test,
    ↪ :build_version)
    IO.puts("Hello world! (build version:
    ↪ #{build_version})")
    IO.puts("Application environment API token:
    ↪ #{api_token}")
    {:ok, self()}
  end
end
```

Rebuilding as above, `BUILD_VERSION="my-version" mix release`, and running yields

```
Hello world! (build version: my-version)
Application environment API token: runtime-token
```

14.5 Logging

Up this point, we have been relying on `IO.puts` for all of our "logging" needs. This is fine for quick and dirty experimenting, but in general it's best use a dedicated logging framework. Lucky for us, Elixir comes with the Logger module and it is incredibly easy to get up and running with it.

To leverage Elixir's Logger library, simply add `require Logger`. at the top of your module. The log functions inside Logger are all macros. Elixir cannot know these functions are macros unless they have been previously compiled, which is why you must always `require` or `import` the Logger module in each file you use logging.

Let's fire up IEx and play around with the module.

```
iex> require Logger
Logger
iex> Logger.info("hello world!")

15:06:05.870 [info] hello world!
:ok
iex> Logger.warning("this is a warning!")

15:07:21.147 [warning] this is a warning!
:ok
```

You can also use structured logging simply by providing a map instead of a string.

```
iex> Logger.info(%{type: "structured", msg: "logging", code:
↪   42})

15:08:10.534 [info] [code: 42, type: "structured", msg:
↪   "logging"]
:ok
```

You can do the same thing with keyword lists.

```
iex> Logger.info([type: "structured", msg: "logging", code:
↪   42])

15:08:10.534 [info] [code: 42, type: "structured", msg:
↪   "logging"]
:ok
```

The Logger module provides seven levels of logging

- :debug – for debugging, don't put critical info in these logs
- :info – typical logs tracking application behavior
- :notice – more important than :info, but not indicating an error state or impending error state
- :warning – indicating abnormal behavior or an impending error state
- :error – something failed or other errors
- :critical – somewhere between :error and :alert
- :alert – action must be taken immediately
- :emergency – system is is about to panic or has panicked

I think these are far too many for the typical application. The problem with having so many error codes is now the developers need to understand the meaning of all seven codes and agree on their uses. For example, it's not clear to me what a :critical error is and how it differs from :alert. What consitutes a :notice?

You can come up with your own system on how to use each of these. But, if you are working with several teams, you will need to communicate this system to all the developers. No matter how skilled of a communicator and/or teacher you are, everyone will have a slightly different understanding of these codes.

In general, I recommend the following:

- :debug - extra logging that will help you understand program state and flow. Use this for logs that would be helpful for debugging the application, but would be too noisy for typical use. This might be something like logging the body of a request.

- :info - use this level to indicate program flow and state. For example, "request received", "request processed", and "sending response". This lets the developer see what happend within the system.

- :warning - use these when something unexpected but noncritical happened. For example, maybe you expected a value to be in the DB, didn't find it, but it's also not problematic.

- :error - something bad happened and needs to be addressed by an engineer. This should generally indicate something is broken and needs to be fixed.

These four levels are sufficient. [1]

Configuration

Production-grade logging libraries, in general, are highly configurable. Elixir's Logger module is no exception. As we've already seen, it's easy to move between standard logging and structured logging. It also could not be easier to start using. You might have also noticed that, by default, mix includes Logger as a dependency in every new project.

Configuration, as you might have guessed, takes place next to your other application configuration in the config/ directory. Use these files to specify how your logs should be formatted, what log level to use, where to store your logs if they are written to a file, and even how often that file should be rotated.

Let's take a look at an example configuration.

```
# config/config.exs

config :logger, :default_formatter,
  metadata: [:mfa]

import_config "#{config_env()}.exs"
```

Here we are adding :mfa (module, function, arity) metadata to every log message. Here's an example log line with this metadata

```
05:19:30.854 mfa=Brdcst.start/2 [info] Started
↪   Brdcst.Supervisor
```

Similarly, we can add line and filename metadata via the configuration

---

[1]So what about the others? Well, use them if you want, but it'll probably end up adding more confusion than clarity. You will inevitably get into a discussion or debate about why someone thinks a log line should be :critical rather than :alert. Maybe that's productive for your organization. In my experience it's not.

```
# config/config.exs

config :logger, :default_formatter,
  metadata: [:mfa, :file, :metadata]

import_config "#{config_env()}.exs"
```

This gives us the follow log format

```
05:20:04.332 mfa=Brdcst.start/2 line=17 file=lib/brdcst.ex
↪   [info] Started Brdcst.Supervisor
```

The logging functions (e.g., Logger.info/2) are macros that wrap
Erlang's logging facilities. One of the advantages of this approach
is we can modify the logging code at compile time. Specifically,
this allows us to completely omit logging calls that meet certain
conditions.

Suppose in production we want to omit all logs below the :info
level. We could use a configuration like this:

```
# config/config.exs

config :logger,
  compile_time_purge_matching: [
    [level_lower_than: :info]
  ]
```

The compile_time_purge_match can take multiple conditions. In
the above example, we are uniformly applying this to all logs. We
can get more specific using the :module and :function specifiers.
For example, suppose we only wanted :error logs from the brdcst
module. At the same time, maybe we are debugging the Applica-
tion.start/2 callback in the Runner module.

```
# config/config.exs

config :logger,
  compile_time_purge_matching: [
    [level_lower_than: :info],
    [application: :brdcst, level_lower_than: :error]
  ]
```

Another useful compile-time option for the Logger module is :al-
way_evaluate_messages. As you might expect from the name, this

option tells Elixir to evaluate the messages inside each log function. This is useful if you are running locally at a different log level than you might run in production and you want to make sure your log messages don't generate an error.

For example, consider the following code:

```elixir
def start(_type, _args) do
  n_children = Application.fetch_env(:brdcst_listener,
  ↪  :n_children)
  Logger.debug("Starting #{n_children} children")
  {:ok, n_children} = n_children

  children =
    for i <- 1..n_children, do: %{
      id: "brdcst_listener_#{i}",
      start: {
        BrdcstListener,
        :start_link,
        [:"brdcst_listener_#{i}"]
      }
    }

  pids = Supervisor.start_link(
    children,
    strategy: :one_for_one
  )

  pids
end
```

On the surface this seems ok. Something like this could very easily make it through code review. If we are running it locally with the logging configuration

```elixir
config :logger,
  compile_time_purge_matching: [
    [level_lower_than: :info]
  ]
```

This will run as expected without issue. However, there is a subtle bug. String.Chars is not implemented for our tuple n_children. Attempting to log it via string interpolation will result in an exception. Adding the line

```elixir
config :logger,
  always_evaluate_messages: true,
  compile_time_purge_matching: [
```

```
    [level_lower_than: :info]
  ]
```

To our config will trigger the exception.

Advanced Configurations

For more advanced logging configurations I recommend checking out
the Logger module documentation on hexdocs (https://hexdocs.pm).
The documentation describes much more advanced configurations
than we will cover here. For example, the Logger module allows you
to configure how logs are written to file, different logging backends,
and so on.

Conclusion

We are finally ready for the grand finale (though, ironically, it's not
the last chapter of the book). We have everything we need to build
a more complex Elixir application. In the next chapter we will build
a multi-service application. One service will interact with the user.
This service will interact with two other services via gRPC and
Kafka. We will also learn how to use Ecto to work with databases.

Chapter 15

Distributed Elixir

15.1 Introduction

Many modern applications, even simple ones, have some degree of real-time interaction. In other cases, like Google Docs, Slack, Figma, and so on, the application is built around real-time collaboration. In either case, whether it's a fast, responsive website, or a smooth, real-time collaborative interaction, you will need to leverage concurrency (probably a lot of it), and you will want your code to run fast. Building these kinds of systems involves overcoming a unique set of challenges, particularly as the load to your system increases and you need to scale out the machines running your software. As these systems grow, they must balance their ability to scale with their ability to fail (paradoxically, these are often in opposition to eachother). Maintaining data consistency and system reliability also become increasingly difficult as the size of your system increases. These are the core problems distributed systems engineers deal with on a daily basis. While a detailed coverage of these topics is out of scope for this book, we will spend this chapter looking at how to build scalable and reliable distributed systems with Elixir.

As soon as you introduce a second system into your application, new and challenging problems start to pop up. In a single program on a single machine every function call happens with minimal latency. Either the call is executed, an exception is thrown and caught, or the application crashes. As soon as you introduce a second system, the context changes quite dramatically.

A call on another server can fail just as a call locally can. One of the challenges is determining whether that call failed, your message to trigger the call got dropped, or the response from the remote call failed. If that remote call changed the state in another system, you now have to consider whether all systems see the same change to that state. This is referred to consistency and there are a number of different consistency models to understand and work within. There are of course other problems like network latency, bandwidth, varying server hardware, and so on. [1] Your software needs to be able to encounter these challenges gracefully.

Fortunately, Elixir is particularly well-suited for distributed systems (as we will see). Being built on top of BEAM gives it excellent fault-tolerance and concurrency. Elixir's actor-based concurrency model makes things like race conditions and deadlocks less common. The OTP encourages developers to build their applications in such a way that they can self-heal after encountering crashes. Elixir's ecosystem contains a number of useful modules for real-time interactions like Phoenix.PubSub and Phoenix channels.

We will spend some time discussing distributed Elixir, and Elixir processes on different machines can talk to eachother. However, we will spend most of the time in this chapter working with Apache Thrift and Elixir. Apache Thrift provides a language-agnostic mechanism for communication over the network. It is a remote procedure call (RPC) style framework, similar to gRPC and Protobuf. Don't worry if none of this makes sense. We will cover what all this means in this chapter. The key things to take away is that Apache Thrift allows us to communicate between servers written in different languages (e.g., Elixir and Python) with a well-typed interface and generated client libraries.

15.2   A Tour of Distributed Systems

Distributed systems is a vast landscape within computer science. It is beyond the scope of this book to cover all of distributed systems, but we will give you a brief lay of the land in this section. We will first give a quick overview of some important theoretical results, followed by a more concrete architectural discussions. In this

---

[1] If you haven't seen the eight fallacies of distributed computing before, they are a quick and instructive read. They are originally attributed to Peter Deutsch and the team at Sun Microsystems. However, there have been many talks and blog posts on them since they were first proposed.

discussion we will cover various system architectures, communication patterns, and data storage.

CAP Theorem

The CAP theorem, first proposed by Eric Brewer, states the following.

> A distributed data store (system) can only guarantee two of the following during abnormal (failure) operation:
>
> 1. Consistency - all nodes have the same updates for all data
> 2. Partition Tolerance - the system can operate even when some parts are unable to talk to others (i.e., a network partition)
> 3. Availability - the system is always available to end users
>
> In the event of a network partition, you must choose between availability and consistency.

This is rather intuitive. A network partition means some nodes are unable to talk to other nodes. In this setting, it makes sense that you must choose either availabilty *or* consistency. If you choose availability, you must accept that some nodes will disagree on updates for some data. Why? Well, during a network partition while maintaining availability we require that all nodes respond to requests. If some of these requests are writes, some nodes will make updates on their respective data without being able to communicate these updates to other nodes maintaining replicas of that data.

Conversely, if we require consistency during a network partition, we must reject some writes. Allowing writes when there exist data replicas across nodes means we would have different views of the data on different nodes. This is an *inconsistent* state, which we don't want to allow. Therefore we must reject writes, which is equivalent to not being fully available.

Figure 15.1 illustrates the CAP theorem.

Processing Architectures

There are three primary patterns when it comes to processing data:

1. Streaming - data is continuously processed as it is received.

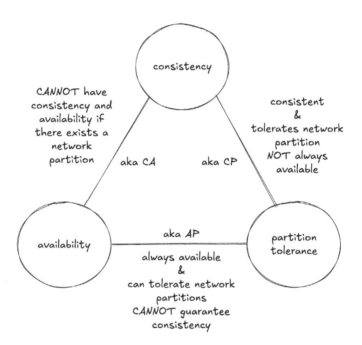

Figure 15.1: Illustration of the CAP theorem

2. Batch - data is collected (i.e., batched) and processed all at once.
3. Lambda - data is streamed through the system but *also* batched to be processed in bulk.

Streaming generally provides the lowest *latency* (the time it takes a single message to be completely processed). Batch processing generally provides the highest *throughput*, or the amount of data processed in a given period of time. This can be a little counterintuitive.

Let's do a thought experiement to better understand the difference. Consider a system, say System A, that can process messages every 0.1 seconds. The latency of System A is 0.1s. Now consider a second system, say System B, that is a batch processing system. Suppose for System B the maximal batch size is 20 pieces of data. Within System B, the communication overhead is 0.1s and the computational overhead is 0.1s. The latency of System B on a single message is 0.2s. If we need data processed as fast as possible, clearly System A wins.

But consider the case we have a backlog of of 100 messages we need processed. Every 0.2 seconds System B can process 20 messages. It will process the entire backlog in 5 seconds. System A, on the other hand, will take 10 seconds to process the entire backlog. This is a scenario where the *average latency* of System A will be slower than that of System B.

Why can batch systems have greater throughout? This typically comes from minimizing data movement, either through optimized communication plans in a distributed system or filling up compute units on a SIMD device like a GPU or TPU.

A lambda architecture utilizes both streaming and batch processing. You use a lambda architecture when you want a fast but approximate answer (the streaming leg of the system) but want an exact answer for later (the batch leg of the system). For example, suppose you have rapidly changing data in a database and you occasionally want to recompute a materialized view. As your streaming data references this materialized view it becomes increasingly out of data (suppose it depends on the streaming data). Every so often you can use a batch job to recompute the view.

The defacto framework for batch processing is currently Spark and to some extent Flink. Most Spark jobs are written in either Python or Scala. As much as I love Elixir, you really shouldn't use it for batch data processing. Don't reinvent the wheel. Leverage the expertise already developed around frameworks like Spark and Flink. You will save yourself and your company headache, heartache, and money.

Communication Patterns

There are two primary communication patterns in distributed systems: synchronous and asynchronous. Synchronous patterns are used when you need an answer as soon as possible. Asynchronous patterns are used when you want to trigger some work but are fine getting the answer later. We've already seen these communication patterns in this book with `GenServer.call/3` and `GenServer.cast/2`. Let's explore these in more depth than we've seen so far.

Synchronous communication occurs when you are trying to fetch something. This could be the frontend fetching a response to a user request. It could also be a backend system fetching data from another backend system. As we saw earlier, we can make synchronous calls within Elixir using `GenServer.call/3`. However, this is limited to Elixir processes. What if we need to send a message to a service written in Python? To do this, we need a different communication protocol. In this chapter we will use Apache Thrift, with is an RPC framework created at Meta.

Asynchronous communication generally happens when you are more interested in the side-effect, rather than fetching data. Asynchronous is also used in the sense of kicking off a request in the background (e.g., `async/await` in Javascript). This type of asynchronous programming is essential for building distributed systems. In the context of distributed system communication patterns, async communication is more often associated with queues and distributed logs.

Kafka is an example of a distributed log. If you are new to Kafka, this is similar to a queue [2], though there is not a strict FIFO guarantee. In this context, a message is sent to a Kafka "topic"

---

[2]It is guaranteed a portion of you reading this are familiar with Kafka, and of that group there is a sub-group squirmming in their chairs yelling internally "KAFKA IS NOT A QUEUE!" Yes, of course you are right, but the distinctions between a queue and a distributed log are unimportant if you are discovering Kafka for the first time in your life. The analogy to a queue is a good mental model for data in/data out.

by a producer (the process that writes the message) and then subsequently processed by a consumer (the process that reads the message). This decouples the rate of writing from the rate of reading, which is the primary distinction between syncrhonous and asynchronous communication models.

Data Consistency Models

There are many different data consitency models ranging from strong guarantees to weak guarantees. Some of these models have rather subtle differences in their semantics. For most engineers though, you really only need to understand two consistency models: strong consistency and eventual consistency.

Strong consistency

This is what you naively might expect when interacting with a system. As soon as you write to the system all reads from that system see the results of that write. It is easy to reason about and there is minimal data loss when there is a failure during a write. This comes a cost, however. Strong consistency has the highest write latency because the data must be replicated to all replicas before the write can be considered a success. This is usually a strong guarantee than you need.

Eventual Consistency

This is more relaxed than strong consistency, giving better write latency. As the name implies, with eventual consistency, reads following a write will *eventually* return the updated value. There may or may not be a guarantee on the time it takes for all reads to return the updated value. This time is the time it takes for the update to propogate through the system. If you've ever had an Amazon shopping cart open on two computers (or a computer and a phone, for example) you have witnessed eventual consistency first hand. You may have noticed if you add or remove an item from the cart on one system it takes a few seconds for the other system to see the update. This is eventual consistency. Most of the time you should reach for eventual consistency.

15.3   System Overview

We will be building a distributed system with several services.

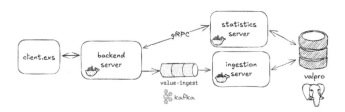

Figure 15.2: Architecture diagram for our system

Figure 15.2 illustrates our system. There are three services, Kafka, and a Postgres database. This is all running in Docker. Our system will take in values at some user-defined interval and process them. This processing is simply computing statistics on the stored values. We will use the name valpro (short for "value processing") in our names below.

Docker

It's unlikely you are reading a book on Elixir and don't know what Docker is. However, if you are that rare swan, Docker is analogous to a virtual machine (though under the hood is *completely* different). It's beyond the scope of this book to dig into how Docker works and the ins and outs of using Docker. For now, it will suffice to maintain the following mental model:

- Think of Docker containers as virtual machines. They *are not* virtual machines, but they look and feel the same.
- Docker images define the container. They are a blueprint of what goes into a container.
- The Dockerfile is the set of instructions used to create the Docker image.

We will use Dockerfiles to create our images. We will then use Docker Compose to run our images as containers.

Go to docker.com and install Docker Desktop on your machine. This will get you everything you need (including Docker Compose) to follow along with this chapter.

Docker Compose

Docker Compose is a tool that comes bundled with the desktop version of Docker. With Docker Compose, you define the services (Docker images) within your system and the Docker Compose tool is responsible for starting all the services up (potentially in the specified order, as we will see in a bit). This is done by first defining your system in a `compose.yaml` file and then running the following command

```
$ docker-compose up -d
```

We will typically use the `-d` flag to run the system in daemon mode. This means the `docker-compose up` command will return immediately and your system will be running in the background.

When you are ready to shutdown the entire system, run the following

```
$ docker-compose down
```

We will always be running these in the root directory of our umbrella project.

For now, create the following `compose.yaml` file.

```
# compose.yaml
version: "3"
```

Postgres

Let's add a Postgres database to our `compose.yaml` file. Why use Docker to run the database instead of using whatever you have installed on your local machine? I find it simpler to work with. The database is easier to nuke. It is trivial to change the DB version. It is clear when it's running and when it isn't. The list goes on. In our case, it's also nice having all our services and database on the same private network (which Docker creates).

Add the following to your `compose.yaml` file:

```
services:
  db:
    image: postgres:16.1
    ports:
      - 5432:5432
```

```
environment:
  - POSTGRES_PASSWORD=postgres
  - POSTGRES_DB=valpro
```

Notice we have added a new top-level key to our YAML file: `services`. All of the services we create will be indented under this key. Here we show the indentation, but in subsequent examples we *may* omit the indentation.

This is creating a new service. Within the Docker Compose file this service is called `db`. If we need to refer to this service within the context of the file, we will just use `db`. The name of the database we are creating is called `valpro` (short for *value processor*). We set the password to `postgres`.

Go ahead and run `docker-compose up -d`. You can verify it is running with the command

```
$ docker ps
```

which will output something along the lines of

```
CONTAINER ID   IMAGE          COMMAND                 CREATED
↪   STATUS         PORTS
↪   NAMES
aa980c839b76   postgres:16.1  "docker-entrypoint.s..."  55
↪   minutes ago  Up 55 minutes  0.0.0.0:5432->5432/tcp,
↪   :::5432->5432/tcp  valpro_umbrella_db_1
```

Kafka

Now that we have some experience with Docker Compose. Let's add Kafka to our list of services. This will be a little more involved, as we will need a Zookeeper service as well as an initialization service that creates our Kafka topic.

Update the `compose.yaml` file with the following services:

```
zookeeper:
  image: confluentinc/cp-zookeeper:latest
  ports:
    - "2181:2181"
  environment:
    - ZOOKEEPER_CLIENT_PORT=2181

kafka:
```

```
image: confluentinc/cp-kafka:latest
depends_on:
  - zookeeper
ports:
  - 9092:9092
expose:
  - 29092
environment:
  - KAFKA_ZOOKEEPER_CONNECT=zookeeper:2181
  - KAFKA_LISTENER_SECURITY_PROTOCOL_MAP=\
    PLAINTEXT:PLAINTEXT,\
    PLAINTEXT_HOST:PLAINTEXT
  - KAFKA_OFFSETS_TOPIC_REPLICATION_FACTOR=1
  - KAFKA_INTER_BROKER_LISTENER_NAME=PLAINTEXT
  - KAFKA_ADVERTISED_LISTENERS=\
    PLAINTEXT_HOST://localhost:9092,\
    PLAINTEXT://kafka:29092
```

This creates two services: ZooKeeper and Kafka. You can think of ZooKeeper as a distributed key-value store. ZooKeeper is no-longer a dependency of Kafka as of version 4.0. So why do we do it this way if we don't actually need ZooKeeper in production? Well, this is the best documented way of getting this configured locally. Confluent (a company that provides managed Kafka on top of other services) *does* provide a local version of Kafka that doesn't require ZooKeeper. However, this version has far less usage, is still considered experimental (as of late 2024), and doesn't seem to have much usage on Stack Overflow. As a result, we use this setup! It really doesn't matter as long as it works since this is just for local development. We are only interested in interacting with Kafka, not a complete production setup.

Ok! So we have our Kafka setup. The environment variables above are just telling the brokers to not encrypt the data, listen locally (and within the Docker Compose network), and where to find ZooKeeper.

Notice in the addresses we use the names of the services. That is, we reach ZooKeeper at `zookeeper:2181`. This is a nice feature of Docker Compose and can greatly simply networking as your services become more complex.

Once you have added these lines to your `compose.yaml` file, run `docker-compose up -d` to make sure everything works. Once you have verified you are up and running with no errors, tear everything down with `docker-compose down`.

One last piece for setting up Kafka is creating the topic we will use. We will use an additional service that starts *after* the Kafka service starts. It then runs a scripts to create a topic in the Kafka service and verifies the topic was created.

```
init-kafka:
  image: confluentinc/cp-kafka:latest
  depends_on:
    - kafka
  entrypoint: ["/bin/sh", "-c"]
  command: |
    "
    sleep 10
    echo -e 'Listing topics'
    kafka-topics \
      --bootstrap-server kafka:29092 \
      --list

    echo -e 'Creating topic value-ingest'
    kafka-topics \
      --bootstrap-server kafka:29092 \
      --create \
      --topic value-ingest \
      --partitions 1 \
      --replication-factor 1

    echo -e 'Created topic. Listing topics:'
    kafka-topics \
      --bootstrap-server kafka:29092 \
      --list
    "
```

One important point from above. Make sure you use single quotes where I use single quotes and double quotes where I use double quotes. If you get the command formatting incorrect it can be difficult to debug.

15.4   Umbrella Projects

We briefly touched on these in an earlier chapter. Umbrella projects are useful when you have internal dependencies you want to share across a number of projects. In our case, we will have two internal dependencies. The first is our database repository. The second is our gRPC client.

Creating an umbrella project is as easy as creating a normal project. The only difference is the addition of the `--umbrella` flag.

```
$ mix new --umbrella valpro_umbrella˙
```

The result looks mostly like the typical projects with a couple of exceptions. The first is there is now lib directory. Instead we get apps. As you might have guessed, this is where our projects will live.

The mix.exs file looks a little different. The project configuration has a key :apps_path instead of the :app key that we are used to.

15.5 Ecto

We will use Ecto to manage our interactions with the database. This means we will use it for defining our schemas, creating and running migrations, as well as interacting with the database. In fact, all database interaction will run through our database module.

Before we get started with Ecto, we need to create our database repo project. From the valpro_umbrella/apps directory, run the command

```
mix new db_repo --module Repo --sup
```

This will give us some additional scaffolding. Specifically, it will create a Repo.Application module within the directory db_repo/lib/repo. This file will contain the scaffolding for a basic Supervisor. Let's add a couple of dependencies we will need to use Ecto. Move inside the db_repo project and open up the mix.exs file. Change your deps definition to include the following two dependencies

```
defp deps do
  [
    {:ecto_sql, "~> 3.12"},
    {:postgrex, ">=0.0.0"},
    {:jason, "~> 1.0"}
  ]
end
```

as usual, once you've made these changes you should run

```
mix deps.get
```

Now let's create the repository to manager the interactions with the database. Run the following command

```
$ mix ecto.gen.repo -r Valpro.Repo
```

This will create some files as well as update the umbrella project configuration. If you navigate to the umbrella root config directory, you should see `config.exs` updated with a placeholder configuration for `:db_repo`. Update is to the below configuration:

```
config :db_repo, Valpro.repo
  database: "valpro",
  username: "postgres",
  password: "postgres",
  hostname: "localhost"

config :db_repo, ecto_repos: [Valpro.Repo]
```

This repository terminology may be new to you. Repositories are a design pattern that attempts to abstract away the database interactions. The idea is the repository manages the DB clients and exposes friendlier APIs to other applications (or internally). There are a number of advantages to this approach:

- It allows you to centralize your database SDKs/dependencies to a single project or service.
- A single package, module, or service manages all the SQL and ORM files. Other packages, modules, or services just interact with the exposed API.
- At scale, it can greatly simplify instrumentation.
- It can simplify error handling, as all your database client code is in one place, instead of scattered across a codebase.

I'm not here to say you should always use a repository. This is the way Ecto does it, so this is the way we will do it.

Anyways, back to the task at handle. Updates your `application.ex` file so that your `Repo.Application` module looks like this:

```
defmodule Repo.Application do
  @moduledoc false

  use Application

  @impl true
  def start(_type, _args) do
```

```
    children = [
      # We added this
      Valpro.Repo
    ]

    opts = [
        strategy: :one_for_one,
        name: Repo.Supervisor
    ]
    Supervisor.start_link(children, opts)
  end
end
```

The key part here is adding `Values.Repo` to the `children` list so that it will be managed by the supervisor.

Database Migrations

At this point we just have a database service but we don't hav the `valpro` database we need. We will use Ecto to create this for us. First, make sure the Postgres database is up and running.

```
$ docker-compose up -d
```

from the umbrella root directory (containing the `compose.yaml` file). Once the database is up and running, navigate back to the `apps/db_repo` directory. Run the following command to create the database:

```
$ mix ecto.create
Compiling 2 files (.ex)
Generated db_repo app
The database for Valpro.Repo has been created
```

If you check Postgres, you should see a newly created database named `valpro`.

We need a table now that we have a database. Let's create a table called `value` which will store the values process. First we will create the migrations.

```
$ mix ecto.gen.migration create_value
* creating priv/repo/migrations
* creating
↪   priv/repo/migrations/20241003193321_create_value.exs
```

We don't need to get crazy with our data model. Our goal is to build a number of services interacting in various ways, not dive deep into databases. Update the `change/0` function in the newly generated migration file to the following:

```
def change do
  create table(:value) do
    add(:key, :string)
    add(:value, :float)
    # The corresponding type here is jsonb
    add(:metadata, :map)

    timestamps()
  end
end
```

The `timestamps/0` function adds to additional fields: `created_at` and `updated_at`. Let's see what happens when we run the migration.

```
$ mix ecto.migrate
11:50:28.814 [info] == Running 20241003193321
↪  Valpro.Repo.Migrations.CreateValue.change/0 forward

11:50:28.816 [info] create table value

11:50:28.829 [info] == Migrated 20241003193321 in 0.0s
```

If you check the tables of the database you should see `value` listed. For example, using `psql`

```
valpro=# \dt
               List of relations
 Schema |        Name        | Type  |  Owner
--------+--------------------+-------+----------
 public | schema_migrations  | table | postgres
 public | value              | table | postgres
```

Let's also create schema in our `db_repo` app to simplify interactions with the database. Create the file `lib/valpro/value.ex` with the following implementation:

```
# lib/valpro/value.ex
defmodule Valpro.Value do
  use Ecto.Schema

  schema "value" do
    field(:key, :string)
```

```
    field(:value, :float)
    field(:metadata, :map)

    timestamps()
  end
end
```

This tells Ecto there is a relationship between a `Valpro.Value` struct and the table `value`. Let's fire up IEx and see what happens when we insert a value into our database.

```
iex> v = %Valpro.Value{key: "hello", value: 42.0}
%Valpro.Value{
  __meta__: #Ecto.Schema.Metadata<:built, "value">,
  id: nil,
  key: "hello",
  value: 42.0,
  metadata: nil,
  inserted_at: nil,
  updated_at: nil
}
iex> Valpro.Repo.insert(v)
<log line omitted>
{:ok,
 %Valpro.Value{
  __meta__: #Ecto.Schema.Metadata<:loaded, "value">,
  id: 1,
  key: "hello",
  value: 42.0,
  metadata: nil,
  inserted_at: ~N[2024-10-03 20:05:05],
  updated_at: ~N[2024-10-03 20:05:05]
 }}
```

And if we query the table in `psql` we see

```
valpro=# select * from value;
id |  key  | value | metadata |       inserted_at       |
↪   updated_at
 1 | hello |    42 |          | 2024-10-03 20:05:05 |
 ↪   2024-10-03 20:05:05
(1 row)
```

Let's take a quick look at how we will query the data. Again in IEx, run the following:

```
iex> Valpro.Value |> Valpro.Repo.all
<log line omitted>
[
```

```
%Valpro.Value{
  __meta__: #Ecto.Schema.Metadata<:loaded, "value">,
  id: 1,
  key: "hello",
  value: 42.0,
  metadata: nil,
  inserted_at: ~N[2024-10-03 20:05:05],
  updated_at: ~N[2024-10-03 20:05:05]
}
]
```

Fantastic! We can also perform queries with a WHERE clause

```
iex> Valpro.Value |>
...> Ecto.Query.where(key: "hello") |>
...> Valpro.Repo.all
<log line omitted>
[
  %Valpro.Value{
    __meta__: #Ecto.Schema.Metadata<:loaded, "value">,
    id: 1,
    key: "hello",
    value: 42.0,
    metadata: nil,
    inserted_at: ~N[2024-10-03 20:05:05],
    updated_at: ~N[2024-10-03 20:05:05]
  }
]
```

Alright, we know enough now to be dangerous. Let's move on to gRPC. You can go ahead and delete the inserted value from the value table. If you aren't sure how to do that, I suggest you treat it as an exercise for the reader. You can use Ecto, psql, or an IDE like JetBrains DataGrip.

15.6   gRPC and Protobuf

gRPC is an RPC [3] framework developed by Google. It provides cross-language RPC support, offering type-safe bindings for client and server in a number of languages. It is used extensively inside Google and benefits from both a deep developer base and active community.

---

[3]RPC, or Remote Procedure Call, is a request-response protocol popular in distributed systems. The core motivation is to "hide" the network call in some sense and make it feel like you are making a local function call. The primary difference is in network latency and alternative failure modes due to the distributed nature of the call.

gRPC works by compiling your Protobuf schema and RPC service definitions into generated code. On the client side, you use this code any time you want to make an RPC to the server. On the server side, it provides simple scaffolding to build out your RPC server.

The message type used by gRPC is Protocol Buffers (Protobuf). Protobuf is a serialization format that is fast, compact, and strongly typed. If you have worked with a C-style language the IDL will feel very familiar.

Setup

First lets create a new project within our umbrella project. Navigate to the the apps/ directory and run the following

```
$ mix new protos
```

This project is just for holding the generated code. All other projects will include this project as an internal dependency.

Navigate into the apps/protos directory and open up mix.exs. Let's add Thrift to this project.

```
deps = [
  {:grpc, "~> 0.9"},
  {:protobuf_generate, "~> 0.1.3"}
]
```

then run mix deps.get.

We will store our .proto files in priv/proto, so let's go ahead and make that directory.

Service Definition

As we mentioned in the Ecto section, the goal of this chapter is not to dive deep in any specific framework. Rather, we are trying to better understand what it looks like when we build a system using various communication technologies. For this section, we don't need to build out some complex RPC service. That would be counterproductive to our goal of building a distributed system in Elixir.

We will keep our gRPC service very simple. There will be a single function, getStats, that returns the predefined set of statistics on our data. There will be two message types. The first is the GetStatsRequest and the second, as you might have guessed, is GetStatsResponse.

Let's go define our service and messages. Create the file priv/proto/statistics.proto with the following content.

```
// priv/proto/statistics.proto
syntax = "proto3";

package statistics;

message GetStatsRequest {
    string metadata_filter = 1;
}

message GetStatsResponse {
    double mean = 1;
    double median = 2;
    double mode = 3;
}

service Statistics {
    rpc GetStats(GetStatsRequest) returns (GetStatsResponse)
    ↪   {}
}
```

Generate the Elixir code by running the following command

```
$ mix protobuf.generate \
  --generate-descriptors \
  --output-path=./lib \
  --include-path=./priv/proto \
  --plugin=ProtobufGenerate.Plugins.GRPC \
  ./priv/proto/statistics.proto
```

You should see a new file in lib/ named statistics.pb.ex. We are adding descriptors to our generated code to aid in debugging later. gRPC has a reflection server that lets you inspect the service and protobuf definitions.

15.7   Buidling the Statistics Server

Alright, now that we have our database repository setup, our gRPC service defined, and Kafka running, let's build out our services. The

first service we will work on is the statistics server. To begin, similar
to what we did in the Ecto section, let's create a new application
in apps with a pre-setup supervisor.

```
$ mix new statistics_server --module Statistics.Server --sup
```

We will need to add both the grpc and db_repo projects as internal
dependencies to this project. Fortunately, this is fairly easy in an
umbrella project. Add the following lines to your deps/0 function
in mix.exs.

```
defp deps do
  [
    {:grpc_reflection, "~> 0.1.0"},
    {:protos, in_umbrella: true},
    {:db_repo, in_umbrella: true}
  ]
end
```

Run mix deps.get to check your internal dependencies and pull in
grpc_reflection.

Let's build out the statistics gRPC server. The first thing we want
to do as implement reflection. This will be useful for debugging our
service later on.

Reflection Server

Let's build the reflection server first, as it is the simplest. Create
the file lib/statistics/reflection/server.ex.

```
defmodule Statistics.Reflection.Server do
  use GrpcReflection.Server,
    version: :v1,
    services: [Statistics.Statistics.Service]
end
```

As we mentioned above, this will enable us to use a tool like grpcurl
to inspect our service once it's up an running.

Statistics Server

When you created the statistics_server application two
files should have been generated for you: lib/server.ex

and lib/server/application.ex.   Let's create a third file:
lib/server/endpoint.ex.

In the server file, we will implement our gRPC service. To start,
let's just have it return a fixed response.

```
# lib/server.ex
defmodule Statistics.Server do
  use GRPC.Server,
    service: Statistics.Statistics.Service
  require Logger

  def get_stats(_request, _stream) do
    Logger.info("got a request")

    %Statistics.GetStatsResponse{
      mean: 42.0,
      median: 42.0,
      mode: 42.0
    }
  end
end
```

This file implements the RPC endpoints we exposed in the service
definition in statistics.proto. Each function defined in that file
has a corresponding function in this file that contains the business
logic. In our case, we only have a single function.

The next step when working with gRPC is to register the service
with the gRPC server. We do this in two parts. The first is to
implement lib/server/endponit.ex. Let's do that now.

```
# lib/server/endpoint.ex
defmodule Statistics.Endpoint do
  use GRPC.Endpoint

  run(Statistics.Server)
  run(Statistics.Reflection.Server)
end
```

Here we are registering two different services. The first is the
service we just implemented, the statistics server. The second is the
reflection server, which allows us to inspect the exposed services
on our gRPC server. This is quite useful for debugging locally and
verifying things are working as expected.

It's worth pointing out that you do this same "registration" step
in every language when implementing a gRPC server. There is the

service definition (Statistics.Server in our case) and it must be registered with the actual gRPC server. The gRPC server is what handles things like accepting and tearing down connections with clients, transport encoding, compression/decompression of data, and so on.

The last step is to update lib/server/application.ex to run our server. We don't have much to do here. All that's needed is to define our child processes. Update children to the following:

```
children = [
  {
    GRPC.Server.Supervisor,
    endpoint: Statistics.Endpoint,
    port: 50051, start_server: true,
  },
  GrpcReflection
]
```

This may feel odd, since we just registered the reflection server in the endpoint. In fact, that registration is just saying "use this API for these RPC calls." In the reflection case there is a separate process that spins up to handle those calls.

Let's run our gRPC service and see if it's working as expected.

```
$ mix run --no-halt
```

Verifying Statistics Server

There are two ways we can interact with the server. The first is through IEx. In the proto application (apps/proto), open up IEx with iex -S mix.

```
iex> {:ok, channel} = GRPC.Stub.connect("localhost:50051")
{:ok,
 %GRPC.Channel{
   host: "localhost",
   port: 50051,
   scheme: "http",
   cred: nil,
   adapter: GRPC.Client.Adapters.Gun,
   adapter_payload: %{conn_pid: #PID<0.193.0>},
   codec: GRPC.Codec.Proto,
   interceptors: [],
   compressor: nil,
   accepted_compressors: [],
```

```
  headers: []
 }}
iex> req = %Statistics.GetStatsRequest{}
%Statistics.GetStatsRequest{
  metadata_filter: "",
  __unknown_fields__: []
}
iex> {:ok, reply} = channel |>
  Statistics.Statistics.Stub.get_stats(req)
{:ok,
 %Statistics.GetStatsResponse{
   mean: 42.0,
   median: 42.0,
   mode: 42.0,
   __unknown_fields__: []
 }}
```

Excellent! Looks like the gRPC service is working. We still need to fill out the database interaction logic, but we will do that a little later.

Another useful tool when working with gRPC is grpcurl. If you are on a Mac you can install it via brew install grpcurl.[4]

You can use grpcurl to list the services and functions available (*if* reflection is enabled). Let's see what services are available.

```
$ grpcurl -v -plaintext localhost:50051 list
statistics.Statistics
```

This gives us the name of the service from the gRPC server's perspective. Now we can list the functions.

```
$ grpcurl -plaintext localhost:50051 list
↪    statistics.Statistics
statistics.Statistics.GetStats
```

This gives us the function we can call. Let's see what happens when we send an empty request to this endpoint.

```
$ grpcurl \
  -plaintext \
  -d '{}' \
```

---

[4]There is also a Docker image for grpcurl. Fetch the image with docker pull fullstorydev/grpcurl:latest and then replace all the grpcurl commands in this section with docker run fullstorydev/grpcurl:latest.

```
    localhost:50051 \
    statistics.Statistics.GetStats
{
  "mean": 42,
  "median": 42,
  "mode": 42
}
```

Exactly what we were hoping for. If you check the terminal running your server you should see some log lines like

```
09:33:02.782 [info] Received v1 reflection request:
↪  {:file_containing_symbol, "statistics.Statistics"}

09:33:02.783 [info] Received v1 reflection request:
↪  {:file_by_filename, "statistics.GetStatsRequest.proto"}

09:33:02.790 [info] got a request
```

Computing Data Statistics

All that is left for the statistics server is to compute the mean, median, and mode of our data. Hopefully everyone is familiar with the mean (the average value). The median of the data is the value in the middle of the sorted data. That is, the value that is greater than half the data and less than half the data. Finally, the mode is the most frequent piece of data.

The first step will be to fetch all data. The second step is computing the above statistics. Fetching the data is easy. Let's create our statistics functions first, so they will be ready when we update get_stats/2 to fetch the data.

Add the following private functions to lib/statistics/server..

```
defmodule Statistics.Server do
  # Other code omitted
  defp mean(vals) do
    Enum.reduce(
      vals,
      0,
      fn x, acc -> x.value + acc end
    ) / length(vals)
  end

  defp median(vals) do
    nums = Enum.map(vals, fn x -> x.value end)
    sorted = Enum.sort(vals)
```

```elixir
    len = length(sorted)
    mid = div(len, 2)

    if rem(len, 2) == 0 do
      # Use the average of the middle two elements whene
      # there are 2
      (Enum.at(sorted, mid - 1) + Enum.at(sorted, mid)) / 2
    else
      Enum.at(sorted, mid)
    end
  end

  defp mode(vals) do
    vals
    |> Enum.map(fn x -> x.value end)
    |> Enum.frequencies()
    |> Enum.max_by(fn {_, count} -> count end)
    |> elem(0)
  end
end
```

In `lib/statistics/server.ex`, update the `get_stats/2` function
with the following body:

```elixir
defmodule Statistics.Server do
  # Other code omitted
  def get_stats(_request, _stream) do
    Logger.info("got a request")

    values = Valpro.Repo.all(Valpro.Value)
    mean = mean(values)
    median = median(values)
    mode = mode(values)

    Logger.info("Computed mean: #{mean}, median: #{median},
    ↪   mode: #{mode}")

    %Statistics.GetStatsResponse{
      mean: mean,
      median: median,
      mode: mode
    }
  end
end
```

Let's build out the ingestion server next.

15.8 Building the Ingestion Server

Before we dive into the implementation of the ingestion server, we should understand what it will do. Recall from our system diagram, the ingestion server sits in between Kafka and the database. As you might guess, the ingestion server will read from Kafka and the write the data to the database.

This means we have two goals for this section:

1. Figure out how to read from Kafka
2. Use `db_repo` to write to the database

Similar to our statistics server, let's start off with a scaffolded supervisor project.

```
$ mix new ingestion_server --module Ingestion.Server --sup
```

We will use Broadway[5] to interact with Kafka. It is an ergonomic, high-level Kafka library that suits our needs without unneccessary complexity. The other popular library, KafkaEx, is slightly more complex but also offers finer-grained features and control. In a production setting you need to choose what's best for your team.

Let's add Broadway to our `deps` and pull it into the project. Update your `deps` as follows

```
def deps do
  [
    {:broadway}, "~> 1.0"},
    {:broadway_kafka, "~> 0.4.1"}
  ]
end
```

and then run `mix deps.get` as usual.

A Note on Terminology

There is some confusing terminology when using Broadway to work with Kafka. In the Kafka world, a *producer* is a process that writes

---

[5]If you are familiar with Kafka Streams, Broadway will feel somewhat familiar. The primary abstraction in Broadway is the pipeline topology. A pipeline is a graph of nodes where each node does some type of processing or batching. Batching nodes simply collect some number of messages before publishing them to some external data sink.

to a Kafka topic. A *consumer* is something that reads from a
Kafka topic. In Broadway word, a *producer* is something that reads
messages from an external source (e.g., Kafka), and passes them to
the Broadway processors within the defined processing graph.

Whether you are coming from Kafka, or potentially going to Kafka
in another language, please always keep in mind that the terminology
we will use with Broadway is very different from everywhere else.

Because of Broadway's design, there is very little code we need to
write to connect to Kafka and start processing messages. Open up
lib/server.ex and add the following start_link/1 implementation.

```
# lib/server.ex
defmodule Ingestion.Server do
  use Broadway

  require Logger

  def start_link(args) do
    Logger.info("Starting Ingestion.Server with args:
    ↪  #{inspect(args)}")

    Broadway.start_link(__MODULE__,
      name: __MODULE__,
      producer: [
        module:
          {BroadwayKafka.Producer,
            [
              hosts: [{"localhost", 9092}],
              topics: ["value-ingest"],
              group_id: "value-ingest-group"
            ]},
        concurrency: 1
      ],
      processors: [default: [concurrency: 1]],
      batchers: [default: [batch_size: 100, batch_timeout:
      ↪  5000]]
    )
  end
end
```

One key point here is we are hardcoding our hosts, topics, and
group_id. This is almost always a bad idea. We will fix this
later in the chapter. Host information should be fetched from and
environment variable. Topics should be stored as constants in a
location that is shared by both the Kafka producer and consumer.

However, we are trying to keep code and complexity to a minimum here, so we will hardcode.

The group_id corresponds to the consumer group. With diving too deep into Kafka, consumer groups are how Kafka tracks offsets within toipc partitions. There can be any number of consumers within a consumer group and they will *not* process the same message. Multiple consumer groups *will* process the same message.

Broadway handles message processing through callbacks. The first callback, Broadway.handle_message/3 is required. The second callback, Broadway.handle_batch/4, is optional. Let's go ahead and implement both.

```elixir
defmodule Ingestion.Server do
  use Broadway

  require Logger

  # start_link omitted

    @impl true
  def handle_message(_, message, _) do
    Logger.info("Received message: #{inspect(message)}")
    {:ok, message}
  end

  @impl true
  def handle_batch(_, messages, batch_info, _) do
    n_msgs = batch_info.size
    Logger.info("Received batch of #{n_msgs} messages")
    {:ok, messages}
  end

end
```

The handle_message/3 function has three parameters

1. processor - the atom that defines the processor
2. message - the Broadway.Message being handled
3. context - a user-defined context that was an argument of start_link/2

Similarly, handle_batch/4 has a similar set of parameters

1. batcher - an atom, similar to processor above
2. messages - the list of Broadway.Messages to be processed
3. batch_info - metadata about the batch
4. context - same as above

All we need in our experiment is message and messages, depending on the function, so we will omit the other arguments.

All that is left is to update the application supervisor to create a process for our Ingestion.Server. Go to lib/server/application.ex and update children to

```
children = [
  {Ingestion.Server, []}
]
```

Now we are ready to fire up the ingestion_service. Make sure you have Kafka running in the background, otherwise there won't be any brokers to connect to (docker-compose up -d if you forgot).

```
$ mix run --no-halt
```

You should see some log messages of Broadway negotiating with the Kafka Broker. Likewise, if you look at the Kafka container logs you should see some logs from the broker assigning the consumer group to the value-ingest topic.

Kafka Message Type

Any time you have data moving over the wire it is a good practice to specify the format of that data. Within the context of a system like we are building, JSON is rarely the right choice.[6] Building distributed systems, especially with a team, requires a lot of coordination. In our case, we need to understand what format we should use when writing to Kafka and what format we should expect when reading from Kafka. While we *could* use JSON, it's a bad idea for two reasons:

1. The reader doesn't know what fields are in the data and there is nothing guaranteeing they won't change.

2. You might counter above by saying it would be specified in the documentation. In my experience, internal technical documentation is *never* as up-to-date as it should be. External facing documentation is a different matter (oftentimes a company's

---

[6]JSON is better suited for responses for web APIs because it is well understood in most languages. You don't have to worry about generating clients, communicating schema files (though the schema should *always* be well documented), and so on.

reputation is affected by said documentation). Hoping that a teammate will update the documentation the same time they make an update to the JSON schema is a recipe for disaster.

Let's go ahead and add a new protobuf schema to the apps/protos project. Create the file priv/proto/ingestion.proto with the following implementation.

```
syntax = "proto3";

package ingestion;

message IngestionMessage {
  string key = 1;
  string value = 2;
  map<string, string> metadata = 3;
}
```

Notice that IngestionMessage mirrors the schema of our database.

Writing to the Database

Each message read from Kafka should be persisted to the database. Let's update the implementation of Ingestion.Server.handle_message/4 to write to the database. The first thing we need to do is add dependencies on protos and db_repo. Update the mix.exs file as follows:

```
# apps/ingestion_server/mix.exs

def deps do
  [
    {:broadway, "~> 1.0"},
    {:broadway_kafka, "~> 0.4.1"},
    {:db_repo, in_umbrella: true},
    {:protos, in_umbrella: true}
  ]
end
```

Now we are ready to update handle_message/4. There are two steps this function must perform:

1. Deserialize the Kafka message data payload into an IngestionMessage protobuf
2. Create a Valpro.Value struct and insert it into the database.

Since we need to handle this for both a single message and a batch of messages, let's create a helper function to handle this for us.

```elixir
defmodule Ingestion.Server do
  defp persist_data(data) do
    msg = Ingestion.IngestionMessage.decode(data)
    Logger.info("Decoded protobuf: #{inspect(msg)}")
    Logger.info("Persisting to db")

    Valpro.Repo.insert(%Valpro.Value{
      key: msg.key,
      value: msg.value,
      metadata: msg.metadata
    })
  end
end
```

We can use this for both `handle_message/3` and `handle_batch/4` as follows.

```elixir
# apps/ingestion_server/lib/ingestion/server.ex
defmodule Ingestion.Server do
  # Other implementation omitted

  @impl true
  def handle_message(_, message, _) do
    case persist_data(message.data) do
      {:ok, _} ->
        Logger.info("Data persisted successfully")

      {:error, changeset} ->
        Logger.error("Error persisting data:
        ↪  #{inspect(changeset)}")
    end

    message
  end

  @impl true
  def handle_batch(_, messages, _, _) do
    Enum.each(messages, fn m -> persist_data(m.data) end)
    messages
  end
end
```

It's a good idea to run `mix compile` as a quick gut check that everything looks roughly correct.

`handle_message/3` must return the given message (possibly transformed) and `handle_batch/4` [7] must return the given messages (possibly transformed). There will be no subsequent processing in our case, so it suffices to simply return the given input.

15.9 Backend Server

At this point we have two services. The ingestion service reads from Kafka and persists the data to Postgres (our database). The statistics service is queried by the backend server, providing mean, median, and mode calculations on our data.

What remains to be done is implement our backend server along with a method of interacting with it. We can think of this as a public API to the world. The natural selection here is exposing a REST API. However, that take us into the land of Phoenix. Phoenix is the de facto web framework in Elixir.

If you have used Ruby on Rails or Django it will feel quite familiar. If you've used either of those frameworks then you'll know just how much material there is within thos frameworks. Phoenix is no different. Entire books can (and have) been written on the Phoenix framework. Rather than try to cram all of that into a section or chapter of this book we are going to skip Phoenix. [8]

Let's start by creating our backend server application. As with the other servers, let's create the application with a supervisor scaffolded for us.

```
$ mix new backend_server --module Backend.Server --sup
```

Our backend needs to be able to write to Kafka as well as make gRPC calls to the statistics service. However, each of these actions will be triggered externally. We will first work on the external

---

[7]We are only implementing `handle_batch/4` here to show you the function and how to use it. This function will never be called in our application because we don't have a batcher in front of our processor in this pipeline. In order for `handle_batch/4` to be invoked, there must be a batching node feeding into it. If you find this material interesting, I encourage you to try and modify our pipeline so that `handle_batch/4` gets called.

[8]This was a point of great interal struggle. I even wrote maybe half of a chapter introducing the key parts of Phoenix. It became apparent to me, as the chapter grew and grew, that this topic would slowly take over the latter half of the book. As a result, I decided to pull the chapter.

interaction. After that is working, we can add in the pieces to make
the gRPC call and writing to Kafka.

Muti-node Elixir

One piece we haven't covered in this book so far is multi-node Elixir.
We will use multi-node Elixir to handle the interaction between
the user and the backend server. There are two advantages of this
approach. It keeps things simple and we will be able to interact
with our system through IEx.

Let's setup up the initialization routine for our backend server. It
will implement the GenServer behaviour, so we can include a use
GenServer at the top. There are two steps the initialization routine:

1. Connect to the Kafka brokers
2. Connect to the statistics gRPC server

Connecting and writing to Kafka requires the package brod. Add
that to your mix.exs file. We will also need to add the protos
sibling project, as we will be interacting with gRPC.

```
# backend_server/mix.exs

def application do
  [
    extra_applications: [:logger, :brod],
    mod: {Backend.Server.Application, []}
  ]
end

defp deps do
  [
    {:broadway, "~> 1.0"},
    {:broadway_kafka, "~> 0.4.1"},
    {:protos, in_umbrella: true}
  ]
end
```

As always, run mix deps.get to fetch and check your dependencies.

For either of these to work we need their respective services running.
Now is a good time to make sure you have both Kafka and the
Statistics Server running in the background.

Let's add the start_link/3 callback to our module.

```
# lib/backend/server.ex
```

```
defmodule Backend.Server do
  use GenServer
  require Logger

  def start_link(args, opts \\ []) do
    GenServer.start_link(
      __MODULE__,
      args,
      opts
    )
  end

end
```

brod requires that we first connect to Kafka (a cluster of Kafka brokers). Once we have established a connection with Kakfa, we must create a producer process, which will handle all the writing to Kafka for us.

Connecting to Kafka requires a few pieces of information.

1. Client ID - this is how Kafka identifies us. It must be an atom.
2. Kafka broker hosts - this is a list of addresses and ports at which we can reach the brokers (localhost:9092 for us).
3. Topic - we need to specify which topic we want the producer to write to.

Update the init/1 callback of your Backend.Server module as follows.

```
# lib/backend/server.ex

defmodule Backend.Server do
  # Other code omitted

  def init(args) do
    {:ok, _} = Application.ensure_all_started(:brod)

    Logger.info("Starting backend server")
    hosts = [localhost: 9092]

    Logger.info("Connecting to kafka")
    :ok = :brod.start_client(
      hosts,
      args.client_id,
      _client_config = []
    )
    :ok = :brod.start_producer(
```

```
      args.client_id,
      args.topic,
      _producer_config = []
    )
  Logger.info("Connected to kafka")

  {:ok, n_partitions} =
    :brod.get_partitions_count(
      args.client_id,
      "value-ingest"
    )

  Logger.info("Found #{inspect(n_partitions)} partitions")

  {
    :ok,
    %{
      client_id: args.client_id,
      topic: args.topic
    }
  }
  end
end
```

You may have noticed the first thing we do is call Applica-
tion.ensure_all_started/2. Interacting with Kafka requires that
brod is completely initialized and running. If we try to connect
before this happens, the connection will fail. This function blocks
until brod is up and running.

The call to :brod.start_client/3 establishes the connection with
the Kafka brokers. The following call to :brod.start_producer
creates a producer process that will write to the specified topic.
We also call :brod.get_partition_count to fetch the number of
partitions in the respective topic.

In most Kafka clients, the partition logic is handled for you. Every
Kafka topic is split into multiple partitions. Usually messages are
written to their respective partition based on the hash of their key.
In the case of Broadway, we must specify the partition. We still
want to use the hash of the key, so we will create a helper function
that helps us do this. In order to convert the hash value to a
partition number, we need the total number of partitions.

We will need to know the client ID, topic, and the number of
partitions when we are writing messages to Kafka. We store these
in the GenServer's state so they are accessible to us in the future.

Let's update our application supervisor to create a child `Back-end.Server` process. Set the children process to the following:

```
children = [
  {
    Backend.Server,
    %{client_id: :backend_server, topic: "value-ingest"}
  }
]
```

It's worth repeating: the client ID *must* be an atom. You will get a vague error and connection to Kafka will fail if it is a string.

At this point you should be able to start your backend server and see it connect to Kafka.

```
$ mix run --no-halt
```

Now is a good time to sort out any bugs or errors you are seeing. Next we will establish connection with the gRPC statistics server.

Upddate the `Backend.Server.init/1` function to connect to the statistics server.

```
defmodule Backend.Server do
  def init(args) do
    # Prior implementation omitted

    Logger.info("Connecting to stats grpc server")
    {:ok, channel} = GRPC.Stub.connect("localhost:50051")
    Logger.info("Connected to stats grpc server")

    {
      :ok,
      %{
        channel: channel,
        client_id: args.client_id,
        n_partitions: n_partitions,
        topic: args.topic
      }
    }
  end
end
```

The `channel` we create stores the connection to the statistics server. We will need to access it every time we want to make a gRPC call to the statistics server, so we need to add it to the GenServer's internal state along with the topic, number partitions, and client ID.

Run the server again and make sure you are able to establish a connection with the statistics server. If it fails, double check that you have the statistics server running in the background.

Now that we are able to initialize our backend server, let's implement our callbacks. There are two scenarios we are going to handle. The first is ingesting new data. The second is retrieving statistics. During ingestion we will write to Kafka. Retrieving statistics requires making an RPC call to the statistics server. Both of these will be triggered by a `handle_call/4` (TODO check arg count). We will implement the ingestion scenario first.

Earlier we mentioned we will need to hash the Kafka key and use that to determine which topic partition we will write to. We will use `phash/2` from Erlang's standard library. This function takes the value to be hashed, along with an integer used to compute the modulus of the hash.

Let's break down what we need to do to write to Kafka.

1. Determine the partition to which we will write using the message key
2. Serialize the message body
3. Send the serialized message to Kafka

Recall from the earlier section where we created the `protos` project. We create a Protobuf called `IngestionMessage` whose purpose was to handle ingesting new data into our system. This is the message value we expect our `handle_call/3` to take. Serializing this message is as simple calling `IngestionMessage.encode/1`.

Add a `handle_call/3` with the following implementation.

```
# lib/backend/server.ex
defmodule Backend.Server do
  @impl true
  def handle_call(
        {:ingest, msg},
        _from,
        %{
          client_id: client_id,
          n_partitions: n_partitions,
          topic: topic
        } = state
      ) do
```

```
    Logger.info("Received ingest call")
    # compute the partition
    partition = :erlang.phash2(msg.key, n_partitions)
    # serialize the protobuf
    bs = Ingestion.IngestionMessage.encode(msg)
    Logger.info("Producing to partition #{partition}")
    # send to kafka
    :ok = :brod.produce_sync(client_id, topic, partition,
    ↪  msg.key, bs)
    {:reply, {:ok, %{}}, state}
  end
end
```

Let's create a helper function, `ingest/1` that takes a map containing the `key`, `value`, and `metadata` we want to ingest. This functio nwill also handle constructing the `IngestionMessage` protobuf correctly so the caller doesn't need to worry about the wire format.

```
defmodule Backend.Server do
  # Other code omitted

  def ingest(m = %{
        key: key,
        value: value,
      }) do
    Logger.info("Ingesting data")

    msg = %Ingestion.IngestionMessage{
      key: key,
      value: value,
      metadata: Map.get(m, :metadata, %{}))
    }

    GenServer.call(__MODULE__, {:ingest, msg})
  end
end
```

Before we test out the backend server, make sure you are running the the ingestion server. If not, open up a terminal, navigate to `apps/ingestion_server`, and run `mix run --no-halt`.

At this point, we should be able to write data to Kafka. We can trigger the writes from IEx. Let's go ahead and give it a try. Start the backend server

```
$ mix run --no-halt
```

and in a separate terminal, attach to an IEx session

```
$ iex -S mix
```

Call ingest/1 from IEx. You should see output similar to the following.

```
iex> Backend.Server.ingest(%{
  key: "hello",
  value: 42
})
[info] Ingesting data
[info] Received ingest call
[info] Producing to partition 0
[info] client :backend_server connected to localhost:9092

{:ok, %{}}
```

Check the terminal running your ingestion server. You should see log output along the lines of:

```
<startup logs connecting to kafka>
[info] Decoded protobuf: %Ingestion.IngestionMessage{
  key: "hello",
  value: 42.0,
  metadata: %{},
  __unknown_fields__: []
}
[info] Persisting to db
[debug] QUERY OK source="value" db=2.6ms...
INSERT INTO "value" ("value", "metadata", "key"...)
```

Looks like it worked! If you query the database you should see a record. Now it's time to add the call to the statistics server. Open lib/backend/server.ex and add the following handle_call/3 implementation.

```
# lib/backend/server.ex
defmodule Backend.Server do
  # other code omitted
  def handle_call(
      :get_stats,
      _from,
      %{channel: channel} = state
    ) do
    Logger.info("Received get_stats call")
    req = %Statistics.GetStatsRequest{}

    {:ok, resp} =
      channel
```

```
    |> Statistics.Statistics.Stub.get_stats(req)

  stats_reply = %{
    mean: resp.mean,
    median: resp.median,
    mode: resp.mode
  }

  {:reply, {:ok, stats_reply}, state}
  end
end
```

The client function is pretty simple:

```
# lib/backend/server.ex
defmodule Backend.Server do
  def get_stats() do
    Logger.info("Getting stats")
    GenServer.call(__MODULE__, :get_stats)
  end
end
```

Let's restart IEx and try it out

```
$ iex -S mix
iex> Backend.Server.get_stats()
[info] Getting stats
[info] Received get_stats call
{:ok, %{mode: 42.0, mean: 42.0, median: 42.0}}
```

Fantastic! Looks like everything is hooked up. We have a fully functioning system at this point. It's alittle annoying we have to open all these terminal session. Let's take care of that in the next section.

15.10 Containerizing Elixir Apps

Right now we have to run each individual application in a separate terminal. This works, but is very hacky annd tedious. It would be better if we could do this all from our `compose.yaml` file.

Before we dig in, though, there is undoubtedly a contingent of you reading this thinking "why the hell would we put our Elixir app into a Docker container?" Indeed, this contingent exists in just about every deployment circle. I actually sympathize with the sentiment. Docker often adds a lot of conceptual overhead and complexity. On top of understanding the code of your system, the system architecture, and all the frameworks, you have to understand Docker, its intricacies, and how to deploy the container (often on Kubernetes). I agree that it's a lot.

However, the reality is, you will see this stuff in your day job at some point. Most of you probably already have. You don't have to like it. You don't have to agree with it. But it's the reality. So rather than fight it or complain about it here, we will just learn it.

Dockerfile

We will use a two-stage build in our Dockerfile. I will only show the Dockerfile for the backend server. The other Dockerfiles are identical, but replacing `backend_server` with the respective application names.

The first part of the file will use `elixir:1.18.1-slim` to build a `prod` release of our application. We will then copy over the build artifact into the second stage, which will service as the final image.

Open up your Dockerfile, `apps/backend_server/Dockerfile`, and add the following

```
# apps/backend_server/Dockerfile
FROM --platform=linux/amd64 elixir:1.18.1-slim AS builder

RUN apt-get update && apt-get install -y \
    build-essential \
    git \
    curl \
    ca-certificates


COPY . /app

WORKDIR /app/apps/backend_server

ENV MIX_ENV=prod
RUN mix deps.get && mix release
```

There are a few things going on here.

- `--platform=linux/amd64` makes it clear we are building for non-ARM, x86-64 linux platforms. With the emergence of Apple's ARM chips, this has become an increasingly important flag.
- We are naming this stage of the build `builder`

- We are creating a prod release by setting MIX_ENV=prod

If you haven't seen this, you are probably wondering why we are doing this. The idea is to create a uniform build environment, identical to the environment in which the program will run. In the second stage, we copy over the build artifacts but not the files we don't need. If we don't use this, espeically if you are on a newer ARM-based Mac, your container will crash upon startup. In fact, even just the difference OSes is enough for your container to not function correctly.

Let's add the second stage to our Dockerfile. Starting where we left off in apps/backend_server/Dockerfile, add the following

```
FROM --platform=linux/amd64 elixir:1.18.1-slim

RUN apt-get update && apt-get install -y \
    build-essential \
    git \
    curl \
    ca-certificates

COPY --from=builder /app/_build/prod/rel/backend_server /app

CMD ["/app/bin/backend_server", "start"]
```

Our build artifacts are all within the app/_build directory. That's all we need to copy over. Before you build, we need to create one last file to prevent our local development from interfering with our Docker builds: the .dockerignore file.

In the umbrella root (the same directory as your compose.yaml file), create a file called .dockerignore and add the following lines:

```
# .dockerignore
_build
deps
```

Now we are ready to check our work. From the umbrella root, run the following command:

```
$ docker build -f apps/backend_server/Dockerfile .
```

Since we are using an umbrella project, we need the umbrella root to be our build context so that all the sibling projects are included in the initial build.

Repeat this process, creating an almost identical Dockerfile in the statistics and ingestion server directories. Make sure to change the `backend_server` references to their respective names.

Running the `docker build` command for all our apps can be tedious. Luckily, we can handle this from Docker Compose. Let's update our `compose.yaml` file so that it can both build and run our services.

Building from Docker Compose

For each of our services we will define the build requirements and the inter-service dependencies. The build context will be the same for each service. The only thing that changes with respect to the build is the location of the Dockerfile. The inter-service dependencies are rather simple.

- `statistics_server` depends on the database
- `ingestion_server` depends on both the database and Kafka
- `backend_server` depends on both the statistics server, ingestion server, and Kafka

Let's start with the statistics service. Add the following lines to your `compose.yaml` file:

```
statistics:
  build:
    context: .
    dockerfile: apps/statistics_server/Dockerfile
  ports:
    - 50051:50051
  depends_on:
    - db
```

The ingestion server looks quite similar.

```
ingestion:
  build:
    context: .
    dockerfile: apps/ingestion_server/Dockerfile
  ports:
    - 50051:50051
  depends_on:
    - kafka
    - db
```

Lastly, the backend server.

```
backend:
  build:
    context: .
    dockerfile: apps/backend_server/Dockerfile
  depends_on:
    - kafka
    - statistics
    - ingestion
```

We can build all of our services with the command

```
$ docker-compose build
```

Before moving to the next section, let's run this an see what happens. You should see a bunch of connection errors. The newly added services aren't able to find or connect to the database or Kafka brokers. We will dig into this in the next section.

Networking

The problem we are hitting is related to how Docker Compose handles networking. Docker Compose creates a private network on the host machine for the containers it manages. Outside of this network, when we make a call to localhost:5432, for example, that gets direct to the running Postgres container. The localhost piece is external to the private network.

Once we move inside the private network Docker Compose has created, we can no longer use the localhost address and instead need to use the service name. The service name in this context is the key in the compose.yaml file. The statistics service has an address of statistics while the ingestion service has an address of ingestion.

Let's create three new configuration files: dev.exs, prod.exs, and runtime.exs. The dev.exs and prod.exs files will contain the different configurations for our database. The runtime.exs file will configure gRPC and Kafka.

Let's start with the database configuration. Move the config for :db_repo from config.exs to dev.exs. Your dev.exs should file should look like this

```
# config/dev.exs
import Config
```

```
config :db_repo, Valpro.Repo,
  database: "valpro",
  username: "postgres",
  password: "postgres",
  hostname: "localhost"
```

And your `config.exs` should look as follows (note the additional line at the end)

```
import Config

config :db_repo, ecto_repos: [Valpro.Repo]

import_config "#{Mix.env()}.exs"
```

The `prod.exs` file will look very similar to the `dev.exs` file, except that we change the host from `localhost` to `db`.

```
# config/prod.exs
import Config

config :db_repo, Valpro.Repo,
  database: "valpro",
  username: "postgres",
  password: "postgres",
  hostname: "db"
```

This is enough to get our Ecto repo configured so that it attempts to connect using the correct address. The changes for Kafka and gRPC will require a little more work. They involve making a few minor application updates.

Let's start with the runtime configuration. Update `runtime.exs` as follows

```
import Config
require Logger

Logger.info("Loading runtime configuration")

config :backend_server,
  statistics_host: System.get_env("STATISTICS_GRPC_HOST",
  ↪ "localhost"),
  statistics_port:
    System.get_env("STATISTICS_GRPC_PORT", "50051")
    |> String.to_integer(),
  kafka_host: System.get_env("KAFKA_HOST", "localhost"),
```

```
    kafka_port:
      System.get_env("KAFKA_PORT", "9092")
      |> String.to_integer()

config :ingestion_server,
  kafka_host: System.get_env("KAFKA_HOST", "localhost"),
  kafka_port:
    System.get_env("KAFKA_PORT", "9092")
    |> String.to_integer()
```

Ingestion Server

Let's start with the ingestion server since it requires fewer changes. We will update `Ingestion.Server.start_link/1` (in `lib/ingestion/server.ex`) to pull the Kafka host and port from the application configuration.

```
# lib/ingestion/server.ex
def start_link(args) do
  Logger.info("Starting Ingestion.Server with args:
  ↪  #{inspect(args)}")

  kafka_host =
    Application.get_env(
      :ingestion_server,
      :kafka_host,
      "localhost"
    )
    |> String.to_atom()

  kafka_port =
    Application.get_env(
      :ingestion_server,
      :kafka_port,
      9092
    )

  # Remaining start_link body
```

Now that we have the host and port values from the configuration, we need to update `Broadway.start_link/3`. Note that, for the sake of brevity, I have omitted some of the `Broadway.start_link/3` configuration. Feel free to refer to earlier in this chapter to see the entire configuration. The only change we are making is updating hosts.

```
def start_link(args) do
  # omitted kafka config from above
```

```
Broadway.start_link(__MODULE__,
  name: __MODULE__,
  producer: [
    module:
      {BroadwayKafka.Producer,
        [
          hosts: [{kafka_host, kafka_port}],
          topics: ["value-ingest"],
          group_id: "value-ingest-group"
        ]},
    concurrency: 1
  ], # prior configuration below this point is unchanged
  )
end
```

This is enough to get the ingestion server running without Kafka
connection errors. If you start this when Kafka is already running,
it should connect without problem. However, if you watch the logs
during a whole-system start (i.e., after running docker-compose up)
you'll notice a number of connection errors. Why is that?

Even though we have a dependency of this service on the Kafka
service in our compose.yaml file, the dependency is not based on
Kafka's internal startup procedures. It is only the order in which
the containers are started. In our case, Kafka takes some time to
startup, negotiate with ZooKeeper, and be ready to accept incoming
connections. Until it is ready, the ingestion server will attempt to
connect and fail. We will see this same behavior with the backend
server.

Backend Server

We will start with fetching the Kafka host and port, the same as
we did with the ingestion server. However, the backend server is
writing to Kafka, rather than reading from Kafka. Instead of using
Broadway, we will use brod, an Erlang framework for interacting
with Kafka. Add the following lines to Backend.Server.init/1 in
lib/backend/server.ex

```
# lib/backend/server.ex
def init(args) do
  {:ok, _} = Application.ensure_all_started(:brod)

  Logger.info("Initializing backend server")

  kafka_host =
```

```
  Application.get_env(
    :backend_server,
    :kafka_host,
    "localhost"
  )
  |> String.to_atom()

kafka_port =
  Application.get_env(
    :backend_server,
    :kafka_port,
    9092
  )

hosts = [{kafka_host, kafka_port}]
end
```

We are pulling in the same host and port info, as we did in the ingestion server. We call `Application.ensure_all_started/1` to make sure `brod` has fully started. We then start the `brod` client with the new host info as follows

```
:ok = :brod.start_client(
  hosts,
  args.client_id,
  _client_config=[]
)
```

The backend server also communicates with the statistics server via gRPC, so we need to update the statistics gRPC host and port info as well. Again, this is just pulled from the application configuration at runtime. Within the same `Backend.Server.init/1` function, before the call to `GRPC.Stub.connect/1` add the following lines and update the `connect/1` call as follows

```
# Note: I am formatting these function calls like this
# to avoid line wrapping in the book...
grpc_host = Application.get_env(
  :backend_server,
  :statistics_host,
  "localhost"
)
grpc_port = Application.get_env(
  :backend_server,
  :statistics_port,
  50051
)
{:ok, channel} =
```

```
GRPC.Stub.connect("#{grpc_host}:#{grpc_port}")
```

Running the System

At this point we are ready to run everythign together. Go ahead and run

```
$ docker-compose up -d
```

Wait a bit and check the services (Docker for Desktop can be useful for this). Most likely you will see the backend server has failed. This is because of repeated failures due to attempting to connect to Kafka. Go ahead and restart it (`docker-compose restart backend` should do the trick).

Now all that is left to do is verify it all works!

Attaching to Running Process

Once you have attached to a shell in the running backend container, you can attach a remote shell to the running application via

```
$ app/bin/backend_server remote
iex(backend_server@37cf0f5c6a79)2>
```

From here, the rest is just as if we were in IEx locally. Let's run `ingest/1` and `get_stats/0` to verify everything is connected and working as expected.

```
iex(backend_server@37cf0f5c6a79)2>
↪   Backend.Server.ingest(%{key: "hello", value: 42.0})

15:35:31.748 [info] Ingesting data
{:ok, %{}}
iex(backend_server@37cf0f5c6a79)3>
↪   Backend.Server.get_stats()

15:35:40.029 [info] Getting stats
{:ok, %{mode: 42.0, mean: 42.0, median: 42.0}}
```

Perfect!

15.11   The Final Challenge

You may have noticed we don't really use the key field in our data other than selecting the partition to write to in Kafka. Similarly, we have the ability to associate metadata with our data, but we never use it. The GetStatsRequest Protobuf gives a hint as to its use. We can use that metadata to filter the stats we want to compute. There are a few fun challenges[9] you can take on.

The purpose of these challenges is for you to spread your wings a bit and try to program some Elixir on your own with minimal direction. This is *by far* the fastest way to learn a language. You have enough background knowledge from this chapter that you should be able to complete these relatively fast. My advice is to read the documentation carefully. Understand what you are trying before you try it. Copying random stuff from Stack Overflow is the fastest way to dig yourself into a hole that is too deep to get out of.

The Challenges

The solutions to these challenges will be in the book's GitHub.

Challenge 1 Update the get_stats RPC call to use the metadata_filter field. Can you do this server-side? Are you able to update the database in such a way that it handles the filter?

Challenge 2 Update the GetStatsRequest to include a filter on the key. The goal is to compute statistics with a given key.

---

[9]For some definition of fun.

Chapter 16

Testing

Testing is an essential part of any software project. It helps you maintain the quality of your code as well as prevent bug regressions. Testing can also be helpful when working through the logic of a function or module.

While I'm far from a Test Driven Development (TDD) zealot, I do find in some cases starting with a test, or at least a conceptual outline of how you would test a function or module, can help you clarify your thinking and your code. For example, if you know you will need to check a database interaction within a test you will immediately start to think about the best way to structure your code to make the test simpler.

The concurrent nature of Elixir makes it easy to introduce subtle bugs. Testing won't solve this problem. But testing can at least help verify things like state management and process behavior.

One of the great features of Elixir is immutability. As we discussed earlier, immutability makes it easier to reason about what your code is doing (or what code someone else wrote is doing). It turns out this feature also makes your code simpler to test. You don't have to worry about state mutation between tests. By default, many functions are pure[1], which makes testing them *far* simpler.

---

[1]Pure functions are functions that *always* give the same output for the same input. For example, the function `add(x: int, y: int): int` is a pure function. On the other hand, a method such as `Counter::increment(x int): int` in a OOP language is not, as it updates some internal state of an

Elixir was designed with testing as a forethought, rather than an afterthought. The core testing facility, ExUnit, is included with the language. It's also prevalent throughout the community (maybe moreso than other communities). Test coverage and clean, simple code are the hallmarks of a good Elixir codebase.

There are three primary tools used for testing in Elixir. ExUnit is the native testing framework with a rich feature set and tight integration with the language itself. Mox is a popular library for mocking. StreamData is a library used for property-based testing [2].

The rest of this chapter will get you up and running with testing in Elixir. As with the rest of this book, the goal is to focus on the 20% of Elixir test mechanics that will cover 80% of your testing usecases.

16.1   Getting Started with ExUnit

ExUnit is Elixir's native testing framework, meaning it is packaged with the language. It is designed to be simple to use but give you powerful testing capabilities. At its core are three key features. It provides assertion and refutation capabilities via `assert` and `refute` (`refute` is equivalent to `assert not`). It provides callbacks for test setup and teardown, like any decent testing framework. It also provide built-in support for asynchronous tests. This might be new to you, depending on where you are coming from. Because Elixir is immutable by default, you don't have to worry about shared mutable state between concurrently running tests like you might in other languages.

Let's create a test project called `testing` to help us explore Elixir's testing facilities.

```
$ mix new testing --sup
```

---

object of type `Counter`.

[2]If you are new to property testing, the basic idea is writing tests to use generators that create data according to the properties of the input arguments to the function being tested. For example, testing `add(x: int, y: int): int` we could manually write a few tests by hand, or we could generate to streams of integers and use them as inputs to our `add` function and verify the result. The latter approach, using streams of integers, is property testing. StreamData helps you generate the test data streams.

We are using the flag here, --sup. If you recall from last chapter, this flag creates a new Mix project with with an OTP application skeleton and sets up a supervision tree for the application. You can see all available flags for mix new using the command

```
$ mix help new
```

You can see there is a directory in our new project called test/. Unsurprisingly, this contains our test files (these are Elixir scripts). There are two files created by default. The first is test_helper.exs, which is used to setup ExUnit (right now it just contains the line ExUnit.start()). The second is testing_test.exs, which contains an exemplar test.

Let's run mix test and see what happens.

```
$ mix test
Compiling 2 files (.ex)
Generated testing app
Running ExUnit with seed: 19175, max_cases: 48

..
Finished in 0.01 seconds (0.00s async, 0.01s sync)
1 doctest, 1 test, 0 failures
```

As you might expect, running mix test runs all of your tests. You can run a specifc file via

```
$ mix test test/path/to/file.exs
```

Or a test for a specific tag via

```
$ mix test --tag <some tag>
```

This won't make much sense now, but we will discuss tags later in this chapter.

You should have a test file corresponding to each Elixir module you create. It is often helpful to have the structure of your test directory mirror that of your lib/ directory, though sometimes it makes more sense to group your tests by function (e.g., test/controllers/, test/models/, etc.). Each test file should have the suffix _test.exs.

A test module consists of two core pieces. You must always include use ExUnit.Case in your module (generally this goes at the top, though not strictly required). Test cases are defined using the `test` macro. You can also add `doctest` followed by the fully qualified module name to have ExUnit run the doctests.

Let's look at the code Mix gives us.

```
# testin/testing_test.exs
defmodule TestingTest do
  use ExUnit.Case
  doctest Testing

  test "greets the world" do
    assert Testing.hello() == :world
  end
end
```

One useful function we have used throughout this book is `IO.inspect/2`. We frequently reach for `IO.inspect/2` when we need to print a data structure (like a list, for example). One of the more useful features of `IO.inspect/2` when it comes to debugging code, which we haven't used much throughout the book, is the fact that it returns its input value in addition to printing it.

That is

```
iex> x = IO.inspect([4, 2])
[4, 2] # <- this is printed from IO.inspect
[4, 2] # <- this is the assignment
iex> x
[4, 2]
```

It is often useful pairing this functionality with the `:label` argument, which adds additional printed context without changing the return value.

For example

```
iex> x = IO.inspect([4, 2], label: "best digits")
best digits: [4, 2]
[4, 2]
iex> x
[4, 2]
```

Starting with Elixir 1.14, there is a new debugging function called `dbg/2`. It is similar to `IO.inpsect/2`, but prints even more info with more context while still returning its argument. Let's look at an example.

```
iex> {a, b} = {4, 2}
iex> x = dbg([a, b])
[iex:2: (file)]
[a, b] #=> [4, 2]

[4, 2]
```

Notice how dbg/2 printed the line number and file (in this case we were inside IEx) along with the variable names we used and their values. Compare this to IO.inspect/2, which replaces the variables with their values.

Before we move on, there is one last useful technique with dbg/2 we should cover, and that is using it to debug pipes.

```
iex> 1..10 \
...> |> Enum.filter(fn i -> rem(i, 2) == 0 end) \
...> |> Enum.reverse \
...> |> Enum.take_random(2) \
...> |> Enum.to_list \
...> |> dbg
[iex:9: (file)]
1..10 #=> 1..10
|> Enum.filter(fn i -> rem(i, 2) == 0 end) #=> [2, 4, 6, 8,
↪    10]
|> Enum.reverse() #=> [10, 8, 6, 4, 2]
|> Enum.take_random(2) #=> [2, 10]
|> Enum.to_list() #=> [2, 10]

[2, 10]
```

Compare this to the IO.inspect/2 equivalent

```
iex> 1..10 \
...> |> Enum.filter(fn i -> rem(i, 2) == 0 end) \
...> |> Enum.reverse \
...> |> Enum.take_random(2) \
...> |> Enum.to_list \
...> |> IO.inspect
[2, 10]
[2, 10]
```

A single call to dbg/2 gives us visibility into the entirety of the pipeline.

One last tool that you will inevitably find useful is pry. You trigger pry by running IEx with the flag --dbg pry. When this flag is enabled, execution will stop at your `dbg/2` calls and you will be able to interact with the code.

16.2   Unit Test Basics

In the prior section we briefly touched on test organization and conventions. Inidividual tests are defined with the `test/2` macro. All tests live in a module, and this module should have the same name structure with the added suffic `Test.` as the module being tested. Test modules live in files whose filename ends with `_test.exs` (an Elixir script).

The test name or description should clearly and concisely describe what is being tested. Avoid superfluous words here. The point of the test name is to communicate to another engineer (perhaps your future self) the goal of the test. This will help them (you) assess whether the test is doing what it is supposed to do.

As with all other test frameworks, the primary modality of specifying a test is through the use of assertions. ExUnit has three major assertions:

- `assert` – assert that something is true.
- `refute` – assert that something is false.
- `assert_raise` – assert that an error was raised.

Within assert, there are two common patterns. The first is the one we are most familiar with: asserting something is true

```
# msg defined here to aid formatting
failure_msg = "actual: #{inspect(actual)} != expected:
↪  #{inspect(expected)}"
assert actual == expected, failure_msg
```

The second is less common, though it should feel familiar at this point: using pattern matching

```
assert {:ok, expected_value} = actual_result, failure_msg
```

Every test gets a context passed to it. This context is a map and can be customized in the module's `setup` block

```
defmodule MyTests do
  use ExUnite.Case
```

```
setup do
    %{
        some_key: "some_value",
        another_key: "another_value"
    }
end

test "context test", context do
    assert context[:some_key] == "some_value"
    assert context[:another_key] == "another_value"
end
end
```

The setup/1 (or setup/2) callback must return either :ok or one of {:ok, a_map}, {:ok, a_keyword_list}, or a_map, where a_map is an arbitrary map (you define) and a_keyword_list is an arbitrary keyword list. Only returning :ok will leave the context unchanged. This setup function gets called before *each* test.

There are two variations for global setup, setup_all/1 and setup_all/2. This callback is only called once, before the tests within the respective test module are executed.

Test context and setup can get quite exotic. See the ExUnit documentation on ExUnite.Callbacks for greater detail and examples.

We can group collections of tests using describe/2. A describe block takes a name (which describes the group) and a collection of tests, which are generally defined within the describe block. The description (the first argument to describe/2) is typically of the form of a fully-qualified name and arity. For example, My-Module.my_function/k, where k here is the arity of the function MyModule.my_function. The expectation is that the tests within this describe block only test this specific function.

```
defmodule MyModuleTest do
  use ExUnit.Case

  describe "MyModule.my_function/2" do

    test "nil inputs" do
      # ...
    end

    test "large inputs" do
      # ...
    end
```

```
    end
end
```

The describe block tests can be executed on their own via

```
$ mix test --only describe:"MyModule.my_function/2"
```

We can also tell Elixir that our tests can run asynchronously via the tag @moduletag: async.

```
defmodule MyModuleTest do
    use ExUnit.Case, async: true
    # your tests...
end
```

Note though that if there is any shared state between your tests that changes, you will end up with hard to debug, flakey tests. As much as possible, try to make your tests pure like your functions.

Pure vs Impure Functions

A pure function is a function that always gives the same output for a fixed input. That is, they are free of any side-effects. We saw earlier that a function like fn x, y -> x + y end is a trivial example of a pure function. In this case, $2 + 1 = 3$ will always be true.

As much as you can, strive for writing pure functions. Because pure functions are free of side-effects, they can safely be run concurrently without fear of race conditions. They are incredibly simple to test since they have no internal state that might change.

Just by writing Elixir code you will end up with a lot of pure functions, due to Elixir's functional nature.

Inter-test Dependencies

It's best to keep your tests small and self-contained. Aside from making your tests easier to write and understand, it also helps reduce dependencies between your tests. Dependencies between your tests can result in cascading failures of a test suite.

16.3 Doctests

In the prior section we saw we can trigger doctests by adding `doctest` `<module name>` in your test module. We briefly saw doctests in chapter 3, though we didn't learn how to write them. We will quickly cover doctests in this section.

Why quickly? Well there isn't much to writing a doctest. They also aren't meant to test your code. You use a doctest to make sure your examples are correct. Writing a doctest is no different than showing someone how to use a function in IEx. The only difference is you can have ExUnit execute this code and verify the output matches the expected output.

A doctest lives in the `## Examples` section of your function documentation (the documentation preceding your function definition that starts with the `@doc` macro). A doctest must be indented 4 spaces from whatever indentation level the `## Examples` header is sitting at. The test definition starts with `iex>` and ends at the end of the line or after the last line starting with `...>`. The expected output comes on the following line.

Let's look at a concrete example. Luckily, Mix gives you a template when you generate your project. Here's the original `lib/testing.ex` file Mix generated for us.

```elixir
defmodule Testing do
  @moduledoc """
  Documentation for `Testing`.
  """

  @doc """
  Hello world.

  ## Examples

      iex> Testing.hello()
      :world

  """
  def hello do
    :world
  end
end
```

Here we have our doctest.

```
iex> Testing.hello()
:world
```

As we've discussed, doctests are simple and not meant for testing functionality. They are really just here to keep our documentation correct.

Suppose we changed our function to the following

```
def hello(name) do
  "hello #{name}!"
end
```

Any unit tests we had around this function would break as soon as we made this change. But the only way we would catch this API change in our documentation is either with a good memory (i.e., remembering you need to update the docs) or your doctests.

There are a few things you will want to watch out for when writing doctests. As you can see, the output of our functions in the test is hardcoded. If you have a function that returns changing output (e.g., a timestamp or random number), this will not be suitable for a doctest. Doctests are also not suitable for illustrating asynchronous code or code with side effects.

16.4   Testing Async Code

Asynchronous code is notoriously difficult to test due to its non-deterministic behavior, timing issues, and the potential for race conditions. Even if you *can* test your async code, it can be even more difficult to debug it when a test fails. As we've learned in this book, the BEAM was designed for building massively concurrent systems.

By default, tests run synchronously. This makes them easy to reason about and avoids any race conditions in the event there is shared state that gets mutated by the tests. You can enable async tests using the module tag :async. Async tests are one of the times I make an exception to my general rule of preferring simple, synchronous code over asynchronous code. Using asynchronous tests forces you to write isolated tests that don't interfere with eachother when run concurrently.

```
defmodule MyModuleTest do
    use ExUnit.Case, async: true # async tests enabled
end
```

ExUnit provides a fair amount of tooling for testing your asynchronous code. For example, from ExUnit.Assertions, you can use assert_receive/2 to assert a message *will* be received (without having to wait for it) or assert_received/2 (note the past tense) to assert that a message was received. For example

```
test "a concurrent test" do
  pid = spawn(fn ->
    receive do
      {msg, pid} -> send(pid, msg)
    end
  end)

  send(pid, {:hello, self()})
  assert_receive :hello
end
```

Here we use assert_receive/2 and everything works. You must be careful when using assert_received/2. Remember, the semantics of this assert are that a message *has* been received, not that it will happen in the future. If we change the to assert_received/2, the test breaks because it ends before the message is actually received.

```
test "a concurrent test" do
  pid = spawn(fn ->
    receive do
      {msg, pid} -> send(pid, msg)
    end
  end)

  send(pid, {:hello, self()})
  assert_received :hello # <-- changed
end
```

Now if we rerun the test, we will see something like this

```
  1) test a concurrent test (TestingTest)
     test/testing_test.exs:10
     Assertion failed, no matching message after 0ms
     The process mailbox is empty.
     code: assert_received :hello
     stacktrace:
```

```
test/testing_test.exs:19: (test)
```

However, adding a `Process.sleep(500)` before we call as-
sert_received/2 will fix the test. This gives the test enough time
to receive the message and make the assertion. Hopefully at
this point you are thinking "this doesn't feel correct..." If so,
you are correct. Building tests that rely on `Process.sleep/1` for
synchronization is generally a terrible idea that will only end in
heartbreak.

ExUnit also provides `ExUnit.CaptureLog.capture_log/2` for capturing log output. `capture_log/2` takes a function as input. It then
executes that function, capturing the log output while the function
executes, and returns that output as a string. It is up to you to
test them in a way that makes sense for your test. The common
approach is to use the match operator `=~`. This operator matches
the string on the left-hand side with the regex pattern on the right.
For example,

```
capture_log(my_fun) =~ "My test log"
```

Care must be taken when using `capture_log/2`. All the logs from
concurrently run tests (that is, when `@moduletag :async` is used)
will be present in the string returned from `capture_log/2`. You can
also specify the for which logs are captured. This is quite useful,
but can lead to subtle bugs in the async setting. If, for some reason,
you have logic in one of your test cases that changes the log level
of `Logger` and you are using `capture_log/2` configured for a specific
log level on another test, the changed `Logger` state could cause your
other test to fail.

Testing a GenServer

Let's work through an example of how we would test a GenServer.
Recall back to chapter 12 where we built a ring buffer server. The
first step was to build a ring buffer module. We then used that
module to handle the core logic of the GenServer. This is not only
good code structure, it greatly simplifies testing the ring buffer
implementation.

For this section, we are going to assume the core logic of the
GenServer is tested somewhere else. That is, we will assume the
`RingBuffer` module has its own set of tests. Instead, we will focus

solely on testing some of the callback functionality.

First we need a toy sever that lets us do some interesting tests

```
defmodule MyServer do
  use GenServer
  require Logger

  @impl true
  def init(_) do
    {:ok, MapSet.new()}
  end

  @impl true
  def handle_call(:hello, {pid, _}, state) do
    Logger.info("received hello call request")
    state = MapSet.put(state, pid)
    {:reply, :world, state}
  end

  @impl true
  def handle_cast({:hello, pid}, state) do
    Logger.info("received hello cast request")
    state = MapSet.put(state, pid)
    {:noreply, state}
  end
end
```

Lets also add some client functions.

```
def start_link do
  GenServer.start_link(__MODULE__, :ok, name: __MODULE__)
end

def hello() do
  GenServer.call(__MODULE__, :hello)
end

def ahello() do
  GenServer.cast(__MODULE__, {:hello, self()})
end
```

Alright, now we are ready to test. We will write two tests, one for GenServer.call/3 and one for GenServer.cast/2. Recall that GenServer.cast/2 always returns :ok, regardless of what happens at the server, so we don't need to test the response. GenServer.call/3, on the other hand, does return a response worth testing. In this case we just need to assert that the response is the atom :world.

In both cases we use Erlang's :sys.get_state/1 function to inspect the GenServer's state.

```elixir
defmodule Testing.MyServerTest do
  use ExUnit.Case
  alias Testing.MyServer
  doctest MyServer

  test "check call" do
    {:ok, pid} = MyServer.start_link()
    resp = MyServer.hello()
    state = :sys.get_state(pid)

    assert resp == :world
    assert MapSet.member?(state, self())
  end

  test "check cast" do
    {:ok, pid} = MyServer.start_link()
    MyServer.ahello()
    state = :sys.get_state(pid)

    assert MapSet.member?(state, self())
  end
end
```

Let's run our tests and see what happens.

```
$ mix test test/my_server_test.exs
Running ExUnit with seed: 153871, max_cases: 20


08:20:42.182 [info] received hello call request
.
08:20:42.184 [info] received hello cast request
.
Finished in 0.01 seconds (0.00s async, 0.01s sync)
2 tests, 0 failures
```

Let's add two tests to check the log output. We are only doing this to play around with capture_log/2. It can be a bad idea to test your log output. There are very specific cases, probably related to error handling, where testing log output makes sense. Logs, by their nature, frequently change, are added or removed by engineers as the codebase evolves.[3] Testing them too closely can result in

---

[3]The only systems I've seen with stable logs are well-established, long-running systems. Otherwise, it is often the case that the logs are often modified. Getting logging right can be tricky. Either the logs are too frequent or not frequent enough. Either they give you too much information (e.g., maybe PII) or not enough information. In my experience, it is rare for a codebase with a

low-value and/or flakey tests. But we are here to learn, so let's add some tests for our logging and see what happens.

```
defmodule MyServerTest do
  use ExUnit.Case
  import ExUnit.CaptureLog
  alias Testing.MyServer

  # code omitted

  test "check log caputre" do
    {:ok, _} = MyServer.start_link()
    logs = capture_log(fn ->
      MyServer.hello()
    end)
    alogs = capture_log(fn ->
      MyServer.ahello()
    end)
  assert logs =~ "received hello call request"
  assert alogs =~ "received hello cast request"
  end
end
```

First we must import the ExUnit.CaptureLog module. Remember, capture_log/2 takes a function as its argument. We are testing both our synchronous and asynchronous functions. You should see the following output after running the new test.

```
$ mix test test/my_server_test.exs:23
Running ExUnit with seed: 473980, max_cases: 20
Excluding tags: [:test]
Including tags: [location: {"test/my_server_test.exs", 23}]

  1) test check log caputre (Testing.MyServerTest)
     test/my_server_test.exs:23
     Assertion with =~ failed
     code:  assert capture_log(fn -> MyServer.ahello() end)
     ↪  =~ "received hello cast request"
     left:  ""
     right: "received hello cast request"
     stacktrace:
       test/my_server_test.exs:26: (test)

Finished in 0.01 seconds (0.00s async, 0.01s sync)
3 tests, 1 failure, 2 excluded
```

high rate of change to have stable logs. At the same time, if the codebase is *not* rapidly evolving, then it probably doesn't need a test that inspects the log output.

There are two interesting pieces here. The first is how we executed this test.

```
$ mix test test/my_server_test.exs:23
```

This is how you run a specific test in a specific file. You specify the filename and append the line number of the test to the end, with a colon in between. As you might guess, in my `test/my_server_test.exs` file, the log capture test we added starts on line 23.

Back to the problem at hand. Why did our second test fail? We can see it was the async function. It seems `capture_log/2` is exiting before our logs are getting printed. As you may have guessed, adding a short sleep gives us just enough breathing room for `capture_log/2` to do its thing. Let's try again, this time using the following capture

```
alogs = capture_log(fn ->
  MyServer.ahello()
  Process.sleep(100)
end)
assert alogs =~ "received hello cast request"
```

This time everything passes. You may have to tune the sleep on your system. Before we move on I want to reiterate that this is not a good test. We are just illustrating how `capture_log/2` works, but that doesn't mean it should be a standard tool in your testing toolkit.

Testing Supervisors

You should thoroughly test your GenServers. They are core to your application. When it comes to Supervisors, you should think carefully about what you want to test and whether it is worth testing. Supervisors are just here to restart a failed process. The `Supervisor` module contains all the testing necessary to make sure this functionality works as expected. You should not duplicate these tests with your own application tests.

So what should you test? You test what you control. In this case, it is the configuration of the `Supervisor`. Is it important your children start in a certain order? Write a test for that. Is it important that all children restart if one child restarts? Write a test for that. Always test what you control.

16.5 Mocks and Stubs

No discussion of testing would be complete without a dicssions of mocking and stubbing. Before we get into the details of using mocks and stubs for testing, we should define them. A *mock* is an object that simulates *external* behavior. A *stub* is used to give predefined responses for a given input. These let you control your external dependencies and make your tests deterministic. They also allow you to isolate your tests, as there is no shared state.

Mocks and stubs are most useful when you are testing a piece of code that interacts with an external API, file system, database, etc. The goal is to isolate the code you own (wrote) from the external dependency. This also lets you simulate errors and edge cases. However, care must be taken when using mocks, as they can lead to brittle tests. It is counter productive to have a suite of tests that take an hour or two to update every time you make a small change to the code being tested. This can be particularly common when mocking databases.

Mox is a popular mocking library. It relies on behaviours for creating mocks. Though we've used standard library behaviours so far, we can also create our own through @callback and @optional_callback . The idea we will use here is to define a boundary within our application using a behaviour. We can then build an actual implementation and a mock implementation for the respective behaviour. Let's build a simple behaviour and see how we can mock it with Mox.

In this example we will assume we are interacting with some external API. Maybe we are interacting with it via an HTTP client, maybe an SDK. The nice thing about using behaviours at the application boundary is we don't really care what the backing implementation is. If we define the boundaries using behaviours we can swap the backing implementation at will.

```
defmodule Testing.ExternalAPI do
  @callback fetch_data() :: {:ok, any()} | {:error, term()}
end
```

Mox is a third-party library, so we will need to update our project's deps in mix.exs.

```
# mix.exs
```

```elixir
defmodule Testing.MixProject do
  use MixProject

  # Other mix.exs content omitted.

  defp deps do
    [
      {:mox, "~> 1.0", only: :test}
    ]
  end
end
```

Notice how we are specifying this is a test dependency. Being explicit like this is great for two reasons. The first, is it keeps your release size down. This is particularly important when using a tool like Docker. The second, which is more of a problem if you work at a large company, is it is one less dependency you have to worry about when the security folks look at the security scans of your dependencies. Nothing ruins a day quite like triaging security scans and adding the same comment over and over that the vulnerability raised by the scanning tool doesn't apply to you.

Anyways, back to the task at hand. Remember to run `mix deps.get` to fetch Mox.

If we wanted to implement this (say, wrapping usage of an HTTP client), it would look something like this:

```elixir
defmodule Testing.SomeAPI do
  @behaviour Testing.ExternalAPI
  require Logger

  @impl true
  def fetch_data() do
    Logger.info("fetching data...")
    {:ok, %{hello: "world"}}
  end
end
```

To tell Elixir we are implementing a behaviour we have to declare it using `@behaviour`. This is a little different from behaviours like `Application`, `GenServer`, or `Supervisor`, which all use use. Those behaviours require use because they inject some code into the calling module. In our case, we just want to implement the behaviour so we use `@behaviour`.

For this chapter, we aren't interested in this implementation but instead how to mock it. There is a fundamental question we must answer when designing with behaviours: how do we specify which concrete implementation should be used by the calling code? The two most common approaches are through application configuration and passing the dependendency in explicitly (i.e., dependency injection). Passing in the dependency is far simpler to use and to understand and should be preferred over application configuration. In this chapter, we will only look at the case of passing in the dependency, rather than relying on application configuration.

We are going to extend our `Testing.MyServer` module to rely on our newly defined (and cleverly named) `Testing.ExternalAPI`. We will pass in the module that defines the implementation of the behaviour. Let's update `Testing.MyServer`'s `init/1` and `start_link/1` functions.

```
def start_link(opts \\ []) do
  GenServer.start_link(__MODULE__, opts, name: __MODULE__)
end

@impl true
def init(opts \\ []) do
  {:ok,
    %{
      pids: MapSet.new(),
      # We are defaulting client_mod to Testing.SomeAPI
      client: Keyword.get(opts, :client, Testing.SomeAPI)
    }}
end
```

Let's add a new `handle_call/3` function that makes use of this client.

```
@impl true
def handle_call(
  :fetch,
  {pid, _},
  %{
    client: client,
    pids: pids
  } = state
) do
  Logger.info("received fetch info request")
  Logger.info("fetching data")
  resp = client.fetch_data()
  Logger.info("fetched data")
  pids = MapSet.put(pids, pid)
  {:reply, resp, %{state | pids: pids}}
```

```
end
```

Our existing tests will fail at this point because we have changed the GenServer state data structure. Let's fix those real quick. We need to change

```
state = :sys.get_state(pid)
```

to the following

```
%{pids: pids} = :sys.get_state(pid)
```

And likewise, we need to change

```
assert MapSet.member?(state, self())
```

to

```
assert MapSet.member?(pids, self())
```

Now our existing tests should all pass. Let's add a new test.

```
defmodule Testing.MyServerTest do
  # Prior code omitted for brevity

  test "check ok fetch data" do
    # TODO: what is client?
    {:ok, pid} = MyServer.start_link(client: ??)
    resp = MyServer.get_data()
    assert resp == {:ok, %{hello: "world"}}
  end

  test "check error fetch data" do
    # TODO: what is client?
    {:ok, pid} = MyServer.start_link(client: ??)
    resp = MyServer.get_data()
    assert resp == {:error, _}
  end
```

We have two new tests, but what do we use for :client here? This is where Mox comes into play. We will create a single mock and setup the expected behavior using Mox.expect/4.

It's generally best to avoid creating mocks individually for each test. The idiomatic approach is to create them either in setup or

in the `test_helper.exs` file. In our case, we will creating them in
`test_helper.exs`.

```
# test/test_helper.exs
ExUnit.start()

Mox.defmock(Testing.MockAPI, for: Testing.ExternalAPI)
```

Depending on what language you are coming from, this may feel
very strange. The call to `Mox.defmock/2` creates a module named
`Testing.MockAPI` that is globally available. We specify the behaviour
being mocked via `:for`, which in this case is `Testing.ExteranlAPI`.

Back in our test file, `my_server_test.exs`, we need to add one
additional line before we can get our tests working.

```
# test/my_server_test.exs
defmodule Testing.MyServerTest do
  use ExUnit.Case
  import Mox
  # other imports omitted

  setup :set_mox_global

  # remaining file content...
end
```

We have to add the line

```
setup :set_mox_global
```

so that the mocks are globally available. If your tests are synchronous, then this isn't needed. Right now, our tests are asynchronous. Mox creates the mocks in the process in which they are
defined (i.e., the process where `Mox.expect/4` is called). Now we
can fix our tests.

```
defmodule Testing.MyServerTest do
  # Prior code omitted for brevity

  test "check ok fetch data" do
    # TODO: what is client?
    {:ok, pid} = MyServer.start_link(
      client: Testing.MockAPI
    )
    resp = MyServer.get_data()
    assert resp == {:ok, %{hello: "world"}}
```

```
end

test "check error fetch data" do
  # TODO: what is client?
  {:ok, pid} = MyServer.start_link(
    client: Testing.MockAPI
  )
  resp = MyServer.get_data()
  assert resp == {:error, _}
end
```

Now these tests should pass.

Refactoring our tests

If you are like me, having to use

```
setup :set_mox_global
```

doesn't sit quite right. So what can we do? Well the reason we need this is we are calling the function via the call `MyServer.get_data/0`, which is just a wrapper on

```
GenServer.call(__MODULE__, :fetch)
```

A better approach would be to put this functionality inside a helper function, say `MyServer.handle_fetch_data/1`, and then we can test this function directly.

```
def handle_fetch_data(client) do
  Logger.info("fetching data...")
  resp = client.fetch_data()
  Logger.info("fetched data")
  resp
end
```

Now we can rewrite our tests as follows.

```
defmodule Testing.MyServerTest do
  # Prior code omitted for brevity

  test "check ok fetch data" do
    {:ok, pid} = MyServer.start_link(client:
    ↪ Testing.MockAPI)
    resp = MyServer.handle_fetch_data(Testing.MockAPI)
    assert resp == {:ok, %{hello: "world"}}
```

```
end

test "check error fetch data" do
  {:ok, pid} = MyServer.start_link(client:
  ↪ Testing.MockAPI)
  resp = MyServer.handle_fetch_data(Testing.MockAPI)
  assert resp == {:error, _}
end
```

Now we can remove the line

```
setup :set_mox_global
```

and our tests will still have access to the mocks. Much better.

Verifying Expectations

One last using `Mox.expect/4` isn't just for returning values for a given input. It also configures the mock to *expect* certain conditions were. That is, the mock expects it will be called with certain inputs. You can verify these conditions using any of the following:

- `Mox.verify!/0` – checks that all expectations within the process were met.
- `Mox.verify/1` – checks that all expectations for the given mock were met.
- `Mox.verify_on_exit!/0` – used with `ExUnit.Callbacks.setup/0` to automatically check expectations were met across all mocks.

What if you want to ensure certain functions *were not* called? Mox provides that functionality as well via `Mox.deny/3`. It works just like `Mox.expect/4`, except you don't specify a return value and calling any of the above verification functions will check that the function specified in `Mox.deny/3` wasn't called.

16.6 Property-based Testing

Up to this point all of our tests have consisted of specific input mapped to a specific output. That is, for a given input we can verify our function works. But what about other inputs? We cannot say. For example, a test like

```
test "check division" do
  assert 2 == MyMath.divide(4,2)
end
```

shows our function works for nice inputs, but it doesn't help
us much when it comes to the more interesting inputs like My-
Math.divide(1,2), MyMath.divide(3,0), or MyMath.divide(1, ep-
silon)[4].

Property-based testing was designed to address these problems. It
still doesn't *prove* our function is correct. Instead, it allows us to
test to some degree of certainty that it is correct. Think back to
our earlier work where we used an algorithm that probabilistically
determined whether a number might be prime or not. It never
guaranteed the number was prime, just gave us increasingly better
odds the longer it ran that number was indeed prime.

StreamData is the de facto standard when it comes to property-
based testing in Elixir. Since it doesn't live in the standard library
we must add it to our test dependencies.

```
defp deps do
  [
    {:mox, "~> 1.0", only: :test},
    {:stream_data, "~> 0.5", only: :test}
  ]
end
```

And as always, we must actually fetch the dependency.

```
$ mix deps.get
```

Property-based tests rely on the StreamData.property/1 (or Stream-
Data.property/3) macro. We will use this macro to define a specific
property we are testing and then use generators to generate a range
of inputs for which we test the given property.

So what is a generator and how does it work? Generators are
streams of data (hence the name StreamData). That means you
can use them with both the Enum and Stream modules and that

---

[4]epsilon (i.e., Nx.Constants.epsilon({:f, 64})) is the smallest floating point number supported by your given hardware. In other words, it is the
decimal value closest to 0 supported by your computer. This is often used in
numerical analysis to determine the accuracy to which floating point numbers
can be compared.

they implement the `Enumerable` protocol. They can be manipulated
and shrunk (e.g., their output modified or limited). We can also
combine them to create a new generators.

For example, StreamData has the `StreamData.integer/0` generator,
which generates integers. There is also the `StreamData.integer/1`
generator, which generates integers from the given range.

We can create our own generator using the `gen` macro. Let's try
our hand at creating our own generator. Suppose we have a `Person`
struct defined as follows.

```elixir
defmodule Person do
  @enforce_keys [:first_name, :last_name, :age]
  defstruct [:first_name, :last_name, :age]
end
```

When creating a generator for this struct we need to consider the
types of values we want to generate. We need a way to generate strings for :first_name and :last_name. We can do this with
`StreamData.string(:utf8)`. What about the age? That is just as
simple. We can use `StreamData.integer(0..120)` (we are assuming
we have no people older than 120). Let's put this together.

```elixir
person_generator =
  gen all first_name <- StreamData.string(:utf8),
          last_name <- StreamData.string(:utf8),
          age <- StreamData.integer(0..120) do
  %Person{
    first_name: first_name,
    last_name: last_name,
    age: age
  }
end
```

This generator could be used in any test where a `Person` struct is
needed.

Before we can dig into property tests, we need some code to test.
Let's create a toy math library to serve as a playground for our property tests. Create a file `testing/math_util.ex` with the following
module.

```elixir
# testing/math_util.ex
defmodule Testing.MathUtil do
  def div(a, b) do
    a / b
```

```
  end

  def factorial(0), do: 1
  def factorial(n), do: Enum.reduce(1..n, 1, &Kernel.*/2)
end
```

We chose these specific functions because their domains are not the entirety of the real number line. Division is only defined for a denominator $d \in \mathbb{R} \setminus \{0\}$ (the non-zero real numbers). Factorial is only defined for $x \in \mathbb{Z}^+$, the non-negative integers[5].

Clearly our functions are problematic. We aren't checknig for a zero denominator in div/2 function and factorial/1 will recurse infinitely for negative input.

Our plan is the following. We can see what is wrong with our existing implementation. The hope is we can implement some property tests and see if they will catch these problems for us. The first step is to create these tests.

Create the file test/math_util_test.exs. Let's start with two tests, one for MathUtil.div/2 and one for MathUtil.factorial/1.

```
defmodule Testing.MathUtilTest do
  use ExUnit.Case
  use ExUnitProperties

  describe "Testing.MathUtil.div/2" do
    test "divides two numbers" do
      check all a <- StreamData.integer(), b <-
      ↪   StreamData.integer() do
        assert Testing.MathUtil.div(a, b) == a / b
      end
    end
  end

  describe "Testing.MathUtil.factorial/1" do
    test "calculates the factorial of a number" do
      check all n <- StreamData.integer() do
        case n do
          0 -> assert Testing.MathUtil.factorial(n) == 1
          n -> assert Testing.MathUtil.factorial(n)
            == Enum.reduce(1..n, 1, &Kernel.*/2)
        end
      end
    end
```

---

[5]This is only partially true. For our purposes we will only consider this limited definition of factorial. However, the Gamma function is the analytic continuation of the factorial function and it *is* defined for negative integers as well as real numbers ($\mathbb{R}$). This function is beyond the scope of this book.

```
      end
   end
end
```

Let's run the first test, "Testing.MathUtil.div/2".

```
$ mix test --only describe:"Testing.MathUtil.div/2"
Running ExUnit with seed: 648064, max_cases: 20
Excluding tags: [:test]
Including tags: [describe: "Testing.MathUtil.div/2"]


  1) test Testing.MathUtil.div/2 divides two numbers
  ↪  (Testing.MathUtilTest)
     test/math_util_test.exs:8
     ** (ExUnitProperties.Error) failed with generated
  ↪  values (after 1 successful run):

        * Clause:    a <- StreamData.integer()
          Generated: 0

        * Clause:    b <- StreamData.integer()
          Generated: 0

     got exception:

        ** (ArithmeticError) bad argument in arithmetic
        ↪  expression
     code: check all a <- StreamData.integer(), b <-
     ↪  StreamData.integer() do
     stacktrace:
       (testing 0.1.0) lib/testing/math_util.ex:3:
       ↪  Testing.MathUtil.div/2
       omitted...
```

We have a failure!. It looks like StreamData found a problem when both the numerator and denominator are 0. This is exactly what we were hoping StreamData would find for us. Let's revise our implementation of `MathUtil.div/2` to the following.

```
# lib/testing/math_util.ex
def div(a, b) do
  case b do
    0 -> {:error, "division by zero"}
    _ -> a / b
  end
end
```

We also need to change the test, since the test is using the expression
a / b.

```
# test/math_util_test.exs
describe "Testing.MathUtil.div/2" do
  test "divides two numbers" do
    check all a <- StreamData.integer(), b <-
    ↪  StreamData.integer() do
      case b do
        0 -> assert Testing.MathUtil.div(a, b) == {:error,
        ↪  "division by zero"}
        _ -> assert Testing.MathUtil.div(a, b) == a / b
      end
    end
  end
end
```

You should see your test pass now if you run

```
$ mix test --only describe:"Testing.MathUtil.div/2"
```

Let's try running our other test.

```
$ mix test --only describe:"Testing.MathUtil.factorial/1"
```

Running this command should cause your terminal to hang. It
seems StreamData has found a case that leads to infinite recursion.
Let's revise our function to handle the case where $n < 0$.

```
def factorial(n) when n < 0, do: {:error, "factorial of
↪  negative number"}
def factorial(0), do: 1
def factorial(n), do: Enum.reduce(1..n, 1, &Kernel.*/2)
```

Now we correctly handle the case where $n < 0$. Let's run our test
again.

```
$ mix test --only describe:"Testing.MathUtil.factorial/1"
Running ExUnit with seed: 565056, max_cases: 20
Excluding tags: [:test]
Including tags: [describe: "Testing.MathUtil.factorial/1"]


  1) test Testing.MathUtil.factorial/1 calculates the
  ↪  factorial of a number (Testing.MathUtilTest)
     test/math_util_test.exs:19
```

```
Failed with generated values (after 0 successful runs):

    * Clause:    n <- StreamData.integer()
      Generated: -1

Assertion with == failed
code:  assert Testing.MathUtil.factorial(n) ==
  ↪  Enum.reduce(1..n, 1, &Kernel.*/2)
left:  {:error, "factorial of negative number"}
right: 0
stacktrace:
  test/math_util_test.exs:23: anonymous fn/2 in
  ↪    Testing.MathUtilTest."test
  ↪    Testing.MathUtil.factorial/1 calculates the
  ↪    factorial of a number"/1
  (stream_data 0.6.0) lib/stream_data.ex:2321:
  ↪    StreamData.check_all/7
  test/math_util_test.exs:20: (test)


Finished in 0.03 seconds (0.00s async, 0.03s sync)
1 doctest, 10 tests, 1 failure, 10 excluded
```

This time it failed, showing the value it failed with was 1 and the error message we see is what we expected

```
{:error, "factorial of negative number"}
```

The problem is the test, not the implementation. Let's fix the test.

```
describe "Testing.MathUtil.factorial/1" do
  test "calculates the factorial of a number" do
    check all n <- StreamData.integer() do
      case n do
        n when n < 0 -> assert Testing.MathUtil.factorial(n)
          == {:error, "factorial of negative number"}
        0 -> assert Testing.MathUtil.factorial(n) == 1
        n -> assert Testing.MathUtil.factorial(n)
          == Enum.reduce(1..n, 1, &Kernel.*/2)
      end
    end
  end
end
```

Now our test passes. We have one final function to fix.

More reading

If you found this section interesting, I encourage you to check out the
paper *QuickCheck: a lightweight tool for random testing of Haskell
programs* by Claessen and Hughes. It was published in 2000 and
introduced the Haskell library *QuickCheck*, which is the inspriation
for Elixir's `StreamData` library. This paper is very approachable (at
least as far as academic papers go).

Chapter 17

Best Practices and Idioms

One of the hallmarks of a good developer is that they write code idiomatically. That is, they write using the idioms of the language in which they are working. For example, factories and utility classes are common in Java, but not so much in Python. Python iteration relies on generators and iterators, avoiding index loops as frequently as possible, while indexing is far more common in languages like C, C++, and Java[1].

This chapter covers some of the core idioms of Elixir. It is *not* meant to be comprehensive. Instead, the goal is to give you 20% of the idioms that will cover 80% of your needs. It is largely taken from Chris Adams' GitHub repo, *elixir_style_guide*[2]. You should absolutely read through everythign in that repo.

Another great resource is the collection of anti-patterns in the Elixir docs themselves[3]. These are very instructive examples of what not to do, why it's wrong, and how to correct it. If you've made it this far into the book, I would consider these required reading in addition to the aforementioned style guide.

---

[1]Of course, modern C++ and Java tend to prefer range-style for-loops rather than loops relying on indexing a collection.

[2]You can find it here https://github.com/christopheradams/elixir_style_guide

[3]You can find them here https://hexdocs.pm/elixir/1.18.1/code-anti-patterns.html

17.1   Naming Conventions

Use snake case for variable and function names, camel case for modules.

17.2   Mix Format

Use `mix format` every time you save.

17.3   Use Pattern Matching

Pattern matching is expected and incredibly useful. Just use it.

```
# Good
{:ok, connection} = MyModule.create_connection()
{:ok, some_data} = MyModule.get_data(connection)

# Better
with {:ok, conn} <- MyModule.create_connection(),
     {:ok, some_data} <- MyModule.get_data(conn) do
  process_data(some_data)
else
  handle_failure()
end
```

17.4   Use with

Leverage `with` pattern matching rather than mutliple nested pattern matching expressions. `with` allows you to match successive expressions, like you would with nested pattern matching, but without the nesting.

In the distributed systems chapter we created a single gRPC channel. Suppose for this example we wanted multiple channels.

```
with {:ok, chan1} <- GRPC.Stub.connect(service1),
     {:ok, chan2} <- GRPC.Stub.connect(service2),
     {:ok, chan3} <- GRPC.Stub.connect(service3) do
  {:ok, %{
    service1_chan: chan1,
    service2_chan: chan2,
    service3_chan: chan3
  }}
else
```

```
{:error, "failed to connect to one or more services"}
end
```

17.5   Pipe Operator

Prefer the pipe operator over nested function calls.

```
# Good
Application.get_env(:hello, :my_num)
|> String.to_integer

# Bad
String.to_integer(Application.get_env(:hello, :my_num))
```

If you aren't used to the pipe operator, this may take a little getting used to.

17.6   Return Status Tuple

This is one of those times where you may encounter people adamantly opposed to this idiom. If you writing a function that may fail, return a tuple that contains the status and the original return value of the function. The status for success should be `:ok` and the status for error should be `:error`.

Here's an example:

```
defp factorial_helper(0, acc), do: 1
defp factorial_helper(1, acc), do: acc
defp factorial_helper(n, acc) do
  factorial_helper(n - 1, acc * n)
end

def factorial(n) when n < 0 do
  {:error, "factorial is only defined for n >= 1"}
end
def factorial(n) do
  {:ok, factorial_helper(n, 1)}
end
```

We write `factorial_helper` in a way that assumes good input values. In the public function, we check input values and use a status indicator in the result to indicate success or failure.

Document Your Code

You should almost always write something for documentation. What is obvious to you now is rarely obvious to you in the future or to your peers. Your future self and your peers will thank you. Always use `@moduledoc` and `@doc`. Indicate deprecated code using `@deprecated` (this emits a warning while `:deprecated` does not). If your docs contain code examples, write them using the doctest format.

Chapter 18

Appendices

Appendix A: BEAM Internals

18.1 Introduction to BEAM

In the introduction to this book we discussed briefly that BEAM and the OTP are what sets Erlang and Elixir apart from other langauges. We listed some features, but we didn't really dig into *what* makes them different and *why* it matters. That is mostly because it's not essential to knowing either of these languages. This is why I have decided to put this background in an appendix, rather than the main text.

That being said, just because something isn't essential doesn't mean it isn't instructive and interesting.

As we learned earlier, BEAM stands for Bogdan/Björn's Erlang Abstract Machine. It is the virtual machine used to run Erlang, Elixir, and other BEAM-compatible languages. BEAM is the successor to JAM (Joe's Abstract Machine), named after Joe Armstrong, one of the co-creators of Erlang.

The BEAM is a virtual machine. It executes your code in two steps. First, the code you write is translated into an intermediate representation known as bytecode. This bytecode is machine and architecture independent. That is, an Erlang or Elixir program compiled on one computer will run on another [1]. The bytecode gets executed by a virtual machine. This virtual machine is a binary

---

[1]Of course this isn't universally true. There are always exceptions. A great exception in this case is when you compile your code with native optimizations. Those are generally not portable across architectures.

installed on a system. Different operatiring systems and different CPU architectures required different versions of the binary.

Among its many features, the BEAM VM excels when it comes to fault-tolerance and concurrency. It provides lightweight processes that are both cheap to create and destroy. Its execution engine provides performant code that is trivially executed across different instances of the BEAM VM. These features are what make the BEAM unique and provide the essence of Erlang and Elixir programs.

18.2   Processes

Processes are independent from one another. Each process has its own heap and message queue. Garbage collection acts on the process level, rather than globally. Processes are also isolated, meaning a failure in one process will not cause another process to fail[2]. There is no shared memory between processes. If data from one process is needed by another, that data is copied to the receiving process's mailbox.

The BEAM scheduler makes sure processes are evenly distributed across CPU cores.

18.3   BEAM Scheduler

Each CPU core gets a scheduler thread. The scheduler threads are responsible for deciding which process is executed. Processes are spread across these threads as evenly as possible. When a process is scheduled for execution it will run until it hits its set number of executed instructions (referred to as *reductions*) or it signals it is waiting for a message. This is called *preemptive scheduling.*

The schedulers try to keep CPU core utilization as high as possible. In this context, idle cores waste CPU resources when there are proceses that need execution. If there is a scheduler thread that doesn't have processes in need of execution (e.g., they are waiting on messages), that thread is able to take work from the other

---

[2]The exception to this is parent processes will crash when a child crashes, depending on whether the parent is trapping exits or supervising the child process.

threads (in most cases). This is referred to as work-stealing . Work-stealing is a common technqiue when you want to maximize resource utilization over a given interval of time.

One area we have not covered in this book is Natively-Implemented Functions (NIFs). These are functions implemented in a low-level language like C or Rust that are callable from Erlang or Elixir. NIFs are *not* preemptable, which means once they execute the scheduler cannot preempt the process and must wait for the NIF to complete. This can wreak havoc on the scheduler algorithm. Stabilized in release 17.3 of the Erlang runtime, the so-called *dirty scheduler* can be enabled. This scheduler allows you to off-load teh scheduling of NIFs to the dirty scheduler, enabling longer NIF execution times without interfering with BEAM-land scheduling. Using the dirty-scheduler means switching OS threads to execute the NIF, so there is a greater overhead when using this feature. In other words, you should only use this if the cost of switching threads makes sense for the time it takes to complete the NIF execution.

18.4   Garbage Collection

As I mentioned in the earlier section on processes, each process has its own heap. These heaps are garbage collected independently of on another. If a process exits before a GC is triggered, then its heap is reclaimed without requiring any garbage collection at all. This means processes that only utilize a small percentage of their heap may never trigger a garbage collection.

The BEAM uses a tracing garbage collector. Garbage collection is triggered when the heap passes a certain threshold. This happens per process rather than globally like it does on the JVM. There are three heaps: the *to* heap, *from* heap, and the *old* heap. During a garbage collection, any data that is still referenced in the *from* heap is copied over to the *to* heap. The BEAM sets a watermark to determine data that should be moved to the *old* heap. Any data below this watermark in the *from* heap will be moved to the *old* heap. The watermark is set to the allocation level of the previous garage collection. This is shown in figure 18.1.

Large binaries are stored off heap and shared across threads. Similarly, atoms are stored off heap and never freed. In other words, atoms last the entire lifetime of your application. This is why you should avoid dynamically creating a large number of atoms.

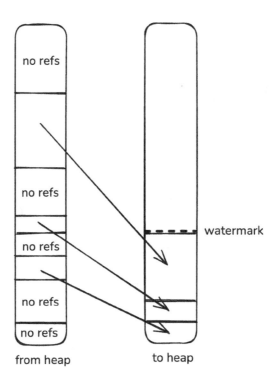

Figure 18.1: Referenced data copied from the *from* heap to the *to* heap

18.5 Compilation

Erlang and Elixir code is compiled to bytecode. This is similar to Java and other JVM-based languages. They bytecode is what is executed by the BEAM VM. This is what enables Elixir to leverage the BEAM VM while offering a more modern syntax from Erlang. The BEAM also supports just-in-time (JIT) compilation.

18.6 Fault Tolerance

One of the guiding philosophies of the OTP is to fail fast. That is, a process should prefer to fail rather than try to handle every possible error. Part of what makes this possible is the design of the BEAM VM. As we discussed earlier, processes are independent. A failure in one process will not impact an unrelated process.

The use of supervisors is one piece of the OTP that makes this philosophy so effective. Supervisors monitor their child processes. They are able to restart failed child processes when they detect a failure and this restart strategy is customizable (as we have learned).

The BEAM VM provides a few other tools for handling errors. One of those tools is links. Links are bidirectional connections between processes. These connections are used when one of the process exits. An exiting process (other than a `:normal` exit) will trigger its linked process to exit with the same signal (or message, if the process is trapping exits, as discussed below). Since links are bidirectional, it doesn't matter which process exits first, the other will follow.

Monitors are another useful fault-tolerance tool. A monitor, once created, will receive a message when there is state chane in the monitored process. Monitors are capable of monitoring both processes and ports. The monitor receives a message when the monitored object, whether it's a process or port, terminates or the connection fails.

18.7 Concurrency

As I have mentioned before, BEAM's concurrency model is often said to follow the Actor concurrency model. This is a good mental model to have, though BEAM's concurrency model was not designed with the Actor model in mind.

As we discussed earlier in this chapter, each process is independent. There is no real concept of shared memory with processes like there is in other languages. Elixir (and Erlang) processes share data through message passing. Each process has its own heap and mailbox. The mailbox is a message queue owned by its respective process. When one process sends a message to another process, that message is *copied* to the mailbox queue. This is in line with Elixir's functional roots. Though we give up some efficiency with the copy (not much), we don't have to worry about concurrent modifications to the same data.

18.8   Performance Tips

There are a few takeaways from this appendix worth keeping in the back of your mind as you work on Elixir code. These will help you keep your code performant and avoid some easy-to-fall-into traps.

Don't create unnecessary processes This is a simple one. Stick to the concurrency you need. Even though processes are lightweight, cheap to create and remove, there is still an overhead to them. More processes increases the load on the schedule. Every new process created takes away execution time from the other processes. This is obvious, of course, but can be easy to forget when you always hear "creating processes is cheap." The overhead of context switching can add up with a large number of processes. Create processes, but do it in a controlled and structured manner.

Use Task and GenServer Lean on the Task and GenServer behaviours for your concurrency needs. These will help you build more reliable and fault-tolerant code. They also force you think a little more carefully about what your code is doing and, more importantly, what it *should* do.

Use NIFs judiciously As I mentioned earlier in this chapter, NIFs can be an effective technique to improve the performance or your code. They can also rapidly destroy the performance of your code. The scheduler works best at a per-process execution time of around 1ms. The scheduler *cannot* preempt a NIF, so it is up to the caller to ensure the NIF doesn't run for too long. If it does, you can see rather sudden and noticeable drops in performance.

Index